D0951985

biscuit

books

The Cuisine of the Sun

Classical French Cooking from Nice and Provence

Mireille Johnston

Illustrations by Milton Glaser

Biscuit Books, Inc.
Newton, Massachusetts

Acknowledgments

I wish to thank Jason Epstein, gourmand par excellence, for his inspired curiosity and his encouragement; Milton Glaser, who can see more and better than all of us; Sono Rosenberg, for her precision, patience and taste; Susan Child, who so generously gave time, imagination and good cheer to the project; and Roberta Schneiderman, for her skillful help in testing the recipes.

Biscuit Books, Inc.
P.O. Box 610159
Newton, Massachusetts 02161

ISBN 0-9643600-4-7 (previously 0-671-70869-4, paper)

Printed and bound in the United States of America

00 99 98 97 96   5 4 3 2 1

Library of Congress Cataloging-in-Publication Data
Johnston, Mireille.
    The cuisine of the sun: classical French cooking from Nice and
Provence / Mireille Johnston. — 1st Biscuit Books ed.
        p.   cm.
    Reprint. Originally published: New York: Random House, 1976.
    Includes index.
    ISBN 0-9643600-4-7 (cloth)
      1. Cookery, French—Provençal style. 2. Cookery—France—Nice.
    3. Cookery—France—Provence.   I. Title.
TX719.2.P75J65   1996
641.59449—dc20   96-35933
                                                     CIP

Contents

The Cuisine of
the Sun

Introduction

I was born in a tall apricot-colored house with green shutters overlooking the sea. When I think of my childhood I remember the bright colors, the sounds, the smells and tastes of Nice. We were constantly sent to the seashore, the garden, or the hills to find ingredients for the kitchen. Along the coast we searched for sea urchins and mussels; in our garden we picked zucchini flowers, tiny eggplants, the tenderest lima beans. In the fields we gathered thyme and oregano; in the woods we searched for blackberries, chestnuts, mushrooms, and pine cones full of pignon nuts. And after a rainfall we would collect snails, wild pink cloves, and genista, whose stems we could suck like candy.

There were lazy afternoons when we would sip orange wine under the fig tree, where all around us would be the scent of lavender, jasmine, and honeysuckle—mingling with the fragrance of fruits that would later be made into preserves—and the endless buzzing of cicadas and bees.

On festive days—a carnival, a visit from a relative, a saint's day—our house was filled with special excitement. Feathers of hens and ducks would fly in all directions; large fish filled with stalks of dried fennel would rest under a layer of lettuce leaves; large platters of seaweed and crushed ice would be piled high with mussels, clams, sea urchins; fruits would be left to marinate in large bowls of rum and sugar; and fresh pasta would be drying on sheets of linen spread on beds, chairs, and tables.

All year long there were special reasons for these ban-

quets. For example, from spring to late summer each village around Nice and each district of the city would celebrate a local saint. These *festins* lasted three days and took place on village squares shaded by large plane, palm, or eucalyptus trees. They were both family and communal affairs. Two days before the *festin*, the kitchens would begin to hum like hives. Walking through the narrow streets, you could actually hear the "chop chop" of Swiss chard being minced for *tourte de blettes*, the pounding of garlic for *aïoli*, and the grating of dry bread to sprinkle on the *farcis*. Traditionally, each housewife had to prepare six big *tourtes* each filled with greens, onions, squash, apricots, walnuts, or honey. The women also made *ravioli* stuffed with beef stew and spinach; *civets* of rabbit simmered in red wine and blood; roast baby goat; and huge platters of *farcis* made with vegetables cooked the same morning they were picked. An invigorating *mesclun* salad was gathered and brought by guests from the neighboring villages.

During the three days, parades, traditional masses, and folk dances alternated with banquets until the last day, when a huge *aïoli—l'aïoli monstre*—was served on the village square and shared by the whole community. And lingering in the houses was the delicious smell of orange rind, garlic, white grapes drying on the beams above, ripe figs on screen trays, and quince preserve simmering on the back of the stove.

Modern life has swept over the Comté de Nice, but things have not changed very much. The dance music is mostly rock now and blue jeans the costume, but the character of the food and ambience has resisted the general leveling of the times.

All this, which is the spirit and heart of this book, evokes not only Nice but all the rest of the South of France. Although Niçois cooking is distinctive in many respects—an almost Oriental way of cooking vegetables in oil, a peculiar mixture of sweet and salty (spinach with raisins, sweet onions with anchovies, carrots with garlic, chicken baked with figs, and so on)—it is inextricably tied to the techniques, ingredient requirements, and esthetics of Provençal cooking. Since I remember and grew to love several Provençal dishes commonly served in Nice, I have included recipes for them as well as for strictly Niçois dishes.

A quick sketch of the character and history of the South of France may help to highlight the eclectic origins of the region's cuisine.

Much has been written about the varied beauty of Provence, and rightly so. There is true kinship between the land and its people, and nothing illustrates this better than its cuisine. It is a resourceful peasant cuisine (though refined by centuries of practice), with powerful basic ingredients— olive oil, garlic, anchovies, and aromatic herbs—to enhance the flavor of fresh vegetables and simple cuts of meat.

The northern Provence of Giono, Cézanne, and Pagnol is ascetic, dry, and secretive. Its olive trees, cypresses, fields of lavender, and rocky hilltops are swept by the mistral. Nevertheless, it is full of unexpected treasures: truffles under the dwarf oak trees, juniper berries, hills of rosemary and thyme. It has deep gorges, woods of chestnut trees, and little villages perched on top of steep hills: Gattières, Châteauneuf, Cabris, Gourdon. Most of the rather dry and highly flavored dishes, such as *aïgo bouido, crespeou, capoun, caillettes, tourte au miel et aux noix,* and *nougats,* come from this region.

To the south is the lush, fertile Provence of Renoir, Matisse, and Picasso. It is well irrigated and offers an abundance of fruits and vegetables. This is where *tian de légumes, artichauts à la barigoule, troucha, salade niçoise* were born.

Finally, along the *côte* there is an explosion of luxuriant vegetation and colors: eucalyptus, mimosa, palm, and orange trees, and roses and jasmine. From Marseilles to Nice to Monte Carlo there are lovely pastel houses, flowered terraces, and brilliant markets. Each town and region varies in history, ambience, and cuisine, and each dish is part of the region's heritage. Yet every village and every cook has a variation on such classics as *bouillabaisse, ravioli,* or *ratatouille.*

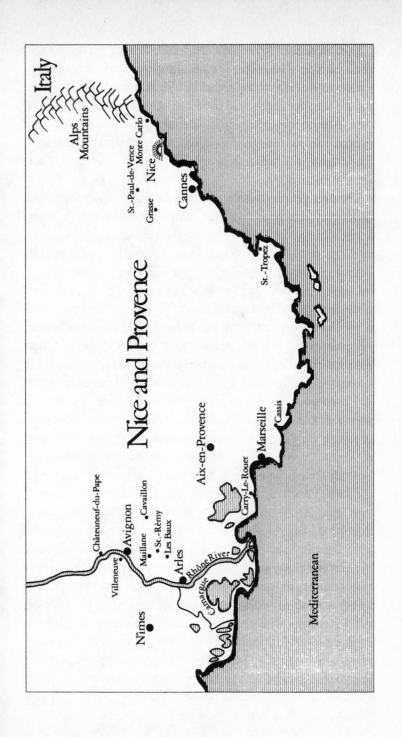

Nice and Provence

Italy

Alps Mountains

St.-Paul-de-Vence
Monte Carlo
Grasse
Nice
Cannes

St.-Tropez

Châteuneuf-du-Pape
Avignon
Cavaillon
Villeneuve
Maillane
St.-Rémy
Les Baux
Arles
Rhône River
Nîmes
Camargue
Carry-Le-Rouet
Aix-en-Provence
Marseille
Cassis

Mediterranean

Provence and Nice have had an extraordinarily tumultuous history. Marseilles was founded by Greek settlers, but it was the Romans who settled the Provincia Romana which was to become Provence. With its deep harbors, its Rhone river, Alpine mountains and Mediterranean shores, the area resisted the successive invasions of barbarians, Arabs, and Franks until the sixteenth century, when it was securely annexed to France.

Though geographically close to Provence, Nice itself has a history that to a large degree is all its own. Like Marseilles, it was founded by Greek settlers and remained a Greek port until the first century, when the Romans formed the province of Alpes-Maritimes and made Nice its capital. During the next centuries the province was swept by barbarian tribes, and then by the Franks and Saracens. In the middle of the twelfth century Nice became a *ville de consulat* and was governed by four consuls, each of whom represented one class of society: a nobleman, a merchant, an artisan, and a peasant. This form of government worked successfully for six hundred years. At the end of the eighteenth century the people of Nice, who had placed themselves under the protection of the Count of Provence, decided to join the House of Savoy. Both François I and Louis XIV attacked repeatedly, but it was not until 1792 that Nice became part of France. In 1814, however, when Napoleon was defeated, Nice again fell under the rule of the House of Savoy. Finally, in 1860, the population voted unanimously to once again become part of France, and it has been so ever since.

That Nice has assimilated its many foreign influences is evident in its cuisine. Settlers, invaders, and tourists all introduced new tastes, techniques, and ingredients. The olive oil and wine came with the Phoenicians. The pasta and ravioli (originally of Chinese origin) came to Nice via Italy. The imaginative use of dried cod was probably inspired by the Portuguese. Stockfish was brought by the Norwegians, and couscous came from the Arabs' former North African colonies.

For the past ten years I have successfully adapted this Southern French cuisine to my American kitchen. I have at times improvised and altered recipes to combine the essence of Niçois and Provençal cooking with what is appealing and practical for the American cook.

The recipes in this book use a wide variety of fresh vegetables, fruits, herbs, seafood, and reasonably priced meat, almost all of which are easily available in the average well-stocked market. Every week the vigilant buyer can find at least two or three perfectly crisp vegetables and as many interesting cuts of meat. To supplement these, I have included a section on mail order stores from which you can obtain quantities of high-quality, relatively inexpensive basic ingredients, such as anchovies, nuts, and spices.

The relaxed nature of Provençal and Niçois cuisine fits nicely with the exuberant, open way in which Americans like to live. The brilliant assortment of flavors and treats can be quickly prepared with imagination and taste. Many of these recipes are perfect for quick yet stylish luncheons and picnics. A number of them can be served as buffet dishes or eaten al fresco with the fingers.

Each recipe is designed for six people, but be generous with your proportions, since many of the dishes are even better served cold or reheated the next day. As you will be happy to discover, several soups, hors d'oeuvres, stews, and gratins are based on a lunch or a dinner served the day before—for example, *boeuf mironton, ravioli, salade de riz, capoun*. As a result, this is an extremely economical way to cook. Also, it is exceptionally healthy. The recipes contain little or no butter, cream, or flour. Instead, the cuisine draws all its strength from the best of natural ingredients and the verve with which they are prepared.

I hope you will come to make these recipes your own and to look upon them as confidences and delights shared with generations of lean, lively Niçois and Provençals who long ago understood that what they enjoy also happens to be what is good for them.

Ingredients

All serious cooks consider their trip to the market the most delicate and decisive part of their culinary preparation. In Niçois and Provençal cooking, the success of a meal depends on the quality of its basic ingredients. In Provence, the shops and open-air markets are places of wonder. All the sinuous narrow streets in Provençal towns lead to the marketplace, which has a fountain in the center, a few benches, and some big plane trees all around it. In the afternoon children run about and adults play *pétanque* or sip *pastis,* but in the morning the whole square is the setting for the market. There are pyramids of fruit and vegetables, bunches of flowers standing in wide pails, dozens of goat's cheese, piles of breads, *bannettes, boules, fougasses.* Here the peasants have brought the small fruits of their labors: a few pounds of green vegetables picked a few hours ago, a basket of figs, a bowl of fresh eggs, a bundle of wild asparagus that were gathered between the olive trees, a couple of rabbits and ducks killed the night before, some cured olives, baskets of snails—some gathered in the fields and fed on rosemary and fennel, some gathered on the salty grass of Camargue.

In Old Nice, shops are like Ali Baba's cave—dark and carefully protected from the flies and bees by strips of colored paper hung from the ceiling. They have large brown paper bags filled with pasta in strange shapes; cloth sacks of corn flour for *polente* and chickpea flour for *socca* are on the floor. On the counter are enormous glass jars of anchovies in rough salt for *bagna cauda* and bowls of *pili pili* (little red peppers) for *rouille* and *couscous*. Whole dried codfish are soaking in tanks of fresh running water, ready for *brandade*. And on the shelves there are bamboo boxes of candied fruits, blue bottles of orange blossom water and cans of olive oil adorned with piquant Niçoises wearing large straw capelines and holding branches of fluffy mimosa. Clusters of sausages, bloodwurst and country hams sway from large hooks. There is pig's caul to wrap *caillettes* and lean salt pork coated with coarsely ground black pepper and wrapped in cheesecloth. There are barrels filled with green, purple, and black olives.

The smells and colors of the French markets have a very special flavor, but I have found shopping in the United States as exciting and inspiring. All the recipes in this book are written from a decidedly American point of view. Basic ingredients are not expensive, and most of what Niçois and Provençal cooking requires can be found in supermarkets throughout the country. Try the two or three supermarkets in your neighborhood and locate the places where the vegetables are the freshest and the butcher is the most cooperative, where they have specials that are indeed special, where the lean salt pork is the leanest, where you can count on genuine Swiss cheese every week, and where there is good olive oil and Spanish saffron. When you go shopping you must always concentrate on the essentials: unbleached flour, meat, fish, fresh vegetables, fresh fruits, good imported Swiss cheese or Parmesan (some American-made Parmesan is very adequate for cooking), garlic, olive oil (Spanish, Italian or French). For authentic items you should explore the shops in Greek, Spanish, and Italian neighborhoods.

For the last ten years in America our confidence in our ability to choose healthy ingredients and in cooking them has been steadily shaken. We are often told children and husbands don't appreciate our efforts. We are told we waste time when we cook from scratch. We find that everything we buy is full of additives. We are offered all kinds of brightly wrapped, partially prepared "time-saving" frozen or dehydrated or processed foods and exotic mixes—convenience food to "liberate" the housewife while satisfying both taste and sight. In the supermarkets the music is so seductive, the display of "time savers" so attractive, that it becomes harder and harder to resist. Of course all these conveniences are very expensive, and of course they are neither nutritious nor very tasty. The excitement remains on the cover. So it is time to choose decisively and enjoy one's food again.

Think of shopping for food as a serious undertaking. You must look, smell, touch, compare, and carefully select all your ingredients. Take an early morning trip to the wholesale market and discover all the unusual foods available in your area, then encourage your butcher, fish market, and vegetable store to stock them for you; or write to the mail order places listed at the end of this book and let the postman deliver your treasures.

The following is a descriptive list of all the basic Niçois and Provençal ingredients, including spices and other flavorings.

Fonds de Cuisine*

Staples to Have in Your Kitchen at All Times

Anchovies–*les Anchois*

Anchovies are used a great deal in Nice—in *bagna cauda, poulet en saupiquet, gigot d'agneau, poisson à la chartreuse*. It's best to buy them packed in salt as sold in Greek, Italian, and Spanish markets; they keep well in the refrigerator. Before using the salt-packed variety, wash the fish thoroughly in cold running water. Cut along the back and pull out the bone; then remove the tail. If

* The stores listed at the end of the book will fill orders for items that are difficult for you to obtain otherwise.

you can't find this type of anchovy, use the kind packed in oil and drain well on paper towels.

Bouquet Garni

This is a small bundle of herbs wrapped in a piece of cheesecloth to enhance the seasoning of soups, stews, and the like. You can use 2 or 3 sprigs of parsley, a bay leaf, and a sprig of thyme (or ¼ teaspoon of dried thyme); for a tastier bouquet garni you may add a stalk of celery and a stalk of fennel. When the dish is ready, remove the bouquet garni.

Bread–*le Pain*

Stale bread, once a stand-by for the frugal housewife, is now a traditional ingredient of many dishes in one of several forms: bread crumbs, croutons, and *chapons*. Sometimes a slice is soaked in milk, which is squeezed out before the bread is used for a sauce or for stuffing. You can buy the so-called French or Italian bread, but home-baked bread is best. I prefer baking my own firm white bread with unbleached flour.

Bread Crumbs–*la Panure, la Chapelure*

Bread crumbs are sprinkled on *farcis* and *tians*. The ready-made kind is uniformly bad, so bread crumbs simply have to be home-made.

To make a supply, either grate a few slices of stale bread or crumble them into a blender and blend at high speed for a few seconds. They will keep for at least two or three days in a jar and for three weeks in the freezer. When kept longer, they will become moldy, but you can still use them if you remove the mold.

Chapons

These are strips (about 2 inches long, 1 inch wide) of stale bread crust rubbed with a clove of garlic. They are added to salads such as *salade mesclun* and *salade niçoise*.

Cheese–*le Fromage*

The traditional accompaniment for soups, *tians,* and pasta in Nice was cheese made from goat's or sheep's milk. Nowadays Swiss or Parmesan cheese is used instead. Keep a large wedge of each, tightly enclosed in plastic wrap, in the refrigerator to grate at the last moment. Never buy "grated cheese"; it will add no flavor to your dish. Domestic Swiss or Parmesan available in the supermarket is perfectly acceptable, but you may choose to buy the imported at a specialty shop.

Ingredients

Soft cheeses, such as Caillé (fresh goat's cheese which is sprinkled with olive oil and can be kept for weeks) or Brous (curdled cheese sprinkled with chopped garlic, pepper, and brandy and kept in a closed jar), have no equivalent here. But I often buy ricotta in the supermarket, although it is made with pasteurized cow's milk and not raw ewe's. I sprinkle it with orange blossom water and sugar and serve it as a light dessert—served this way, it is very close to the Brousse du Roves.

Chickpeas–*les Pois Chiches*
Italian, Spanish, and Greek markets sell them dried. You boil them with a bouquet garni and a few vegetables and then use them in soups, salads, hors d'oeuvres. But most supermarkets sell them canned, which are infinitely quicker to prepare, although a little less firm and tasty.

Chickpea Flour–*la Farine de Pois Chiches*
It is sold in the ethnic markets and by mail order. We make *socca* with it, as well as *panisses* and soups.

Couscous
This crushed grain is available in most health food stores, the gourmet section of supermarkets, and by mail order.

Corn Meal–*la Farine de Maïs*
We make *polente* with it. Every supermarket has corn meal; buy the stoneground kind if possible.

Croutons–*les Croûtons*
We use them as a garnish for *brandade* or *poulet en saupiquet,* with *anchoïade,* and with soups. To make them, cut slices of good, firm homemade bread in cubes or triangles and place in a 350° oven for 4 minutes. Turn them over, sprinkle with a little olive oil, and bake 3 more minutes.

Dried Cod–*la Morue Sèche*
Dried cod can be kept in a dry corner of your kitchen or in the freezer. It is sold in three forms. The dried whole fish (bone, skin, and tail) requires about two days of soaking in cold water, with the water changed several times a day. Dried filleted cod, often sold in pound packages, requires an overnight soaking and four changes of water. Frozen fillets will require only about four hours' soaking with four changes of water.

Always ask your fish dealer how long his particular dried codfish should soak and follow his instructions. Most fish markets sell it, but for the tastier, drier kind you will probably have to go to Italian, Spanish, or Greek markets. Buy a great amount, since so many of Nice's light, tasty, inexpensive dishes can be made from it—*estockaficada, morue en raïto, aïoli,* and so on. The Chinese *tai tze* salt cod is very dry and perfect for *estockaficada.*

Flour–*la Farine*
Always use unbleached flour, available in most supermarkets or by mail order.

Garlic–*l'Ail*
Since we need great quantities of garlic in *aïoli, agneau à l' aillaide, oeufs à l'ail,* we buy it in a wreath and hang it in a dry place in the kitchen. Red garlic (usually from Mexico) is tastier and stronger than the white. All supermarkets carry some garlic in the vegetable department. Remember that a garlic clove cooked whole is much less strong than a minced or crushed one.

Gherkins–*les Cornichons*
Used in hors d'oeuvres, with *boeuf mironton* and in various sauces, they can be bought in gourmet and specialty stores. They are easy to make at home. Choose very small (about 2-inch long) cucumbers, all roughly the same size. Wash and dry carefully and place them in a bowl. Sprinkle with salt and let stand for twenty-four hours, tossing them from time to time. Place them in a jar with a few pearl onions, a few cloves, a garlic clove, and a sprig of tarragon. Boil enough white vinegar to cover them and pour it over the vegetables. Let stand overnight. In the morning pour the vinegar into a pan and boil it again. Let the vegetables soak in it a second night. Repeat the boiling and soaking. The fourth day the gherkins are ready to use. Keep in a closed jar.

Lean Salt Pork–*le Petit Salé*
Sautéing in salt pork is the essential first step in making stews and fish dishes, such as *loup farci.* Always choose the leanest and keep a large piece in the refrigerator. Most supermarkets and all pork butchers sell good salt pork. Try to find some that is free of nitrate and nitrite.

Nuts–*les Noix; les Noisettes; les Pignons; les Amandes*
Walnuts are used for sauces (*sauce aux noix,* for example), or cookies (*les petits biscuits aux noix*). Pine nuts, often labeled "pignole" here, are used in *tourte de blettes* and are cooked with spinach. Almonds are used in ice cream and cookies such as *soupirs aux amandes.* French bitter almonds are not sold in the

Ingredients

United States, so I add some almond extract for the authentic flavor. Nuts can be purchased in every supermarket but are usually much cheaper and fresher bought by the pound in the ethnic markets. Always keep them frozen for freshness—they need no defrosting time.

Oil–*l'Huile*

I usually use half peanut oil and half olive oil for cooking or for mayonnaise and *aïoli,* since the olive oil is too potent. For salad dressing and seasoning, of course, I use only olive oil. There are delicate yellow olive oils and heavy, green, fruity ones. Many good brands of imported olive oil are sold here. Experiment, then buy your favorite by the gallon, which is proportionately cheaper. Keep in closed dark bottles. Refrigerate if you use it slowly. (See pp. 292–94 for description of oils, harvesting, and refining.)

Olives–*les Olives*

The little black or dark purple olives of Nice are sold only in specialty or gourmet shops. Use them unpitted. If you cannot find them, buy oil-cured black olives (available in Italian, Spanish, and Greek markets, delicatessens, and many supermarkets) and pit these, using an olive-pitter (*dénoyauteur*).

Orange Blossom Water–*l'Eau de Fleur d'Orangers*

This flavoring is used in desserts (*glace à la fleur d'orangers*), with vegetables (*épinards aux pignons*), or with fresh ricotta cheese. It is available here in dark blue bottles in specialty stores and some "apothecaries" (because it is supposed to put angry babies to sleep) and through mail order.

Parmesan Cheese

Freshly grated Parmesan is sprinkled on *soupe au pistou, soupe de pêcheurs, pâtes aux oeufs, farcis,* and numerous other dishes. Grate the cheese finely at the last minute so it is light and fresh. Never use the commercial grated Parmesan, which is dry and either tasteless or sour.

Pepper–*le Poivre*

White pepper made from the ripe berries of the pepper plant has a little stronger flavor than the black, which is made from the dried under-ripe berries. But the major difference is color—add white pepper to dishes that should have a pale color and black to others. Peppercorns are sometimes added to a simmering liquid and then removed when the dish is done. For sprinkling, always use peppercorns to make freshly ground pepper.

Pork Caul, or Lace Fat–*la Crépine*

This thin fatty membrane is sold by the pound in German, Italian, Chinese, and Spanish butcher shops. If you cannot find it, substitute thin slices of bacon. We use it for *caillettes* and to cover *terrines*.

Salt–*le Sel*

Kosher salt is coarse and tasty; I use it with *pot-au-feu* and also in cooking. *Sel gros* is excellent for cooking and is available at some shops, but it tends to be expensive. Since the amount of salt used depends on individual preference, I recommend tasting each dish at least twice to check the seasoning adequately.

Swiss Cheese–*le Gruyère*

The domestic brand sold in all supermarkets is very good. Grate it fresh and sprinkle on soups, pasta, and stews. Always keep a large piece, tightly wrapped, in the refrigerator.

Vermouth

The dry white vermouth made in the United States is good in sauces. The red sweet vermouth is acceptable for *raïto* sauces. Take a sip of your vermouth before using, since cooking intensifies its flavor—whether good or bad.

Vinegar–*le Vinaigre*

Whether red or white, wine vinegar is available everywhere. Find one you like and keep a few bottles on hand. Or else make your own.

Wine–*le Vin*

I use California red Burgundy to make stews, and either a dry white wine or a dry white vermouth for fish, lamb, or chicken sauces. Always taste before using it and keep a few bottles of your favorite wines in your kitchen for cooking.

Les Épices et les Aromates

Spices and Flavorings

Anise Seed–*les Graines d'Anis*

Anise has a flavor somewhat like that of licorice. The seeds are used in pastry (*biscuits à l'anis*), with fish (*loup farci à la niçoise*), and with pork.

Basil–*le Basilic*

Although there are some sixty kinds of basil, the two most common in the United States are those with small leaves having a strong peppery flavor and those with large leaves that are milder. Basil is easy to grow and can be frozen (in a plastic bag). You can make a purée of it with olive oil and grated cheese in a blender. This will keep for a month in the refrigerator covered with a little olive oil or it can be frozen. Add fresh crushed garlic to the purée at the time of using (garlic acquires an unpleasant taste when frozen). Basil goes well with eggplant (*caviar provençale*), pasta (*pâtes au pistou*), tomatoes (*salade niçoise*), and soup (*soupe au pistou*). It is an excellent garnish and can be mixed with fresh mint before sprinkling on vegetables. Basil finely chopped with anchovies is delicious on raw tomatoes, hard-boiled eggs, and grilled fish.

Bay Leaf–*le Laurier*

The California bay leaf is stronger than the French one but very good. Use it in stews (*daube Avignon, ratatouille*), soup (*aïgo bouido*), fish (*gigot de mer*), and rice (*riz aux herbes*).

Capers–*les Câpres*

Capers are the buds of the caper bush. They are kept in vinegar or salt and used in hors d'oeuvres, with meat (*boeuf mironton, porc à la sauge et aux câpres*), and sauces (*sauce piquante*).

Cayenne Pepper

This strong red pepper is used in sauces (*rouille, couscous* sauce), and fish dishes.

Chives–*la Ciboulette*

We use the narrow, long leaves, finely chopped, in omelets (*troucha*), with pasta (*pâtes à la verdure*), and vegetables (*févettes à la laitue*).

Ingredients

Cloves–*le Clou de Girofle*

We stick one clove in a large onion, sauté the onion on all sides and add it to *pot-au-feu* or chickpea soup to give color and flavor. Cloves also flavor *boeuf à la niçoise*.

Coriander–*la Coriandre*

The round seeds of coriander look like peppercorns. This spice must be used with discretion because it is powerful. It is used in marinades and with pork, and is a must in hot sauce for *couscous*.

Cumin Seed–*le Cumin*

Quite a powerful spice, delicious with *capoun* and in *couscous*.

Curry Powder–*le Curry*

Used in *poulpes provençales* or *merlan aux moules*. Can be made at home by blending coriander, cumin, fennel seeds with cloves, cinnamon, mustard, ginger, and ground nuts.

Fennel–*le Fenouil*

This is a marvelous, savory herb. The dried stalks of wild fennel are used to stuff broiled fish or to make a bed for cooking fish. They are used in soups (*soupe de pêcheurs, bourride, bouillabaisse*), in court bouillon, in pork dishes (*rôti de porc provençale*), and with snails (*escargots provençale*). However, it is quite difficult to find dried fennel stalks here, so I use fresh fennel (found in some supermarkets and in Italian or Spanish markets) or even dried fennel seeds. The taste and smell of lamb or fish barbecued over fennel or rosemary twigs are glorious. If you cannot find such twigs, sprinkle the meat with dried rosemary leaves and fennel seeds about an hour before broiling.

Juniper–*le Genièvre*

These little black berries are used to stuff birds (as in *chacha au genièvre*), to marinate game, and to flavor *pot-au-feu provençale* and some *pâtés*. Juniper jelly is delicious on toast or mixed with a light herb tea instead of honey.

Melissa–*la Mélisse*

This unusual mint makes a delicious cordial, *l'eau des Carmes,* and a tea which is supposed to cure indigestion.

Mint–*la Menthe*

This is used chopped in *salade niçoise* (with or instead of fresh basil), *brochettes de Nice,* and *pâtes à la verdure*. It is lovely as a garnish for *glace à la fleur d'orangers* or *tian de rhum,* or

Ingredients

sprinkled on fruit salads. Brewed as a tea, it is supposed to re-kindle an honest man's passion and a pretty woman's vigor!

Nutmeg–*les Noix de Muscade*

Buy whole nutmeg and grate what you need at the last moment with a sharp knife. Use in *gnocchis,* with vegetables (*papeton d'aubergines*), seafood and fish (*moules aux épinards, brandade*), and meat (*boeuf mironton*).

Orange Rind–*le Zeste d'Orange*

Use a potato peeler to pare only the thin orange-colored rind and hang it in your kitchen to dry. (It's an essential in a well-stocked Niçois kitchen.) Use it in meat dishes (*boeuf à la niçoise, daube d'Avignon, estouffade, gardiane*) or in soups (*soupe de pêcheurs, bouillabaisse*).

Parsley–*le Persil*

This is the most commonly used of all herbs. Italian parsley, flat-leaved, is the most savory and will keep in a plastic bag in the refrigerator. Because parsley is rich in vitamins A and C, which heat destroys, add it, finely minced, at the last minute. Try to grow it (you might have a hanging basket in the kitchen), since there is constant use for it—sprinkled on black olives, in omelets, in sauces, and in most meat and fish dishes. Always chop it as finely as possible with a *hachoir* (see Techniques and Tools, p. 21) so that it is almost a paste.

Rosemary–*le Romarin*

This is a very strong herb, so use it cautiously. I enjoy cracking the dried needle-like leaves between my teeth, but if you do not, wrap them in a piece of cheesecloth to remove after cooking. Rosemary is used with lamb (*daube d'Avignon, brochettes de Nice, agneau à la niçoise*), soup (*bouillabaisse*), and fowl (*poulet en gelée*).

Techniques and Tools

There are seven ways of cooking: boiling, roasting, broiling, sautéing, frying, stewing, and braising (which means cooking in a closed pan with less liquid than when stewing). So one can endlessly seek utensils to help one master each method. With the proliferation of shops offering intriguing items, one can collect equipment forever. But so far as traditional Provençal cooking is concerned, it requires no more than four pans: an earthenware *poêlon,* which has a handle; a *poêle,* or frying pan; a *fait-tout,* a deep casserole made of cast iron, copper, or earthenware, which can be tightly closed; and a *tian* for gratin dishes.

There are basically only two techniques in Southern French cuisine: one is sautéing in oil; the other is simmering over a low flame. The first is quick and decisive—meat or vegetables are quickly seared over high heat in order to seal in the juices and therefore the natural flavor. The second method involves slow cooking, which tenderizes the meat and vegetables as they simmer in liquid in a covered pot or pan.

In addition, there are special techniques that I mention elsewhere in the book, such as making pasta, preserves, and so on; I have chosen to describe these in connection with specific recipes.

The equipment to prepare my repertory of dishes is not very extensive. I have a plain functional kitchen which looks and feels like a kitchen. It is honest and practical. My herbs are in glass jars and I never keep them more than a year.

Sugar, flour, and rice are in big Pyrex containers on an easy-to-reach shelf above the working counter. I keep vegetables and fruits in wide baskets. The grater, sieve, kitchen shears, Mouli food mill, and wire whisk hang on pegs on the wall. The mortar and pestle are within easy reach. I have an assortment of pretty baskets in which I serve *beignets,* fresh fruits, fried whitebait. I have cheerful earthenware and bright paper napkins for *socca, beignets,* snails. I serve wine in glass pitchers, water in earthenware pitchers, and oil and vinegar in individual glass cruets.

The following is a list of the basic equipment in my kitchen—equipment that I use constantly in preparing Niçois and Provençal dishes.

Casserole–*la Cocotte, le Fait-Tout*
The best of the cast-iron casseroles is the *Doufeu* (which means gentle fire). It comes either round or oval and is sold almost everywhere in the United States. It has a recessed cover, which I fill with water so that the stew bastes itself as it cooks. The evenly distributed heat makes it perfect for *boeuf à la niçoise, daube d'Avignon,* and *ratatouille.*

Cheesecloth–*la Mousseline*
Used to line a sieve before straining soups or sauces.

Chopping Board–*la Planche à Hacher*
Narrow board with a handle (with a hole so that it can be hung in a convenient spot). I use it not only for chopping vegetables and meat but also as an aid in slicing such foods as terrines so that each slice remains firm and intact—I hold the board perpendicular to the terrine resting on a platter or another board and press it against the terrine as I cut each slice.

Colander–*le Passoire*
The three-legged stand makes this convenient for draining pasta and vegetables.

Conical Sieve–*le Chinois*
Made of strong aluminum mesh so you can purée food by pushing it through with a spoon or pestle.

Double Boiler with a Steamer–*la Couscoussière*

This is primarily used to prepare couscous but is also useful for reheating meat or fish and to cook fragile vegetables, such as asparagus. The top part is perforated.

Frying Pan–*la Poêle à Frire*

I use this wide pan only for frying and clean it with paper towels and rough salt. Aluminum or stainless steel pans are the best.

Gratin Dish–*Tian*

A somewhat shallow oval or square ovenproof dish made of earthenware, china, or Pyrex.

Garlic Press–*le Presse Ail*

Made of aluminum. I use it to press garlic directly onto the dish I am preparing.

Kitchen Shears–*les Ciseaux*

Snipping with scissors is still the best way to cut chives, basil, squid, cooked chicken livers.

Mincer and Chopper–*le Hachoir*

Curved stainless steel blade with two wooden handles. Perfect for mincing parsley, garlic, and onion, it is also useful for chopping meat, salt pork, etc.

Mortar and Pestle–*le Mortier*

The traditional marble mortar with four round ears and its big wooden pestle are so expensive in the United States that I would advise the purchase of the widely available vitrified porcelain mortar and its matching porcelain pestle.

Mouli Food Mill–*la Moulinette*

This wonderful machine has three interchangeable discs and is indispensable for making purées, sauces, and soups. It gives more texture than the blender, and it can retain such rough parts of food as fruit seed and fish skin.

Pepper Mill–*le Moulin à Poivre*

Used to grind fresh peppercorns on dishes in preparation and also on food at the table.

Rotary Grater–*le Mouli-Fromage*

Has three cylinders for grating cheese, nuts, and chocolate.

Techniques
and Tools

Salad Maker–*le Mouli-Julienne*
Has five steel discs, which grate, shred, and slice all vegetables and even chocolate.

Salad Bowl–*le Saladier*
The bowl should be of china or glass, not wood (garlic, vinegar, and olive oil have lasting flavors that would cling to wood). Glass is best because it gives the most appetizing effect. To evenly distribute the dressing I gently toss the greens with my hands.

Saucepan–*la Sauteuse*
Made of copper, stainless steel, or aluminum; has low straight sides.

Skewers–*les Brochettes*
The best kind is flat, not round. Skewered pieces of meat or vegetable will not twirl or slip off if you use two flat skewers to secure each row of them.

Stockpot–*la Marmite*
The heavy aluminum kind is best. The pot is used to prepare *pot-au-feu, pâtes aux oeufs, ravioli niçoise,* and other similar dishes.

Tart Pan–*la Tourtière*
Used for *tourte aux noix et au miel* and *tourte de blettes.* It has a loose bottom for easy removal.

Terrine–*la Terrine*
This type of casserole is made of porcelain or eathenware. It has a lid that fits snugly and has a small hole that allows steam to escape. It is used with the lid for making *terrine de campagne* and without the lid for making *tians.*

Tongs–*les Pinces*
Used for turning over pieces of meat or fish as you sauté them.

Wooden Spoon–*la Cuillère en Bois*
The long handle is helpful in stirring food cooking on the stove.

Les Soupes

Soups

Provence and Nice offer an abundance of delicious soups. They are pungent and fresh, and depend on the bounty of each season. Some constitute a whole meal in themselves: *pot-au-feu provençale, soupe au pistou, bouillabaisse.* Some, such as *aïgo bouido,* are light and cleansing. Although the ingredients are varied, there are only two ways to start a Niçois or Provençal soup. Either you sauté the meat or vegetables in olive oil, then add the liquid (broth, wine, or water), or you put all the ingredients in boiling water to start with and then cook them together slowly over low heat.

Pistou is the only soup we eat cold as well as hot; all other soups are served hot. Most are served with croutons or freshly grated Swiss or Parmesan cheese and garnished with fresh herbs.

There are four types of soups:
—**Les soupes maigres** (or *potages de santé*), made with combinations of beans, zucchini, potatoes, squash, tomatoes, chickpeas, spinach, sage, or garlic. Examples: *aïgo bouido, soupe de courges, soupe au pistou.*
—**Les soupes grasses,** made with meat and bones. *Pot-au-feu* is the classic example.
—**Les soupes au bâton** (so called because they were stirred with a stick), made with chestnut or chickpea flour. *Fournade* is an example.
—**Les soupes de poissons,** made with fish or shellfish. Examples: *soupe de pêcheurs, bouillabaisse, bourride, soupe de moules.*

Always make these soups in generous quantities. They will keep two or three days in the refrigerator and some will freeze well. In any case, you will find them to be more than "something to take the chill out of your children."

Aïgo Bouido
Herb and Garlic Broth

This light and pungent soup is full of virtues. It is even said that *"Aïgo bouido sauva la vido"*—*Aïgo bouido* will save your life. It is the perfect soup to serve the day after a rich meal. For a more substantial version, you may add cheese, vermicelli, or even egg yolks.

For 6 people:

5 *cups water*
6 *whole garlic cloves, peeled*
2 *2-inch pieces dried orange rind*
2 *bay leaves*
5 *fresh sage leaves, or ½ teaspoon dried sage*
2 *sprigs thyme, or 1 teaspoon dried thyme*
4 *ounces vermicelli (optional)*
  salt
  freshly ground pepper
1 *tablespoon olive oil*

Heat the water in a large pot until it boils. Add the garlic, orange rind, bay leaves, sage, and thyme, and boil for 20 minutes.* Strain through a sieve.

Add the vermicelli if you wish, and cook it until it is soft—about 5 minutes. Turn off the flame. Add the salt, pepper, and olive oil.

Variation:
If you want a richer soup, beat 4 egg yolks and pour in a little of the hot soup to warm them before adding them to the pot. Stir in ½ cup grated cheese and serve at once.

* The broth may be prepared in a slightly different way: Sauté garlic cloves in hot olive oil for 3 minutes; add the water, herbs, and spices and, 10 minutes later, the vermicelli, and then cook for 5 more minutes.

Bourride

A Creamy Garlic Fish Soup

This unctuous, savory cream soup is a tradition in the South, from Marseilles to Monaco. Since either whiting and bass or cod are available year round in the United States, you may serve this soup in any season.

The chunks of fish are removed from the soup and served separately. I like to serve the fish as a second course after the soup, but most Niçois prefer having everything arrive on the table at the same time. Choose a bright crockery dish, since both the soup and the fish have a pale color.

For 8 people (you must make this recipe for at least that many):

4½ pounds of three different fish in any
  proportions (choose among striped
  bass, ocean perch, whiting, pollack,
  haddock, cod, flounder, halibut)
  1 whole leek, chopped
  1 large onion, chopped
  1 carrot, chopped
  2 tablespoons olive oil
1½ cups dry white wine
1½ cups water
  3 2-inch pieces of orange rind
  1 teaspoon dried fennel or anise
  1 teaspoon thyme
  2 bay leaves
    salt
    freshly ground white pepper
  3 slices good white bread for making
    Croutons (p. 12)
  5 egg yolks
  2 cups Aïoli (p. 75)
    sprigs of parsley

Fillet the fish (do not discard the heads and bones) or ask to have this done at the fish market. Stew the leek, onion, and carrot in the olive oil for about 15 minutes, or until they are soft. Add the fish heads and bones only, then the wine, water (more if necessary),

Soups

25

orange rind, fennel or anise, thyme, and bay leaves. Bring to a boil and skim off the froth. Simmer uncovered for 30 minutes. Strain into a pot, pushing as much of the bits of fish through as possible.

Cut the fish fillets into 2-inch-square pieces. Bring the soup stock to a boil, reduce to a simmer, and put in the heavier pieces of fish first, adding the lighter, more delicate ones later. The whole cooking time should be about 6 minutes for the entire batch.

Meanwhile, warm a platter in the oven, set at 200°. Place the fillets on the platter and pour a ladleful of warm broth over them. Seal with aluminum foil and keep the fish warm in the oven. Reserve the soup.

Prepare *aïoli* sauce. Put 8 tablespoons of this in a bowl and slowly add the egg yolks, stirring gently. Refrigerate the rest of the *aïoli* to use later. Prepare the croutons.

Reheat the stock over a low flame. Beat half of it very slowly into the *aïoli*-egg mixture with a wooden spoon, then pour this mixture back into the rest of the soup (be sure the flame is low or the soup will curdle). Keep stirring and cook until the soup has thickened enough to coat a spoon as with custard. When the soup has been reduced to a velvety texture, ladle it onto the croutons and serve as a first course.

As a following course, remove the foil from the platter of fish, garnish with parsley and serve with the bowl of chilled *aïoli*.

Variation:
Serve the soup over both the fillets of fish and the croutons, and pass the bowl of *aïoli* separately.

Soupe de Carottes
A Delicate Carrot Soup

This light and refreshing soup is easy to prepare in any season. If you use big winter carrots, add a lump of sugar during cooking.

For 6 people:

> *1 quart water*
> *salt*
> *1 bay leaf*
> *4 large or medium-sized carrots*
> *1 large potato*

>   *1 large onion*
>   *freshly ground black pepper*
>   *1 tablespoon olive oil*
>   *1 tablespoon chopped parsley (optional)*
>   *2 slices firm white bread for making*
>   *Croutons (p. 12), optional*

Bring water to a boil and add salt and bay leaf. Peel and slice the vegetables, then add them to the boiling water and simmer for 15 minutes. Pass through a Mouli food mill into a saucepan. Add salt and pepper (and sugar if desired), and check the seasoning.

Heat for 3 minutes. Sprinkle with olive oil and serve.

You may serve the soup on croutons and sprinkle it with parsley at the last minute to add color, but I like the very simple, un-adorned version.

Soupe de Courges

Zucchini or Pumpkin Soup

This is a light, delicious soup, whether it is made with zucchini in the spring or pumpkin in the fall. Select very crisp vegetables, since the flavor of the soup depends on the freshness of the ingredients. Pumpkin is sweeter and thicker than zucchini, so you will need more salt, pepper, and water for pumpkin soup.

For 6 people:

>   *10 zucchini or a 3-pound pumpkin, diced*
>   *2 tablespoons olive oil*
>   *4 large onions, chopped*
>   *1 garlic clove, peeled*
>   *1 cup cooked rice (4 tablespoons, raw)*
>   *1 teaspoon sage*
>   *2 to 4 teaspoons salt*
>   *1 to 1½ teaspoons freshly ground black*
>   *pepper*
>   *3 to 4 cups water*
>   *1 tablespoon raw olive oil*
>   *½ cup cheese, freshly grated*
>   *2 tablespoons chopped fresh mint leaves*
>   *or parsley*

Peel and dice the zucchini or pumpkin (discard seeds). Heat the olive oil in a cast-iron pan, add the onions and cook them until they are transparent—about 5 minutes. Add the zucchini or pumpkin and the garlic clove. Cook for 30 minutes more.

Add the rice, sage, salt, and pepper. Pass the mixture through a Mouli food mill. Add enough water for the consistency you like and check the seasoning.

Serve piping hot after adding a dash of olive oil and a garnish of cheese and mint or parsley.

Fournade

A Creamy Chickpea Soup

This is one of the simplest and most economical soups you can ever make. You can prepare it at the last minute. It is rather thick and should be stirred with a wooden spoon while cooking (in the mountains this kind of soup was called *soupe au bâton*). A great treat for children.

> For 6 people:
>
> 2 *cups chickpea flour*
> 2 *quarts water*
> *salt*
> *freshly ground white pepper*
> 2 *bay leaves*
> 1 *clove, or a pinch of ground cloves*
> *a pinch of freshly ground coriander*
> 4 *tablespoons olive oil*

Combine the chickpea flour and water in a large bowl, and beat with an egg beater until the mixture is fairly smooth. Pour into a saucepan and heat over medium flame. Add salt, pepper, bay leaves, clove, coriander, and 2 tablespoons of the olive oil. Simmer, gently stirring, for about 10 minutes. The soup will quickly thicken. Add more water if you wish. Check the seasoning and add the remaining olive oil just before serving. This soup reheats well.

Soupe de Lentilles

Lentil Soup

This is a hearty soup, perfect for a cold winter night. It seems to improve with each reheating, so make a good amount of it.

For 6 people:

1½ cups raw lentils
2 tablespoons olive oil
1 onion, chopped
1 tomato, peeled and quartered, or ⅓ cup drained canned tomatoes
2 carrots, chopped
2 garlic cloves, peeled and crushed
1 teaspoon dried thyme
2 bay leaves
salt
freshly ground black pepper
4 cups water
3 slices good white bread for making Croutons (p. 12)
1 tablespoon sherry

Wash the lentils in cold water and drain in a sieve. Heat the oil in a heavy pot and cook the chopped onion until soft. Add the tomato, carrots, garlic, thyme, bay leaves, salt, pepper, and lentils. Add water and bring to a boil. Cover and simmer 1 to 2 hours. Cooking time will depend on the size of the lentils (they should be tender but not mushy).

Prepare the croutons, cutting them into ½-inch cubes. Place them in each soup plate or at the bottom of the soup tureen. Remove the bay leaves from the soup, add sherry to it and pour over the croutons. Serve immediately.

Soupe de Moules

Mussel Soup

This light and delicately flavored soup is one of the quickest to prepare. Since mussels are available all year round in America, you may enjoy it often.

For 6 people:

> 6 *pounds mussels, preferably small*
> 4½ *cups water*
> 1 *tablespoon olive oil*
> 1 *garlic clove, unpeeled*
> 1 *large onion, minced*
> 1 *bouquet garni (p. 11)*
> *salt*
> *freshly ground white pepper*
> ½ *teaspoon saffron*
> 1 *cup fine vermicelli*

Scrub the mussels thoroughly with a wire brush. Remove the beard with your fingers and place the mussels in a large bowl of cold water. Wait 2 minutes, then discard all the mussels that are open—they are not fresh.

Boil ½ cup water in a heavy-bottomed pot and add the mussels. Cook them covered for 5 minutes, tossing from time to time with a slotted spoon. Turn off the flame. Place a piece of cheesecloth over a sieve and pour the mussel broth through it. Reserve the broth and the mussels.

Heat the olive oil in a large skillet. Crush the garlic clove with your fist on a board and add this, the onion, and the bouquet garni. Cook for 5 minutes. Add salt, pepper, and the mussel broth, and stir carefully for 5 more minutes. Add the saffron, crushing it between your fingers over the soup.

Pour this mixture into a soup kettle and add 4 cups of *hot* water (using some to rinse the skillet). Bring to a boil and add the vermicelli. Cook for another 15 minutes.

Check the seasoning and add the mussels just before serving.

Soupe de Petits Pois

Fresh Pea Soup

This is a refreshing hot-weather soup. Most supermarkets have a good supply of fresh peas, which are quite large by French standards but are often tender and tasty. Choose very fresh and smooth pea pods, because you will use the pods also for this soup.

For 6 people:

>   1½ pounds fresh peas
>   2 large onions
>   3 carrots
>   ⅓ cup lean salt pork
>   2 tablespoons peanut oil
>   bouquet garni (p. 11)
>   water to cover
>   a pinch of sugar
>   salt
>   freshly ground black pepper
>   1 tablespoon olive oil
>   3 slices firm white bread for making
>   Croutons (p. 12)

Wash the peas and shell them. Keep all the pods that are firm and green. Snap and pull each pod as you would tough celery fibers, and discard the transparent linings. Prepare the croutons, cutting them into triangles.

Peel and chop the onions, carrots, and salt pork. Heat the peanut oil in a cast-iron pan. Add the chopped ingredients, the bouquet garni, peas and pods. Cover with cold water and bring to a boil. Lower the flame and cook for 30 to 40 minutes. Add sugar and salt and pepper to taste.

Just before serving, remove the bouquet garni, add the olive oil, and garnish with the croutons.

Variation:

If you want a more elegant soup, pass it through a Mouli food mill to make a fragrant, velvety *crème de petits pois*. Garnish it with croutons, cut in cubes. Frozen peas are acceptable for this version of the soup.

Soups

31

Soupe au Pistou

Vegetable Soup Flavored with Basil Paste

Pistou refers to the paste consisting of crushed garlic, basil, cheese, and olive oil which is added to a dish just before serving. This soup is enjoyed in Italy as well as in the South of France. The best time to prepare it is summer or fall, when there is the greatest variety of fresh vegetables. However, since carrots, onions, turnips, cabbage, celery, dried white (Great Northern) beans, and potatoes are available all year round, you can alway make this soup if you keep *Pistou* (p. 86) in the freezer.

This is a wonderful soup—strong in flavor, yet very light. It can be served hot or cold with equal success.

For 6 people:

1 *pound white (Great Northern) beans,*
   fresh or dried
1/2 *pound fresh or frozen lima beans*
1/2 *pound green beans*
6 *potatoes*
5 *onions*
5 *carrots*
3 *pink turnips or 1 yellow turnip*
5 *zucchini*
1/2 *cup lean salt pork*
1 *leek*
1/2 *head green cabbage*
1/2 *bunch celery*
1 *tablespoon olive oil*
2 *quarts water*
2 *bay leaves*
   a pinch of sage
   salt
   fresh ground black pepper

If you use dried white beans, parboil them for 1/2 hour. Shell and blanch the lima beans if they are fresh. String the green beans or snap off both ends and cut into 1-inch pieces (put a handful at a time on a board and chop roughly with a large knife). Peel and dice the potatoes, onions, carrots, and turnips. Dice the zucchini (unpeeled) and the salt pork. Coarsely chop the leek, cabbage, and celery.

Heat the olive oil in a large heavy-bottomed pan. Add the onions and cook over a medium flame for 5 minutes, then add the salt pork, potatoes, leek, carrots, sage, and as much of the other vegetables as the pan will hold. Sauté for 5 more minutes.

Bring a large pot of water to a boil and add the contents of the pan, along with the rest of the vegetables, bay leaves, and salt and pepper. Simmer uncovered, for 40 minutes. Check the seasoning and continue cooking slowly for 1 hour more, or until the vegetables are just tender.

Pistou*

2 to 3 cups fresh basil, to taste
4 to 6 garlic cloves
1/2 to 1 cup Swiss, Parmesan, or Romano
    cheese
1/2 cup olive oil
 a pinch of kosher salt

While the soup is simmering, prepare the *pistou*. Rinse and dry the basil leaves, and shred them with kitchen shears. Peel and crush the garlic cloves. Grate the cheese.

Place the garlic, basil, and salt in a large mortar and pound vigorously with the pestle until you have a paste. Add the cheese, then the oil, stirring vigorously with the pestle until smooth. (A blender simplifies the process: Put in the basil, cheese, garlic, and olive oil and turn on high speed for a few seconds. Stop and stir with a spoon, then blend again. Do this two or three times until you have a smooth paste.)

Add the *pistou* to the soup a moment before serving and stir. You may want to serve the soup with a small bowl of grated Romano, Parmesan, or Swiss cheese.

*You can double the amount of garlic or double the whole recipe for the paste according to your taste. This recipe corresponds only to my own preferences.

Soupe de Pois Chiches à la Sauge

Chickpea and Sage Soup

This is a hearty winter soup. For this recipe I always use canned chickpeas. They taste as good as dried ones and are infinitely more convenient.

For 6 people:

2 *onions*
2 *carrots*
1 *tomato, fresh or canned*
1 *garlic clove*
5 *heads Boston or iceberg lettuce (Boston is preferable)*
4 *teaspoons olive oil*
salt
1 *teaspoon dried sage*
freshly ground black pepper
6 *cups water*
1 *16-ounce can chickpeas*
3 *slices firm white bread for making Croutons (p. 12)*

Chop the onions, carrots, and tomato; peel and crush the garlic clove. Rinse and *mince* the lettuce.

Heat 3 teaspoons of the olive oil in a cast-iron frying pan or enameled casserole dish. Add the onions and sprinkle with salt. Add the carrots, garlic, tomato, lettuce, sage, pepper, and water. Simmer for 25 minutes.

Drain and rinse the chickpeas under cold water, and add to the soup. Cook for 5 minutes, then pass the mixture through a Mouli food mill. Check the seasoning. Cut the bread into triangles and make croutons.

Just before serving, add 1 teaspoon of olive oil to the soup and stir. Pour over the croutons and serve immediately.

Soupe de Pêcheurs

A Rich Fish Soup

This great fish soup is the base for the renowned *bouillabaisse*, and is made of the cheapest possible ingredients: fish heads and bones. Those of striped bass, red snapper, or whiting will make the best soup, since they are not oily. Either use the head and bones left over from a broiled fish dinner or ask for them at your fish dealer's, where you might get them for nothing.

You can use this recipe as a base and add crabs, a whole firm fish, vermicelli, pasta or croutons, and cheese to make it more substantial. Serve it with a chilled dry white wine.

For 6 people:

1 *fish head (snapper or bass) or 2 whit-*
    ing heads
1 *or 2 fish backbones*
    salt
    freshly ground black pepper
1 *tablespoon flour*
2 *medium-sized potatoes*
2 *medium-sized onions*
7 *teaspoons olive oil*
2 *fresh tomatoes, quartered, or ⅔ cup*
    drained canned tomatoes
1 *teaspoon thyme*
3 *2-inch pieces orange rind*
1 *bay leaf*
1½ *quarts water or 3 cups water mixed*
    with 3 cups dry white wine
½ *teaspoon Spanish saffron (do not*
    use the powdered kind)
1 *garlic clove, peeled and crushed*
3 *slices good white bread for making*
    Croutons (p. 12)
½ *cup Parmesan or Swiss cheese, freshly*
    grated
½ *cup very thin vermicelli (optional)*

Rinse and dry the fish head and bones. Sprinkle them with salt, pepper, and flour and set aside. Peel and dice the potatoes. Peel and grate the onions or mince them finely.

In a heavy frying pan, heat 6 teaspoons olive oil and add the onions. Sauté gently for 3 minutes, add the fish head and bones and sauté another 3 minutes. Add the potatoes, tomatoes, thyme, orange rind, bay leaf, salt, and pepper and cook for 5 minutes. Add the water or wine and water and bring to a boil. Simmer for 30 minutes.

Crush the saffron between your fingers over the soup. Cook the soup for another 2 minutes.

Place a Mouli food mill over a pan and pour two ladlefuls at a time of the soup mixture into it. Add broth whenever necessary. After the soup mixture is entirely ground, put it in a sieve over a large bowl and force it through with a pestle. Discard the residue left in the sieve.

Reheat the soup over a medium flame. Add the garlic, 1 teaspoon olive oil, salt, and pepper to taste. Add more saffron if desired.

Cut the bread into triangles and make the croutons. Serve the soup over croutons sprinkled with the cheese.

Variation:
If you want a more substantial soup, add the vermicelli 10 minutes before serving.

Les Hors-d'Oeuvre

Appetizers

In the Midi there is no cocktail hour. We may nibble on olives or toasted almonds with *pastis* (a licorice drink served with iced water) or a chilled glass of herb-flavored vermouth, but hors d'oeuvres are served at the table and are part of the meal.

The French are highly conscious of the need for a delicate balance between the courses. The flavors and textures must complement each other. And in the South of France, with such a colorful array of fruits, vegetables, and aromatic herbs, this is particularly important. Thus, before a hearty *boeuf à la niçoise* or *pot-au-feu provençale* a light but tasty *anchoïade* might be served. Or a rich *terrine de campagne* might precede a vegetable main course such as *artichauts à la barigoule*.

However you compose your meals, remember always that they must be a feast for the eye as well as the palate. No hors d'oeuvre, no matter how simple, should be served without a garnish, and the variety of what you can offer is as limitless as your imagination. As long as this first course is tasty, light, and enticing, call it an hors d'oeuvre.

You might prepare a basket of raw vegetables with a bowl of *bagna cauda, caviar provençale,* or *aïoli* to dip them in, a platter of prosciutto ham surrounded by sections of a ripe cantaloupe, crisp pieces of *socca,* tomatoes filled with *sauce verte,* marinated sardines, yellow and red peppers sprinkled with garlic and parsley, raw whiting with wedges

Appetizers

of lemon, or an assortment of raw oysters, clams, and mussels garnished with lemon slices and buttered homemade bread. And finally, you may serve an endless variety of salads, raw fennel with vinaigrette sauce, warm chickpeas, cold mussels, and, of course, the queen of Niçois salads and hors d'oeuvres —*la salade niçoise.*

Anchoïade

Anchovy and Garlic Spread

Here are two recipes for *anchoïade,* a spicy anchovy and garlic spread to be served on dry toast. The first is a powerful, concentrated version served hot; the second is creamy and served cold.

If possible, use the kind of anchovies packed in rough salt.

For 6 people:

Anchoïade I

- 20 anchovy fillets
- 2 garlic cloves, crushed
- 1 tablespoon red wine vinegar or lemon juice
  freshly ground black pepper
- 4 tablespoons olive oil
- 6 slices good white bread or 12 slices "French" bread

Mash the anchovies in a mortar (or use a blender or food processor for this). Add the garlic, vinegar, and pepper, and dribble the oil in very slowly so the sauce does not separate. Sprinkle the slices of bread with olive oil, place on a cookie sheet and toast under the broiler for 2 to 3 minutes, or until slightly crisp. Turn them over, spread them with the anchovy paste and return to the broiler for 3 to 5 minutes. Cut each slice into 4 triangles and serve immediately while piping hot.

To garnish, you might sprinkle the triangles with crushed garlic and arrange them attractively on a platter with lemon slices, white and red radishes, chopped parsley or chives, and black olives.

Anchoïade II

        24 *anchovy fillets*
         2 *garlic cloves, peeled*
         2 *egg yolks*
         4 *tablespoons olive oil*
            freshly ground black pepper
         6 *slices good white bread*

Mash the anchovies and garlic in a mortar. Add egg yolks and mix
well. Very slowly beat in the oil and add pepper to taste. Sprinkle
the slices of bread with olive oil and toast lightly under the broiler
for 2 to 3 minutes. Cut into triangles while they are still hot. Let
them cool, then spread with the anchovy paste.

Suggestions for garnishing: chopped parsley or chives, a hard-
boiled egg passed through a sieve, a grated onion, small black
olives from Nice, or sliced radishes.

Caviar Provençale
Eggplant, Lemon, and Garlic Purée

This refreshing, piquant purée is served on toast as an appetizer.
It also makes a wonderful dip: Place it in half a scooped-out raw
eggplant or in a brightly colored bowl and surround it with 2-inch
sticks of cucumbers, fennel, celery, and carrots, along with whole
white radishes and cherry tomatoes, or with potato chips. It is
delicious served with a vermouth or chilled white wine.

        For 6 people:

         3 *eggplants* (*about 1 pound each*)
         3 *garlic cloves, crushed*
       1/3 *cup olive oil*
            juice of 1 lemon
            salt
            freshly ground white pepper
         1 *tablespoon chopped onion* or *parsley* or
            basil or *anchovies*
            Croutons (*p. 12*)

Heat the broiler and turn it down to low. Slice the eggplants in half lengthwise. Place them 2 inches below the flame for about 50 minutes, turning once. When they become very soft, scoop out all the flesh (discard skins). Remove the seed strips and press the pulp through a Mouli food mill into a bowl. Add the garlic. Slowly beat in the olive oil, lemon juice, salt (a fair amount is needed, so taste to make sure), and pepper. Cover with plastic wrap and chill.

To serve, sprinkle with chopped onion, basil, parsley, or anchovies. Prepare triangular croutons and arrange them around the bowl along with raw vegetables or potato chips.

Citrons, Courgettes, Concombres, Oeufs, et Tomates à la Tapenade

Lemons, Zucchini, Cucumbers, Hard-Boiled Eggs, and Tomatoes Filled with a Garlic, Anchovy, Olive, Tuna, and Lemon-Juice Mixture

1 egg, hard-boiled, sliced in half lengthwise
1 tomato, sliced in half
1 cucumber, sliced in half lengthwise
1 zucchini, sliced in half lengthwise
1 lemon, cut in half
1 garlic clove
2 anchovies
2 tablespoons capers
2 tablespoons tuna
6 olives, pitted
3 egg yolks, raw
½ teaspoon thyme
juice of 1 lemon
2 tablespoons chopped parsley
pepper

Remove the yolk from the hard-boiled egg and scoop out the pulp from the tomato, cucumber, zucchini, and lemon. Reserve the yolk.

Whirl all the remaining ingredients in the blender to make the filling. Stuff the egg, lemon, and vegetable halves with the filling and sprinkle with the egg yolk passed through a sieve. Chill.

Crudités et Bagna Cauda

Raw Vegetables Dipped in a "Warm Bath" of Garlic,
Anchovies, and Olive Oil

This recipe has all the best qualities of Niçois cooking: it is fresh,
colorful, easy to prepare, and light. It is perfect for an outdoor
buffet.

Choose among the vegetables suggested, but do not include any
that is not tender and fresh—no frozen food.

> *romaine, leaves separated*
> *watercress, cut in 2-inch pieces*
> *broccoli, only the peeled stalks*
> *endive, small, sweet whole leaves*
> *celery hearts, cut in strips*
> *cauliflower, florets separated*
> *scallions, whole or sliced lengthwise*
> *spinach, with stems*
> *cucumbers, peeled, seeded and cut in strips*
> *fennel bulbs, cut in strips*
> *radishes (white and red), whole, with
>   leaves if possible*
> *mushrooms, whole, with stems*
> *carrots, peeled and with some stem left on*
> *zucchini, unpeeled and cut lengthwise into
>   1-inch-thick sticks*
> *cherry tomatoes, whole*
> *Italian green peppers (small), seeded and
>   quartered*
> *baby purple artichokes, whole or cut
>   lengthwise*
> *asparagus (preferably very small), pared*
> *baby lima beans*
> Bagna Cauda (p. 76)

Wash, clean, and prepare a variety of the vegetables listed. Arrange them attractively in a long, shallow basket or on an earthenware dish or several plates. Sprinkle with cool water, cover with
foil and chill. Serve with *bagna cauda* kept warm in an earthenware or chafing dish heated by a candle. Guests will dip the
vegetables in the sauce as with fondue.

Appetizers

43

Variations:

Although *bagna cauda* is the sauce traditionally served, you will find that *crudités* are delicious with any of the following sauces: *Pistou* (p. 86), *Sauce Piquante* (p. 84), *Aïoli* (p. 75), *Rouille* (p. 89), *Sauce Ravigote* (p. 88), *Sauce Verte* (pp. 91–92), or *Bagna Rotou* (pp. 76–77).

Mousse d'Aubergines Froide
Eggplant Dip

This pungent mousse is wonderfully versatile. You may fill halves of tomatoes with it or serve it as an appetizer in a brightly colored bowl with sticks of cucumber, zucchini, and fennel for dipping. Since the mousse is so dull in color, sprinkle it with parsley and always serve it in a colorful dish. You can mound it in an eggplant shell if you scoop the insides out of an eggplant for the recipe instead of using it whole, skin and all. The mousse is better made a day ahead and left in the refrigerator.

For 2 cups:

> 3 *large* (*3-pound*) *eggplants, unpeeled*
> *and sliced as thinly as possible*
> *salt*
> 2 *anchovies*
> 2 *tablespoons olive oil*
> 2 *onions, grated or very finely chopped*
> 3 *garlic cloves, crushed*
> *freshly ground black pepper*
> 2 *tablespoons parsley or basil, chopped*
> *juice of* 1/2 *lemon*

Sprinkle the eggplant slices with salt. Toss and let stand for 1 hour. Preheat oven to 375°. Wash the anchovies, fillet, and cut them in small pieces. Rinse and dry the eggplant slices. Sprinkle with olive oil and bake in an oiled baking dish for 1½ hours, or until soft. Pass the eggplant through a Mouli food mill.* Add the

* If you put the cooked eggplant and the chopped ingredients into a blender the texture will be more "pasty," but the taste will be equally good.

onion, garlic, anchovies, and salt and pepper to taste (it should be highly seasoned). Chill.

Before serving, sprinkle on the parsley and lemon juice, and if you like, a few drops of olive oil.

Oeufs à l'Aillade

Hard-Boiled Eggs Filled with Garlic, Capers, and Anchovies

This is made in a jiffy and is a flavorful way to stuff hard-boiled eggs. Boiled garlic cloves are mild and have an interesting texture.

For 6 people:

- 6 *eggs*
- 10 *garlic cloves, peeled*
- 3 *anchovies, filleted*
- 3 *teaspoons capers*
- 3 *tablespoons olive oil*
  dash of red wine vinegar
  salt
  freshly ground black pepper
- 1 *tablespoon minced parsley or basil*
- 2 *teaspoons cayenne pepper*
  sprigs of parsley or watercress

Place the eggs and garlic cloves in a pan of cold water, bring to a boil and cook for 10 minutes over medium heat. Peel the eggs and cut lengthwise. Let the garlic cloves cool, then place them in a mortar. Add the fillets, capers, and yolks of the hard-boiled eggs. Pound with the pestle and reduce the mixture to a paste. Slowly beat in the olive oil as you would for a mayonnaise. Add vinegar, salt, pepper, and parsley or basil.

Fill the egg-white halves with the mixture and sprinkle with cayenne pepper (more for color than for the taste). Garnish with parsley or watercress. Chill and serve.

Oeufs et Légumes
à la Mayonnaise Orange

Hard-Boiled Eggs, Tomatoes, Cucumbers, and Zucchini Filled with
Saffron Mayonnaise

>   3 *eggs, hard-boiled*
>   3 *firm tomatoes, cut in half*
>   3 *small, crisp cucumbers, peeled*
>   3 *small, crisp zucchini, peeled*
>   1 *cup* Mayonnaise Orange (*p. 82*)
>   *mixture of chopped mint, basil, and
>   parsley*

Cut the eggs lengthwise and remove the yolks. Scoop out some of
the pulp from the tomato halves and turn upside down to let them
drain (try to remove as much water and seeds as possible without
wasting too much of the pulp). Cut the cucumbers and zucchini
lengthwise and remove seeds. Prepare the *mayonnaise orange*.

Fill the vegetable shells with the mayonnaise and sprinkle with
chopped herbs and the yolks, which have been passed through a
sieve. Chill. An attractive way to serve is to arrange the vegetable
shells on a bed of watercress or lettuce leaves.

Note: You can also use *Sauce Verte* (pp. 91–92) as a filling.

Pan Bagna

A Niçois Sandwich

This is a sandwich sold in the streets of Nice, like pizza in Italy,
and may be one of the best you've ever tasted. It is prepared there
with 3-inch-thick round breads. Perfect for children and picnics.
It is best prepared at least 1 hour before serving.

For each person:

> 2 slices good French bread or whole
>   wheat bread, a wide round roll, or a
>   lightly toasted hamburger bun
> 1 garlic clove, peeled
> 1 tablespoon olive oil
>   about 1 teaspoon red wine vinegar
>   salt and pepper
> ½ onion, sliced
> 1 firm tomato, sliced with skin left on
> 3 white or red radishes, sliced
> 2 anchovy fillets, chopped
> 1 tablespoon tuna (canned in oil or
>   water)
>   a few leaves of basil or mint

Rub the bread with a peeled garlic clove. Sprinkle both slices of
bread with olive oil and vinegar, sprinkle with salt and pepper,
then pile all the other ingredients on one slice and crush the garlic
clove on top. Cover with the other slice and weight the sandwich
down for 2 to 3 minutes with a heavy plate so that the insides are
pressed together (this is one sandwich that tastes best soggy).

Paniers et Barquettes au Thon et aux Anchois

Cucumbers, Tomatoes, and Lemons Filled with Tunafish, Anchovies, and
Capers

For any recipe where vegetables and fruits are filled with a sauce
and served as a cold hors d'oeuvre, make sure they are crisp and
very fresh. Remove as little of the pulp as possible when you remove the seeds from such vegetables as tomatoes, zucchini, and
cucumbers. Always serve on a green bed—watercress or crisp
lettuce.

For 6 people:

    3 *eggs*
    6 *anchovy fillets*
    ¾ *pound canned tuna (preferably canned*
        in oil; if canned in water, discard
        the water) or canned sardines
    ⅓ *cup capers*
        juice of 2 lemons
    4 *tablespoons olive oil*
        pepper
        salt
    3 *large tomatoes*
    3 *large lemons*
    2 *small, firm cucumbers*
    3 *tablespoons whole capers*

Hard-boil the eggs and let them cool. Peel and press them through
a sieve into a bowl. Chop the anchovies, tuna (or the sardines),
and capers, and press through the sieve into the same bowl. Stir in
lemon juice and oil. Add pepper to taste before adding any salt.
The mixture will have a coarse consistency. (All its ingredients
can be put in a blender and puréed, but it will lose in taste what it
gains in smoothness.)

Cut the tomatoes in half and let them drain upside down. Cut
the lemons in half and remove the insides; clean them with a very
sharp knife so the shells will be completely free of pulp. Peel the
cucumbers and cut them in half lengthwise. Remove the seeds and
drain them upside down.

Stuff the lemon and vegetable shells with the fish-egg mixture
and top each shell with a few capers. Chill until ready to serve.

Pissaladière
Onion Tart

Whether you serve this crisp, light tart as a first course for a dinner
or as the main offering for a light lunch or picnic, it is a simple but
elegant dish to enjoy at any time of the year. In Nice there are
many variations of the *pissaladière*. Each pastry shop, each marketplace, each bakery, each home has its own version. Some have

more crust, others have more onion purée; some are heavy with anchovies and olives, while others are mild and sweet. This version, which is my grandmother's, is the one I prefer, but feel free to adjust the seasonings to your own taste, since that is part of the tradition of this dish.

For 6 people:

Onion Purée

12 (about 3 pounds) medium-sized yellow onions
2 tablespoons olive oil
2 garlic cloves, peeled and crushed
1 bay leaf
1 teaspoon thyme
freshly ground black pepper
½ teaspoon salt

Peel and mince the onions (since you must make a purée, it is important that the onions be minced very finely). Warm the olive oil in a large frying pan. Add the onions, garlic, bay leaf, thyme, pepper and salt (the salt draws water from the onions, preventing them from turning brown). Cover tightly and simmer gently *over the lowest flame* for 1 to 1½ hours, or until the onions have completely dissolved into a pale purée. Remove from heat and squeeze the onions gently to one side of the pan with a slotted spoon, drawing off the liquid, which you will use for the crust.

Crust

¼ teaspoon dry yeast
¼ cup lukewarm water
liquid from onions (at least 1 tablespoon—if there is not enough, add olive oil)
1 teaspoon salt
1 cup unbleached flour
1 teaspoon olive oil

Dissolve the yeast in water in a large bowl. Let stand 5 to 10 minutes, preferably in a warm place. Stir in the onion liquid, salt, and flour and mix well. Knead on a floured board for 20 minutes, or until the dough is soft and smooth. Place in a greased bowl and turn it over. Cover with a damp cloth.

Appetizers

Turn on the oven at 300° for about 30 seconds. Put in the dough and shut off the heat. Let it rise there until it has doubled in bulk —about 1 hour. Punch it down. Sprinkle with olive oil and knead it in the bowl for 3 minutes. Re-cover with a damp cloth and let it rise again in the oven for 10 minutes. Remove the dough.

Preheat the oven to 375°. Oil an 8 x 13-inch baking pan or a fluted round French tart pan if you have one. Roll out the dough with a rolling pin on a floured board and then, with your hands, stretch it along the sides of the pan so that the crust is ¾ inch high up the sides. Taste the onion purée to check for seasoning and spoon it into the crust.

Garnish
---

6 *anchovy fillets*
1 *tablespoon olive oil*
12 to 18 *small black olives from Nice, or*
        pitted, large oil-cured black ones,
        quartered

If the baking pan was used, arrange the anchovy fillets on top of the tart in a lattice pattern; if the French pan was used, arrange the fillets like the spokes of a wheel. Sprinkle the top with olive oil and bake at 375° for 1 hour, or until the dough has separated from the sides of the pan and is golden and crisp. Remove from the oven and dot with olives. This tart tastes best warm and reheats very well.

Plateau de Hors-d'Oeuvre Variés

A Platter of Cold Appetizers

For an interesting hors d'oeuvre you can assemble on a platter various dishes such as vegetable salads (fennel, tomato, chick-pea, green bean), shredded raw carrots (seasoned with olive oil, lemon, and little black olives), marinated fish, rice salads, *brocoli au vin blanc,* and *champignons en citronnette.*

You can also present on a large tray a colorful array of vegetables, lemons, and hard-boiled eggs filled with delectable mixtures on a bed of watercress such as:

Sardines au Vinaigre

Sardines Marinated in Red Wine Vinegar and Spices

This vigorous hors d'oeuvre can also be made with fresh anchovies, herring, or smelts. It is better after two days in the refrigerator and will keep up to a week there.

For 6 people:

　3　*pounds fresh sardines*
　1　*fennel bulb, cut in sticks, or 3 table-spoons fennel or anise seeds*
　　　freshly ground pepper
　1　*cup red wine vinegar*
2½　*cups water*
　2　*tablespoons peppercorns*
　1　*teaspoon coriander*
　　　half a nutmeg, freshly grated
　3　*bay leaves*
　4　*teaspoons salt*
　　　a few sprigs of watercress or parsley

Wash the fish and discard the heads. Fillet the fish (sardines may be left whole if they are small enough) and drain on paper towels. Put the fresh fennel between every two fillets or sprinkle the fillets with fennel or anise seeds. Season with salt and pepper and place the fish in a shallow baking dish.

Put the vinegar, water, peppercorns, coriander, nutmeg, bay leaves, and salt in a saucepan. Bring to a boil, simmer for 5 minutes, then pour while hot over the fillets and let them cool. Cover and refrigerate.

Appetizers

To serve, carefully lift out the fish with two spatulas onto a platter. Garnish with watercress or parsley.

Note: If there are any leftover sardines, dip them in a light batter (see *Beignets de Légumes*, pp. 175–76) to make sardine fritters—delicious served with *salade mesclun*.

Saussoun

Almond and Fennel Anchovy Spread Served with Croutons

An unusually refreshing spread on toast, a fine dip for raw vegetables, and a fragrant sauce for *Pâtes aux Oeufs* (p. 216).

> 2 to 3 tablespoons olive oil
> 1 cup finely chopped almonds
> 12 anchovy fillets, chopped
> 1 fennel bulb, chopped
> 2 leaves fresh mint or basil, minced (optional)
> 6 slices firm white bread
> fennel leaves, finely chopped

Using a mortar and pestle* and adding a little olive oil, mash the almonds, anchovies, fennel, and mint or basil to make a paste. Mash only a portion of these ingredients at a time, transferring each batch of paste to a bowl.

Toast the slices of bread under the broiler, turn them over and sprinkle with a little olive oil and let them cool. Thickly spread the toasted bread with the paste and cut each slice in four triangles. Sprinkle with fennel and serve.

Variation:
If you use this sauce with warm pasta, add 3 tablespoons of olive oil to the sauce, stir, and pour over the pasta.

---

* If a food processor is used, start with the almonds or the fennel.

Socca

Chickpea Flour Pancake

Every morning the streets of Nice are full of men carrying large round trays of *socca* on their heads (wrapped with handkerchiefs) to the marketplaces and shouting *"Tout caud"* (It is hot). The fragrance of small pieces of *socca* wrapped in brown paper cones mingles with the smell of fresh fruits and vegetables to give the open-air market a truly wonderful atmosphere.

Socca is quick and easy to prepare at home. Chickpea flour is sold in Greek, Spanish, and Italian markets as well as mail order shops. Children love *socca* for snacks, and it is a delicious appetizer, cut in small pieces and wrapped in bright paper napkins to accompany a chilled rosé, vermouth, or dry white wine.

For 6 people:

> 2/3 *cup chickpea flour*
> 3 *tablespoons olive oil*
> 1/2 *teaspoon salt*
> 1 *cup water*
> *freshly ground black pepper*

Mix the flour, oil, salt, and water, in a bowl. Stir well and let stand for 1 hour (at room temperature or refrigerated).

Preheat oven to 400°. Oil a round, shallow pan and pour on the batter—it should be very thin, about 1/8 inch thick. Put the pan under a moderate broiler as close to the flame as possible. After 5 minutes, sprinkle a little olive oil on the top and broil for 5 to 10 more minutes until it is crisp and golden, with the consistency of a thick crêpe or pancake. Sprinkle with salt and freshly ground black pepper. With a spatula, slide it onto a serving plate and cut it into 2 x 2-inch wedges. Serve on small plates with forks or on paper napkins—a bit messy, but so delicious.

Tapenade

Anchovy, Olive, Garlic, and Capers Spread

This fragrant mixture can be served in many ways. Surrounded by raw vegetables or potato chips, it is a delicious dip. Spread on thin Croutons (p. 12) it is a savory spread. As a filling for raw tomatoes, it becomes *Paniers et Barquettes* (p. 47). Diluted with about 3 tablespoons of olive oil, it can be tossed with warm *Pâtes aux Oeufs* (p. 216) and become an interesting sauce.

For 6 people:

> ½ cup black olives from Nice or oil-cured black olives,* pitted
> 6 anchovy fillets, cleaned, rinsed, and drained
> 1½ tablespoons capers
> 1 garlic clove, peeled and crushed
> juice of 1 lemon
> 4 tablespoons olive oil (*possibly more*)
> freshly ground pepper
> 2 tablespoons fresh basil, finely chopped (*do not use dried basil*)

Place the olives in a blender† with the anchovy fillets, capers, garlic, lemon juice, olive oil and pepper. Turn on high speed for a few seconds. Stir, and check if the mixture is too thick and needs more oil. Pour into a bowl and check the seasoning (if it is too salty add ½ teaspoon of sugar). Add the basil. Cover with plastic wrap and keep in the refrigerator until ready to use. It will keep about ten days.

---

* If you use oil-cured olives, add 1 tablespoon or more of canned tuna oil to reduce the saltiness.

† You can use, instead of a blender, either a mortar and pestle or a Mouli food mill. But I find the blender satisfactory, as well as time-saving, for this recipe.

Tomates à la Brandade

Tomatoes Filled with a Dried Cod Mousse

    3 tomatoes
    6 tablespoons Brandade (*pp. 102–3*)
    2 tablespoons chopped parsley

Cut the tomatoes in half and scoop out some of the pulp. Turn them upside down and let them drain.

Fill the tomatoes with the *brandade* and sprinkle with parsley.

Suggestion for serving:
Arrange the stuffed tomatoes on a bed of watercress or crisp lettuce leaves.

Tomates et Courgettes au Caviar Provençale

Tomatoes and Zucchini Filled with an Eggplant, Lemon, and Garlic Purée

    3 tomatoes
    3 zucchini
    1 cup Caviar Provençale (*pp. 41–42*)
    1 tablespoon grated onion
    1 tablespoon minced parsley

Cut the tomatoes and zucchini in half. Scoop out some of the pulp from the tomatoes and the seeds from the zucchini. Turn the zucchini and tomato halves upside down and let them drain. Fill the vegetable shells with *caviar provençale* and garnish with onion and parsley.

An attractive way to serve is to arrange the stuffed vegetables on a bed of watercress or crisp lettuce leaves.

Terrine de Campagne

A Hearty Country Pâté

A good terrine contains many textures and flavors. This one alternates three contrasting layers: the first consists of marinated strips of veal, chicken, and ham; the second, chopped sautéed chicken liver; and the third, ground pork mixed with egg and seasonings. Terrines can, of course, be very rich and grand and their ingredients can include marrow, butter, cream, cognac, truffles, pistachios, and goose or duck liver. This recipe is for a simple peasant terrine, lean and spicy, delicious served with sour gherkins, a tart green salad (dandelion, arugula, romaine, or watercress), and wine. It is excellent as the first course for a hearty winter meal or as the main course for a summer picnic or buffet.

The recipe is designed for a 1½-quart terrine with a lid, but you can substitute a loaf pan.

> ½ pound veal, cut roughly into 4-inch strips
> 1 pound chicken breasts, boned and diced
> 3 slices ham
> 1 onion, chopped
> 2 garlic cloves, crushed
> 1 bay leaf
> 3 sprigs thyme, or 1 teaspoon dried
> 1 cup dry white wine
> 1 tablespoon brandy
> 6 peppercorns, crushed with a mallet
> 1 teaspoon salt
> ½ pound chicken livers
> 1 tablespoon olive oil
> ½ pound ground pork or ham
> ½ pound salt pork, finely minced
> 3 eggs
> 2 tablespoons port or sherry
> ½ teaspoon thyme
> 2 teaspoons salt
> 1 pound salt pork, cut in strips, or caul
> 2 4-inch slices bacon or salt pork
> 4 bay leaves
> sprigs of parsley or watercress

Mix and marinate overnight the first eleven ingredients.

Sauté the chicken livers in olive oil until firm. Chop and set aside. In a bowl, mix the pork or ham, salt pork, eggs, port or sherry, thyme, and salt. Line a terrine or loaf pan with three-quarters of the salt pork strips or caul. Preheat the oven to 350°.

Assemble the pâté in the following order, packing down each layer: half of the pork or ham mixture, the marinated sliced ham, all the chicken livers, half of the liquid from the marinade, the marinated veal strips, and the remaining pork or ham mixture. Put bay leaves on top and pour the rest of the marinade over the pâté. Seal completely with the remaining salt pork strips. Seal with aluminum foil and place the terrine in a pan of hot water 1½ inches deep. Bake for 2 hours.

Remove from the oven and set 2 to 5 pounds of weights (stones, irons, tiles, etc.) on top of the foil-covered pâté.* (Cover the entire surface with weights. This squeezes out the excess fat and juice so that the pâté will slice well and have the proper consistency.) Refrigerate at least 5 hours.

Remove the weights and gently lift out the pâté with two spatulas and place on a platter. Trim the fat—you may remove it all, if you wish—and cut a few slices of terrine with a big, sharp knife with the help of a chopping board (see technique for using this on p. 20). Cut 3 or 4 little clover shapes out of a slice of bacon or salt pork with kitchen shears and arrange them in a pattern, along with the bay leaves, on the uncut part of the pâté. Surround the pâté with parsley or watercress.

This is delicious with a full-bodied red wine, a chilled dry white wine, or a cool dry rosé.

Note: This pâté is a bit crumbly. To make it smoother, you can add more eggs, salt pork, and some bread, but it then becomes heavier and somewhat dull.

---

* If you make pâtés often, it is well worth cutting a piece of plywood or cardboard to fit the dimensions of the terrine and wrapping it in aluminum foil. Weights can be put on top of it to press down evenly.

Les Salades

Salads

In Nice, salads can be served either as an hors d'oeuvre, an accompaniment, or the main part of a meal. There are two kinds of salads: the cool, tart, crisp green salads, such as watercress, lettuce, and dandelions, and the warm salads made with vegetables, rice, meat, or fish.

The dressing is usually a simple vinaigrette. In a large glass or china bowl, a clove of garlic is crushed, salt and red wine vinegar, and then the oil and freshly ground black pepper are stirred in.

Good red wine vinegar and pure olive oil (the Extra Vierge label means a pure oil extracted from the olives without the use of chemicals or heat) are essential to a good vinaigrette. You may make it thicker with mustard or the yolk of a hard-boiled egg by adding them first to the vinegar, and then thinning the mixture with the oil.

Vary the texture of your salads and work with whatever you have at hand—raw vegetables, cooked vegetables, leftover fish, shellfish, cooked meat, tuna, rice. Served warm, they will enhance the flavor of the vinaigrette. The whole spirit of Southern cooking is in such imaginative and highly flavorful mélanges.

Some salads will keep in the refrigerator. They can be life savers by making up for a dish ruined at the last minute. They are perfect for an improvised meal.

Salade Amère

Dandelion Salad

You can pick dandelion leaves in the country, along roads, or buy them in a number of good vegetables markets in summer. Always pick the youngest, most tender leaves—when they are old they are tough and bitter.

> 40 *young dandelion leaves*
> ⅓ *cup olive oil*
> 2 *tablespoons red wine vinegar*
> *salt*
> 2 *garlic cloves, peeled and crushed*
> *freshly ground black pepper*
> 1 *egg yolk, hard-boilèd*
> 6 to 12 *strips of stale bread crust for making* Chapons (*p. 11*)

Wash and dry the dandelion leaves. Wrap them in a towel and refrigerate for at least 20 minutes so they become cold and crisp.

Mix olive oil, vinegar, garlic, salt, and pepper to make the dressing. Prepare the *chapons,* and sprinkle a little dressing on them. Pass the yolk through a sieve.

Place the dandelion leaves in a salad bowl, pour the dressing over them and toss with your hands. Sprinkle the sieved egg yolk over the leaves and arrange the *chapons* around the edge of the bowl.

Asperges Vinaigrette

Warm Asparagus Dipped in Vinaigrette

This appetizer is eaten warm—like *crudités et bagna cauda*—so that the full flavor of both the asparagus and the vinaigrette is enhanced. Each person should be served his or her own plate for mixing a little vinaigrette in which to roll the asparagus with the fingers.

Salads

For 6 people:

24 *asparagus*
   olive oil and red wine vinegar in small
      serving cruets
   salt shakers
   pepper mills

Wash and chop off the heavy ends of the asparagus. Pare with a
vegetable peeler. Tie the stalks in two bundles and cook them in a
large pot of boiling salted water for 10 minutes, making sure not
to overcook (asparagus should be firm).

Remove the strings and serve on a folded napkin in a basket or
on a platter, along with two or three sets of cruets, pepper mills,
and salt shakers set on a tray.

Salades Blanches
Warm Bean, Cauliflower, and Potato Salads Dressed with a
Spicy Vinaigrette

The secret of these salads is that the sauce is added when the
vegetables are warm. It is quickly absorbed and the salads steam
with the powerful fragrance of olive oil, herbs, scallions, anchovies,
and garlic.

Cauliflower or potato salad can be made in less than half an
hour. If you use dried beans (Great Northern beans, lentils, or
chickpeas) for a salad, you must let them soak overnight and then
cook them the next day for about 1½ hours.

For 6 people:

Dressing for All Three Salads

Simply mix and stir the following ingredients:

½ *cup parsley, minced (reserve 2 table-*
      spoons for garnishing the salad)
3 *scallions, finely minced*
6 *anchovy fillets, minced*
⅓ *cup olive oil*
2 *tablespoons red wine vinegar*

1 teaspoon tarragon
  a few drops of Tabasco sauce
3 garlic cloves, crushed
1 teaspoon freshly grated nutmeg
1 teaspoon salt or more, according to
  your taste
  freshly ground white pepper

Bean Salad

1 pound dried white (Great Northern)
  beans or lentils or chickpeas
5 cups cold water
2 carrots, sliced in half
2 onions, sliced in half
2 whole cloves
  bouquet garni (p. 11)
  salt
2 tablespoons chopped parsley or chives

Soak the white beans, lentils, or chickpeas in a large pan of cold water overnight (read instructions on the package before soaking —they might require less time).

About 1½ hours before you are ready to serve this dish, place the beans in a large pot of water with the carrots, onions (stuck with the cloves), and the bouquet garni. Bring to a boil. Add salt and cover. Simmer for 1 to 1½ hours. (The beans should be tender but retain their shape). Meanwhile prepare the dressing.

Drain the beans. Discard the other vegetables and broth, or you may use them later for soup. Put the warm drained beans in a warm glass or earthenware bowl and pour the dressing over them. Toss gently and sprinkle with parsley or chives. Serve warm.

Cauliflower Salad

2 large heads cauliflower
2 tablespoons parsley or chives

Rinse the cauliflower under cold water and cut out any bruised spots. Separate the florets and blanch them in salted water for 10 to 15 minutes. Do not overcook—they should remain crisp. Meanwhile prepare the dressing.

Place the warm cauliflower in a large glass or earthenware bowl and pour the dressing over it. Sprinkle with parsley or chives, toss very delicately and serve warm.

8 large potatoes
2 tablespoons parsley or chives

Boil the potatoes in a pot of salted water for 20 minutes, or until tender. Meanwhile prepare the dressing.

Holding each hot potato with a kitchen towel or an oven mitt, peel them, then slice them ½ inch thick and place them in a warm shallow dish. Pour the dressing over them and sprinkle with parsley or chives. Toss gently and serve warm.

Brocoli au Vin Blanc

Blanched Broccoli Simmered in White Wine and Herbs

Broccoli is very popular in Nice, and is often served in warm dishes. This chilled preparation may be part of your *plateau de hors-d'oeuvre variés*. It will keep in the refrigerator, covered with plastic wrap, for a few days.

For 6 people:

1 to 2 bunches (about 4 heads) broccoli
water to cover
salt
½ cup dry white wine
4 tablespoons olive oil
5 scallions, minced
2 tablespoons parsley, minced
2 garlic cloves, crushed
juice of 2 lemons
2 teaspoons thyme
1 tablespoon peppercorns

Wash the broccoli, pull off the leaves, cut off the tough base of the stems, and pare the stems with a vegetable peeler. Blanch in a large pot of salted water for 10 minutes. Rinse under cold water and drain. Cut in 2-inch pieces.

Put the wine, olive oil, scallions, parsley, garlic, lemon juice, thyme, and peppercorns in a pan, and simmer, covered, for 20 minutes. Add the broccoli and cook, uncovered, for 2 minutes more (the broccoli should be slightly crisp).

Check the seasoning and pour in a shallow dish. Serve at room temperature or slightly chilled.

Champignons en Citronnette

Sliced Mushrooms with Lemon and Olive Oil Sauce

This tart, delicate dish can be part of a *plateau de hors-d'oeuvre variés*. It may accompany a roasted leg of lamb or a baked fish.

The mushrooms must be very fresh, firm, and cream-colored. You can keep this dish, covered with plastic wrap, for about a week in the refrigerator.

For 6 people:

> 20 (*about 1½ pounds*) *2-inch-wide fresh*
> *mushrooms*
> ½ *cup olive oil*
> *juice of 2 lemons*
> *salt*
> *freshly ground white pepper*
> 2 *teaspoons minced fennel leaves or*
> *parsley*

Wipe the mushrooms carefully with a moist towel and cut off the tips of the stems. Slice the mushrooms as thinly as possible and place them in a bowl. Pour the olive oil and lemon juice over them, add salt and pepper to taste, and toss gently. Cover with plastic wrap and chill for at least 3 hours.

Sprinkle with fennel leaves or parsley before serving.

Champignons en Marinade

Mushrooms Marinated with Lemon, Bay Leaves, and Garlic

This dish is best when prepared a day ahead.

For 6 people:

- ⅔ *cup olive oil*
- ½ *cup water*
  - *juice of 2 lemons*
- 3 *bay leaves*
- 3 *garlic cloves, peeled*
- 5 *black peppercorns*
- 1 *teaspoon salt*
- 1 *pound small fresh mushrooms (about 20)*

Bring everything *but the mushrooms* to a boil in a large, heavy saucepan. Simmer for 10 minutes. Strain carefully and put the broth back in the pan.

Wash the mushrooms and chop off the base of the stems but do not slice. Simmer them in the broth for 5 to 10 minutes, or until tender, and let them cool in the marinade. Cover and refrigerate for 1 to 2 days.

Serve chilled or at room temperature.

Salade de Haricots Verts

Warm Green Bean Salad with Vinaigrette

This can, of course, be eaten cold as part of a *plateau de hors-d'oeuvre variés.*

For 6 people:

- 2 *tablespoons red wine vinegar*
  - *salt*
- ⅓ *cup olive oil*
  - *freshly ground black pepper*

Les Salades

                    1 *garlic clove, crushed*
                    2 *pounds green beans*
                  1/2 *cup parsley, minced*

Prepare the vinaigrette: Mix the vinegar and salt, and add olive oil, pepper, and garlic.

Snap off the tips of the beans and wash them in cold water. Steam or cook, uncovered, in boiling salted water for 15 to 20 minutes—do not overcook. Pour the beans into an earthenware bowl.

Add the vinaigrette and toss immediately. Sprinkle with parsley and serve.

Variation:
I often boil 3 to 5 small new potatoes, unpeeled and quartered, along with the green beans. The potatoes become quite mushy after absorbing the vinaigrette, so it is less elegant a dish—but so tasty.

Maïs en Salade

Corn Simmered in White Wine, Served Cold

Everywhere in France, corn is used for feeding animals, but in Nice it is prepared in many exciting ways for human enjoyment. We use it in *polente,* eat it cold with vinaigrette and with little shrimp, or prepared in the following manner (this dish looks lovely in a *plateau de hors-d'oeuvre variés*).

                  For 6 people:

                  1/3 *cup olive oil*
                    6 *scallions, minced*
                    2 *garlic cloves, peeled and sliced in half*
                      juice of 1 lemon
                    1 *tablespoon peppercorns*
                      salt
                    2 *bay leaves*
                    1 *teaspoon thyme*
                    1 *16-ounce can corn, drained*
                  1/2 *cup dry white wine*

Salads

Heat the olive oil in a heavy-bottomed pan and add the scallions, garlic pieces, lemon juice, peppercorns, salt, bay leaves, and thyme. Cook over a high flame for 5 minutes. Lower the flame and add the corn and wine. Simmer, uncovered, for 5 more minutes. Chill for at least 3 hours.

Salade Mélangée aux Noix

Mixed Greens and Walnut Salad

For 6 people:

- 2 tablespoons red wine vinegar
- 1 teaspoon Dijon mustard
- 2 teaspoons salt
- 1/3 cup olive oil
- 1 teaspoon freshly ground black pepper
- 1/2 cup coarsely chopped walnuts
- 4 firm endives, quartered lengthwise
- 1 bunch watercress

Prepare the vinaigrette in a bowl: Mix vinegar, mustard, and salt, then add olive oil, pepper, and walnuts.

Wrap the endives and watercress in a kitchen towel and refrigerate them. When ready to serve, put the greens in a salad bowl, pour the vinaigrette over them, and toss gently with your hands.

Salade de Moules

Fresh Mussels with an Herb Vinaigrette

This is a perfect summer meal, light and enticing. Be sure to serve it with plenty of good bread and a cool, crisp white wine.

For 6 people:

>6 *pounds mussels (there will be about*
>>*12 in a pound, but only about 10*
>>*will be fresh)*
>1½ *cups water*
>1½ *cups dry white wine (California*
>>*Chablis is perfectly good)*
>3 *bay leaves*
>⅓ *cup olive oil*
>2 *tablespoons red wine vinegar*
>2 *large onions, grated or very finely*
>>*minced*
>½ *cup chopped Italian parsley*
>1 *teaspoon chopped fresh tarragon, or*
>>*½ teaspoon dried*
>2 *tablespoons capers or chopped French*
>>*gherkins*
>>*freshly ground black pepper*
>>*salt*

Scrub the mussels with a strong brush, remove the beards, and leave them in cold water for 10 minutes. Throw away all the mussels that are not firmly closed.

Bring the water, wine, and bay leaves to a boil in a large, heavy casserole. Add the mussels and cook, tightly covered, over high heat 4 to 6 minutes, shaking the pot two or three times so that the mussels cook evenly. When all the shells are open, remove the mussels with a slotted spoon and discard the shells. Boil the broth in the casserole to reduce it to about ½ cup and strain it through wet cheesecloth. Check to make sure there is a minimum of sand.

Combine the oil, vinegar, onions, parsley, tarragon, capers, pepper, and salt (if mussels are excessively salty, use only a small amount), and toss with the cooled mussels. Add the mussel broth slowly and taste to check the seasoning. Toss well and chill for at least 1 hour. Check the seasoning again before serving.

Salads

Salade Nicoise

Vegetable, Tuna, Egg, Anchovy, and Olive Salad

This is the ultimate salad—a feast of feasts—eaten only in the spring or summer when tender fresh vegetables are ripe and abundant. There are many adulterations of this salad—some of which use meat, leftovers, and potatoes—but there is only one classic *salade niçoise,* and its ingredients are listed below. Use the freshest *raw* vegetables, never frozen or canned.

For 6 people:

   6 *firm half-ripe tomatoes*
   1 *cucumber, peeled and sliced*
   1 *head Boston lettuce or 3 heads Bibb lettuce, each leaf cut in half*
 ½ *pound very young fresh lima beans*
   6 *small purple artichokes (from California, and found in Italian markets), quartered*
   1 *fennel bulb, sliced in ¼-inch strips*
   2 *green peppers (Italian preferably), seeded and sliced*
   6 *small white onions or half a Spanish onion, thinly sliced*
     a handful of white or red radishes with stems
   3 *hard-boiled eggs, cut in half lengthwise*
 10 *anchovy fillets, cut in thirds (1 8-ounce can tuna in oil may be substituted)*
     handful of small black olives, unpitted, or oil-cured big black olives, pitted
   6 *to* 12 Chapons (*p. 11*)
 ¾ *cup olive oil*
 ¼ *cup red wine vinegar*
     salt
     freshly ground black pepper
 10 *leaves fresh basil or mint, chopped*
   2 *garlic cloves, peeled and crushed*

Wash and quarter the tomatoes (do not peel them), salt lightly and let them drain upside down on a board for 10 minutes. Peel and slice the cucumber, drain on a paper towel for 10 minutes. Prepare the other vegetables and the eggs, anchovy fillets, and olives. Prepare the *chapons*.

To make the vinaigrette, mix the oil and vinegar, season to taste with salt and pepper, and add the garlic and basil or mint.

Arrange the vegetables, eggs, anchovy fillets, and olives attractively on a shallow dish and surround with lettuce leaves and *chapons*. Pour the vinaigrette over everything and bring the dish to the table without stirring it. Just before serving individual portions, toss delicately but thoroughly.

Pois Chiches Marinés

Chickpeas Simmered in White Wine and Herbs

Chilled, this pungent dish can be part of a *plateau de hors-d'oeuvre variés*. Served at room temperature, it can accompany plain meat or broiled fish.

For 6 people:

- *3 tablespoons olive oil*
- *5 small white onions, grated or minced*
- *2 teaspoons thyme*
- *1 garlic clove, peeled and crushed*
- *salt*
- *1 teaspoon peppercorns, roughly crushed*
- *½ cup dry white wine*
- *juice of 2 lemons*
- *1 20-ounce can chickpeas*

Heat the olive oil in a heavy-bottomed pan. Add the onions, thyme, garlic, salt, and peppercorns and sauté for 5 minutes. Add the wine and lemon juice and bring to a boil. Lower the flame and simmer for 5 minutes.

Drain and rinse the chickpeas. Add them to the pan and cook, uncovered, for 5 minutes over low heat.

Serve either at room temperature or chilled.

Salads

69

Pois Gourmands en Marinade

Snow Peas Simmered in White Wine

This dish can be served on a platter of hors d'oeuvres and eaten cold. It is also a lovely accompaniment to cold fish, chicken, or meats; it can also be part of a buffet.

For 6 people:

- 3 *pounds fresh snow peas (you may use frozen, but it is not as good)*
- 3 *tablespoons olive oil*
- 4 *to 6 small onions, chopped*
- 2 *garlic cloves, minced*
- ½ *cup white vermouth*
  juice of 2 lemons
- 2 *teaspoons thyme*
- 1 *bay leaf*
- ½ *cup water*
  salt
  freshly ground black pepper

Snap off the stem ends of the snow peas, pull out the strings and wash them carefully. Heat the oil in a large cast-iron pan and sauté the onions with the garlic. Cook until golden, then add the snow peas, vermouth, lemon juice, thyme, bay leaf, water, and salt and pepper. Wait until simmering begins, then cover and cook for 20 minutes, or until only a quarter of the liquid remains.

Remove bay leaves, pour into a bowl and refrigerate at least ½ hour before serving.

Salade de Riz Variée

Rice Salad with Assorted Meats and Vegetables

Les Salades

This is a wonderful way to use leftover chicken, shellfish, fish, beef, or vegetables. Be sure that the rice is fluffy, with each grain well separated.

For 6 people:

1 cup raw rice (3 cups cooked)
2 cups chopped, cooked fish, chicken,
    beef, shrimp, mussels, squid, slivers
    of fennel bulb, chopped green pep-
    pers, or blanched peas
2 celery stalks (without leaves), diced
1 cucumber, peeled, seeded, and diced
1 head Boston lettuce or 2 heads Bibb
    lettuce
8 tablespoons olive oil
1 teaspoon Dijon mustard
2 tablespoons red wine vinegar
2 teaspoons salt
    freshly ground white pepper

Cook the rice in a kettle of salted water. Drain well. Pour it in a bowl and add 2 tablespoons olive oil, tossing lightly with a fork until all the rice is well coated. Combine all the ingredients except lettuce in a large bowl and toss gently with two forks.

Wash and dry the lettuce leaves. Scatter them on a shallow serving dish and mound the rice mixture on top. Serve at room temperature. (This can be prepared a day ahead and kept, covered with plastic wrap, in the refrigerator.)

Tian Rouge

Cold Red Pepper and Tomato Gratin

This brilliant, layered gratin must be prepared at least 2 hours ahead of time so it can be served cold. It is most inviting on a hot day.

For 6 people:

½ cup Italian parsley, chopped
⅓ cup fresh basil, chopped
1 tablespoon dried thyme
2 to 3 red bell peppers
2 tablespoons olive oil
6 large, firm tomatoes
  salt
  freshly ground black pepper
1 tablespoon capers
2 tablespoons bread crumbs (preferably
  homemade)

Preheat the broiler to 400°. Mix together the parsley, basil, and thyme. Wash the red peppers, leaving the stems on. Brush them with oil and put under the broiler close to the flame. Turn frequently with tongs until they are evenly blistered all over. Remove and wrap in a wet towel for 15 minutes. Peel off the skin under cold running water with a small sharp knife and discard stems and seeds. Dry and cut into 1-inch strips.

Wash the tomatoes and slice each into 4 round pieces. Oil an earthenware or enamel casserole dish and cover the bottom with a third of the tomato slices. Sprinkle with a quarter of the herb mixture and salt and pepper. Cover with a layer of half of the pepper strips. Repeat the layering until these ingredients are used up. Sprinkle the top with capers and bread crumbs and dribble with olive oil before baking for 20 minutes.

Chill well before serving.

Salade Verte

Fresh Green Salad with Vinaigrette

You can choose from a variety of cultivated greens, such as:

arugula (also called rocket or roquette)
Bibb lettuce
Boston lettuce
chicory
endive

> *escarole*
> *fennel*
> *leaf lettuce*
> *romaine*
> *watercress*

or wild or semi-wild greens, such as:

> *dandelion leaves*
> *field lettuce, or lamb's tongue*
> *purslane*

Always follow the same process in preparing the greens: Remove any wilted leaves; wash and dry the greens carefully; break into pieces with your hands; put leaves between kitchen towels and refrigerate until ready to serve.

Prepare *Vinaigrette* (pp. 92–93). Put the greens in a large glass, china, or earthenware bowl, add vinaigrette, and toss *with your hands*. Add *Chapons* (p. 11) and serve.

Variations:
Salade de Noël, to accompany the Christmas turkey, is made with the tenderest celery leaves and the thick lower part of the stalks a few fresh truffles, anchovy fillets, and seasoned with newly pressed olive oil.

Salade de Pâques, to accompany the Easter leg of lamb, consists of crisp Boston lettuce seasoned with vinaigrette and garnished with hard-boiled eggs quartered lengthwise.

Salade mesclun (from the Niçois *mescla,* to mix) is a strong, bitter, invigorating salad made with dandelion, arugula, field lettuce, purslane, and watercress seasoned with vinaigrette and garnished with garlicky *chapons.*

Lastly, you can, of course, prepare endless variations of *salades composées* (mixed greens) using such combinations as endives and fennel bulbs or watercress, or endive and Boston lettuce—all seasoned with vinaigrette.

Salads

Les Sauces

Sauces

French haute cuisine may boast about its three thousand sauces, but in Nice we do not want it said that *"la sauce fait passer le poisson"* (it is the sauce which makes the fish bearable).

In our cuisine the ingredients must speak loud and clear, not smothered by heavy sauces that may drown out their natural flavor. As Curnonsky, "the prince of gastronomes," said, "Cuisine is when food tastes of what it is."

The other basic difference from haute cuisine is that Niçois and Provençal sauces are not based on butter, cream, or flour but on oil and vegetables. Most of the sauces are cold, and accompany meat, fish, and vegetables. They are used to fill halves of hard-boiled eggs and lemon, tomato, and cucumber "boats"; and as dips to accompany a basket of *crudités* (trimmed raw vegetables).

The sauces can be grouped into four kinds:
—sauces made with a vinaigrette base
—sauces made with a homemade mayonnaise base
—sauces made with a tomato base
—sauces with special flavors, such as walnut sauce and
   anchovy butter

These sauces are an essential part of Niçois cuisine because they are extremely versatile and can transform leftovers into hors d'oeuvres or simple dishes of vegetables into delightful feasts.

Aïoli
Garlic Mayonnaise

This wonderful sauce has been called "the butter of Provence," "the soul of the South," "cream of sun," and it is indeed as heady as it sounds. It can be served with a basket of raw vegetables and hard-boiled eggs or as part of an *aïoli monstre,* with snails, squid, dried cod, tuna, and a splendid array of vegetables. In all cases, it is superbly invigorating. Only water should be served with this potent sauce, but a vigorous red wine is acceptable.

This is a sauce which cannot be made successfully in a blender. Mortar and pestle are as essential to *aïoli* as crisp, fresh garlic.

For 6 people:

> 8 to 10 *garlic cloves*
> 2 *egg yolks at room temperature*
> *salt*
> 1½ *cups oil (half peanut and half olive*
> *oil) at room temperature*
> *juice of 1 lemon*
> *freshly ground white pepper*

Peel the garlic cloves (make sure they are firm and without any green in the center). Place the egg yolks in the mortar and slip a kitchen towel under it to prevent it from slipping when you use the pestle.

Crush the garlic through a garlic press into the mortar. Add the salt and pound with the pestle until the garlic, salt, and yolks have turned into a paste.

Slowly start pouring the oil in a steady flow, stirring constantly with the pestle. Keep stirring steadily until you obtain a thick, shiny, firm sauce. Add the lemon juice and pepper and stir for another minute. Cover with plastic wrap and refrigerate until ready to use.

Note: If the *aïoli* curdles (that is, the oil and egg yolk separate), empty it in a bowl. Put a fresh yolk in the mortar, add 1 tablespoon of warm red vinegar or lemon juice and 1 teaspoon of mustard and stir vigorously. Then slowly add the curdled *aïoli.* Beat steadily until you have a smooth sauce. Add the lemon juice and pepper and beat for another minute.

Sauces

Bagna Cauda
A Warm "Bath" of Anchovies, Garlic, and Olive Oil

This sauce is a delectable accompaniment to crisp raw vegetables (see *Crudités et Bagna Cauda,* p. 43). It can be heated and poured over room-temperature leftover slices of meat (from an abundant *pot-au-feu,* for instance) to make a zesty dish.

> 12 *whole anchovies*
> 3 *slices of bread, with crust removed*
> 3 *tablespoons milk*
> 2 *garlic cloves*
> 1 *cup olive oil*
> ½ *teaspoon freshly ground black pepper*
> 1 *tablespoon butter*

Wash the anchovies and fillet them (discard the backbones and tails). Place the bread in a bowl, pour the milk on it, and mash it with a fork. Squeeze out the excess liquid and set aside.

Place the anchovy fillets in a mortar or bowl and mash them with a pestle or fork. Pass the garlic through a garlic press and add to the anchovy paste. Add the bread paste, and stir and pound. Slowly beat in the olive oil and pepper to make a smooth sauce.

Heat the butter in a small saucepan over a low flame. Add the anchovy-and-bread mixture. Heat gently while stirring, making sure not to let it smoke.

Pour into a flameproof pot and place over low heat. The guests will dip the vegetables in the warm sauce either with fingers or with a fork (as for fondue).

Bagna Rotou
A Vinaigrette with Anchovies, Garlic, and Herbs

You may serve this cold sauce with a basket of trimmed raw vegetables, with leftover meat or shellfish, or with cooked warm or cold vegetables.

2 tablespoons red wine vinegar
  salt
6 tablespoons olive oil
  freshly ground black pepper
1 onion, grated
1 tablespoon finely chopped basil
3 tablespoons finely chopped parsley
4 anchovy fillets, chopped (canned either
    in oil or in rough salt)
2 garlic cloves, peeled and crushed
  salt

Mix the vinegar and salt in a bowl. Add the oil and pepper, then the rest of the ingredients. Taste to check the seasoning before serving.

Beurre d'Anchois

Anchovy Butter

This is a traditional Niçois recipe for a sauce that is spread on grilled fish, such as red mullet and bass, or on broiled meat. It keeps well, refrigerated or frozen, and can transform a last-minute hamburger or boiled potatoes into a flavorful treat.

This recipe may lack Niçois integrity because it uses butter instead of the always favored olive oil, but it is delicious.

12 whole anchovies (canned either in oil
    or in rough salt)
1 pound butter, softened at room tem-
    perature
  juice of 2 lemons
  freshly ground white pepper

Rinse the anchovies and fillet them (discard the backbones and tails). Cut the anchovy fillets into small pieces with scissors or a knife. Mash to a paste in a mortar and gradually add pieces of butter and lemon juice. When the paste is light and soft, add it to the rest of the softened butter and blend thoroughly. Add pepper and taste—you may wish to add more lemon juice or a good deal of pepper (as I do).

Sauces

Roll the anchovy butter in the shape of a thick sausage about 2 inches in diameter. Wrap it in a piece of waxed paper and refrigerate or freeze until ready to use.

Note: Place a ½-inch-thick slice of anchovy butter on a grilled fish, a slice of broiled meat, a lamb chop, or a hamburger just before serving. Or sprinkle little pieces of it on boiled or sautéed potatoes; toss gently and serve at once.

Citronnette
A Lemon and Mustard Vinaigrette

This is a lovely sauce to use with broiled fish or on delicate lettuce or a tender boiled artichoke.

> *1   teaspoon Dijon mustard*
> *   juice of 1 lemon*
> *6   tablespoons olive oil*
> *   freshly ground black pepper*
> *½   teaspoon crushed fresh coriander*
> *   salt*

Place the mustard in a bowl and slowly beat in the lemon juice and then the oil until smooth. Add pepper, coriander, and salt, stirring constantly.

Coulis
A Warm Tomato Sauce

This tomato sauce is briskly cooked to avoid any bitter taste, and is delicious served with *Pâtes aux Oeufs* (p. 216), *Papeton d'Aubergines* (p. 199), or *Beignets de Légumes* (pp. 175–76).

Poured into a jar and covered with 1 tablespoon of olive oil, it will keep for a week in the refrigerator.

> 2 onions, minced
> 5 pounds very ripe tomatoes
> 2 tablespoons olive oil
> 2 garlic cloves, minced
> ½ cup chopped parsley
> 1 teaspoon dried thyme, oregano, or tar-
>   ragon
>   bouquet garni (p. 11)
> 3 lumps sugar
> 10 fresh basil leaves (omit if unavailable
>   —do not use dried basil)
>   salt
>   freshly ground pepper

Squeeze the minced onions in a towel to remove excess moisture. Quarter the tomatoes and pass them through a Mouli food mill.

Heat the olive oil in a heavy-bottomed pan, add the onions, half of the garlic, the parsley, thyme, and bouquet garni. Cook for 10 minutes, or until the onions are soft.

Place the tomato purée in a heavy-bottomed pan over a moderate flame. Add the sugar and simmer, uncovered, for 10 minutes. Pass through a sieve to get rid of the excess liquid.

Pour the thickened tomato purée into the onion-and-herb mixture and cook, uncovered, for 5 minutes. Remove from the flame and add the basil, the remaining garlic, salt, and pepper. Discard the bouquet garni.

Variation:
You may add ¼ cup of dry white vermouth to the sauce while it is simmering for the last 5 minutes.

Sauce Dorée

Tomato, Vinegar, and Herb Sauce

This tawny sauce is good with boiled meat, broiled fish, cold shrimp, or cold chicken. It will keep up to two days in the refrigerator.

For 1⅓ cups (enough for 6 people):

    1 *cup* Mayonnaise (*pp. 81–82*)
    ½ *cup red wine vinegar*
    2 *bay leaves*
    ½ *teaspoon nutmeg, freshly grated*
    2 *tablespoons tomato sauce* (*homemade
       or canned*)
    1 *tablespoon cognac*
    salt
    freshly ground black pepper

Prepare the mayonnaise and set aside.

Pour the vinegar in a pan, add the bay leaves and nutmeg, and simmer for 5 minutes. Let it cool. Remove the bay leaves.

With a wire whip, beat the vinegar, tomato sauce, and cognac gradually into the mayonnaise. The mayonnaise will become softer, but it will regain its firmness when chilled. Add salt and pepper and chill.

This sauce needs lots of salt and pepper, so after the sauce has been chilled, check the seasoning before serving.

Sauce Jaune et Verte

A Light Vinaigrette with Lemon, Garlic, and Herbs

This fragrant cold sauce is wonderful with either warm or cold broiled fish. To serve fish cold, spoon the sauce over it while it is still hot—as it cools, the fish will absorb the sauce deliciously.

For 6 people:

⅓ cup red wine vinegar
    salt
⅔ cup olive oil
    freshly ground white pepper
 3 large lemons, peeled with all mem-
    brane removed, and thinly sliced
½ cup chopped parsley
½ cup chopped fresh tarragon or fresh
    basil, or 1 teaspoon dried
 2 garlic cloves, peeled

Place the vinegar in a bowl, add the salt and stir. Add the oil, pepper, lemon slices, parsley, and tarragon or basil. Crush the garlic cloves through a press into the bowl and stir.

Mayonnaise
The Basic Recipe

Homemade mayonnaise is so good and so easy to make that you can learn to make it *"les yeux fermés"*—that is, practically with your eyes closed. A blender or a food processor will, of course, make the task even easier. Mayonnaise can be used with cold meat, cold fish, and vegetables, or as a dip. It is also the base of innumerable other sauces.

To make 2 cups of mayonnaise:

By Hand

 2 egg yolks
 1 teaspoon Dijon-type mustard
 2 cups oil (half peanut, half olive oil)
    about 2 tablespoons lemon juice or red
      wine vinegar
    salt
    freshly ground pepper

Have all ingredients at room temperature. Slip a kitchen towel under a small bowl to prevent it from sliding when you beat too vigorously. Put egg yolks and mustard into the bowl and begin beating with a wire whip. After a minute or so, slowly add the oil in a thin stream while continuing to beat. When the mayonnaise begins to thicken, you may add the oil a bit more rapidly, but always beat well after each addition. When the mayonnaise is firm, add the lemon juice, salt, and pepper and beat well.

Cover with plastic wrap and refrigerate. It will keep for about four days.

Note: If the mayonnaise curdles (the yolks separate from the oil), place a new yolk in another bowl, add 2 teaspoons mustard, and stir well. Slowly add the curdled mixture, stirring constantly until it is firm and thick and silky. Add salt, pepper, and half the juice of a lemon—or less if you prefer thicker mayonnaise.

With a Blender

2 whole eggs
1 teaspoon Dijon-type mustard
juice of 1 lemon
2 cups oil (half peanut, half olive oil)
1 teaspoon salt
freshly ground white pepper

Place the eggs, mustard, lemon juice, and 1 tablespoon of the oil in the blender. Cover and blend on low speed for 2 minutes. Uncover; set at low speed again and slowly add the rest of the oil in a steady flow. When the sauce has thickened enough, add salt and pepper. Check and correct the seasonings. Pour into a bowl, cover with plastic wrap, and refrigerate until ready to use.

The following recipes are essentially the basic *mayonnaise* with the addition of special ingredients.

Mayonnaise Brune

1 cup mayonnaise
2 whole anchovies, filleted, rinsed, and chopped
2 tablespoons finely minced parsley

Mayonnaise Orange

1 cup mayonnaise
1 to 2 teaspoons curry powder or saffron powder (season to taste)

Mayonnaise Ravigote

1 cup mayonnaise
2 hard-boiled egg yolks, passed through a
  sieve
1 tablespoon chopped parsley
1 tablespoon chopped chives
1 teaspoon capers
1 teaspoon dried tarragon

Mayonnaise Tartare

1 cup mayonnaise
2 tablespoons chopped gherkins
2 tablespoons chopped capers
2 tablespoons chopped parsley

Mayonnaise Verte

1 cup mayonnaise
2 tablespoons finely chopped parsley
2 tablespoons finely minced chives

Note: The Cuisinart food processor makes a good egg-yolk mayonnaise in seconds. The mayonnaise machine is a lot less expensive and makes either the whole-egg or yolk variety; essentially, it's a jar with a plunger, simple and easy to use.

Sauce à la Moutarde

A Good Vinaigrette with Mustard and Herbs

This is served with cold meat, mussels, or boiled vegetables, such as artichokes, carrots, potatoes, green beans, or cauliflower.

For 6 people:

4 tablespoons Dijon mustard
2 tablespoons red wine vinegar
  juice of 1 lemon
6 tablespoons olive oil
  salt
  freshly ground pepper
1 tablespoon finely chopped parsley
1 tablespoon finely chopped mint, basil,
    tarragon, or chives

Put the mustard in a bowl and, with a fork, slowly beat in the vinegar, lemon juice, and olive oil. Keep stirring as you add salt, pepper, and the herbs. Stir well.

Sauce aux Noix
A Walnut, Garlic, and Olive Oil Sauce

This is wonderful with freshly made *pâtes aux oeufs* (p. 216) or lean *ravioli* (made with squash, rice, and cheese) or plain, boiled rice.

Make sure your walnuts are perfectly crisp and fresh (the best way to keep them is to freeze until ready to use).

For 6 people:

½ cup walnuts, chopped
1 garlic clove, crushed
2 tablespoons olive oil
2 tablespoons warm water
  salt

Place the walnuts in a mortar, add the garlic, and pound with a pestle until you have a smooth texture. Stirring constantly, add the olive oil slowly and steadily. Add the salt and the warm water. The result should be a smooth sauce.

Sauce Piquante

A Warm Wine and Vinegar Sauce with Tomatoes, Shallots, and Gherkins

Sauce Piquante I

This is a rather rare item in Niçois cooking: a warm sauce. It is used with leftover meats or vegetables.

For 6 people:

- 2 tablespoons olive oil
- 4 shallots, chopped
- 2 tablespoons red wine vinegar
- 1/3 cup dry white wine
  freshly ground pepper
- 3 tomatoes, peeled and chopped, or 1 cup canned
- 1 garlic clove, crushed
  salt
- 4 gherkins, chopped
- 1/3 cup capers

Heat the oil in a heavy-bottomed pan and add the shallots, vinegar, wine, and pepper. Boil for 5 minutes, then add the chopped tomatoes, garlic, and salt. Cook over low heat for 15 minutes and remove from heat. Stir in the gherkins and capers.

Sauce Piquante II

This is a brisker version, which gives leftovers a new life. It is a good accompaniment for *poche de veau farcie,* and with any cold vegetables, meat, or fish.

For 6 people:

- 2 whole anchovies, filleted
- 1 onion
- 1 garlic clove
  a pinch of salt
- 2 tablespoons red wine vinegar
- 6 tablespoons olive oil
- 3 tablespoons parsley, chopped
  freshly ground pepper

With a pair of kitchen shears, finely cut the anchovies into a bowl. Grate the onion directly into the bowl and crush the garlic through a garlic press also into the bowl.

Dissolve the salt in the vinegar, then stir in the olive oil, garlic, anchovies, onion, parsley, pepper, and salt. Check the seasoning—it should be highly flavored.

Pistou

Basil, Garlic, Olive Oil, and Cheese Sauce

Never use just-picked basil for this; let the fresh leaves rest for one day to lose some of their moisture. The proportions for this sauce are not definitive, as the pungency of the basil varies. Small leaves are stronger in flavor and the taste is influenced by where it was grown. So test to see what your basil is like and adjust the amounts of the other ingredients accordingly.

You can keep this sauce, covered with a little olive oil in a jar in the refrigerator, for months. You can also make a *pistou* base (using basil, parsley, and a little oil) without completing the sauce and freeze it flat in a tight plastic bag; when you need it you can break some off and add the garlic and cheese.

For 6 people:

3 to 5 cups day-old basil leaves (preferably the small-leaved variety) finely shredded with kitchen shears
1/2 cup chopped parsley
1 teaspoon salt
freshly ground black pepper
3 garlic cloves, peeled and crushed
1/2 cup freshly grated Parmesan or Swiss cheese
3/4 cup olive oil

Mortar and Pestle Method
Put a little of the basil, parsley, salt, pepper, garlic, and cheese in the mortar. Pound to a smooth paste and slowly pour in the olive oil (do a little at a time to make the pounding easier—it will take

about 15 minutes to make it all into paste). If the consistency is too thick, you may add more olive oil.

Blender Method
Place a third of all the ingredients except the cheese in the blender and blend at high speed. Stop and scrape down the sides now and then. When the purée is smooth, put it in a bowl or refrigerator jar and purée the rest in two more batches. Add the cheese (this must be freshly grated in order to give the proper texture to the sauce, which becomes too smooth when made in the blender).

Sauce Raïto

A Warm Tomato, Wine, and Onion Sauce

A variety of fish can be simmered in this fragrant sauce: dried cod, whiting, fresh cod, halibut, belly fish. Since the traditional *vin cuit* is hard to prepare, here we have replaced it with a sweet red vermouth or a rich red wine.

For 6 people:

- 2 *tablespoons olive oil*
- 3 *onions, finely chopped*
- 2 *cups good red sweet vermouth or red wine (taste carefully)*
- 1 *cup water*
- 4 *fresh tomatoes, or 1 1/3 cups canned, chopped*
- 6 *cloves garlic, peeled and crushed*
- 2 *teaspoons thyme*
- 2 *teaspoons oregano or savory*
- 3 *bay leaves*
  salt
  freshly ground pepper
- 1/2 *cup unpitted little black olives from Nice, or pitted oil-cured Greek or Italian olives*
- 2 *teaspoons chopped capers*
- 2 *tablespoons chopped parsley*
- 3 *tablespoons chopped gherkins*

Heat the olive oil in a heavy-bottomed pan, add the onions and cook slowly for 20 minutes until soft. Add the vermouth or wine and the water. Stir and boil for 5 minutes, then add the tomatoes, garlic, thyme, oregano or savory, bay leaves, salt, and freshly ground pepper. Reduce heat and simmer, uncovered, for 1 hour. It should be quite thick.

Remove from the heat. Discard the bay leaves and pass the mixture through a Mouli food mill. Check the seasonings (the sauce should be pungent) and correct them if necessary. Add the olives, capers, parsley, and gherkins and cook for an additional 5 minutes.

Note: Check your red vermouth before using it. A good red wine is often better in a *raïto* sauce than a mediocre red vermouth. I prefer red wine myself.

Sauce Ravigote
Vinaigrette with Gherkins, Capers, and Onions

This is a good sauce to serve with cold chicken, turkey, shrimps, mussels, vegetables, or beef.

For 6 people:

  a pinch of salt
  2 tablespoons red wine vinegar
  6 tablespoons olive oil
  freshly ground pepper
  3 tablespoons finely chopped chives,
      parsley, or tarragon
  1 onion, peeled and grated
  2 gherkins, finely chopped
  2 tablespoons capers

Dissolve the salt in the vinegar. Stir in the olive oil, pepper, herbs, onion, gherkins, and capers.

Rouille

A Thick Cayenne Pepper and Garlic Sauce

For 6 people:

Rouille I

4 *garlic cloves*

2 *teaspoons cayenne pepper or Tabasco sauce to taste*

1 *slice good white firm bread, preferably homemade, sprinkled with a little milk, then squeezed to a paste*

4 *tablespoons olive oil*
 salt
 freshly ground white pepper

Peel the garlic cloves and press them through a garlic press into a mortar. Add the cayenne pepper or Tabasco sauce and the bread paste. Stir with a fork or pestle and slowly add the oil. Season with salt and pepper, correct the seasoning, and pour the sauce into a bowl. Cover and keep in the refrigerator until ready to use.

Rouille II

4 *garlic cloves*
 salt

2 *egg yolks*

1 *cup olive oil*

½ *teaspoon saffron*

1 *teaspoon cayenne pepper*
 juice of half a lemon (*optional*)

Make sure all ingredients are at room temperature and the garlic cloves are firm and crisp.

Peel the garlic cloves and crush them through a press into the mortar. Pound with the pestle, sprinkle with salt and pound some more—after a few minutes the garlic should turn into a paste. Add the yolks (the mixture will become sticky). Add the oil slowly, stirring constantly as in making mayonnaise. When the sauce is firm, add the saffron, cayenne pepper, and salt to taste. If you find it too heavy, add the juice of half a lemon before serving and stir.

This sauce can be kept for 24 hours in the refrigerator covered with plastic wrap.

Note: You may use a blender to make the sauce, but first crush the garlic cloves and salt into the mortar and pound into a smooth paste. Put 2 *whole* eggs in the blender jar and a little more salt if you think it's needed (the sauce should be heavily seasoned). Cover and blend at high speed for ½ minute. Add the garlic paste. Cover again and blend for about 1 minute and then start pouring in the oil very slowly while blending at high speed. When the sauce is smooth and firm, remove from the blender and add cayenne and saffron. Check the seasoning—you may want to add more salt.

Sauce Tartare
A Vinaigrette with Hard-Boiled Eggs, Mustard, and Gherkins

This lovely sauce has a rich texture and is wonderful served with cold fish or leftover beef meat. It can also be used to fill hard-boiled-egg and tomato halves.

For 6 people:

⅓ *cup chopped basil* or *mint* or *parsley*
½ *cup chopped cornichons (see*
   Gherkins, p. 13)
3 *hard-boiled eggs*
1 *tablespoon Dijon-type mustard*
⅔ *cup olive oil*
   juice of 1 lemon or 2 tablespoons red
   wine vinegar
½ *cup capers*
   salt
   freshly ground pepper

Place the herbs and gherkins on a kitchen towel (cloth or paper) and squeeze them well to extract as much moisture as possible. Peel the eggs and remove the yolks.

Place the yolks in a large bowl, mash, add the mustard, and stir. When the mixture is smooth, slowly add the oil, beating constantly. When the sauce is firm, add the lemon juice or the vinegar. Sieve the egg whites. Stir into the sauce the gherkins, capers, salt, pepper, and egg whites.

Note: This sauce cannot be made in a blender because its essence is its rough texture. A blender would turn it into a paste.

Sauce Tomate
A Raw Tomato Sauce

This delicious cold sauce is light and fresh. Truly superb with cold dishes.

> For 6 people:
>
> 5 *pounds ripe tomatoes, peeled*
> 2 *large onions, quartered*
> 2 *garlic cloves, peeled*
> 3 *tablespoons chopped fresh basil*
> 3 *tablespoons coarsely chopped parsley*
> 3 *tablespoons olive oil*
>   *salt*
>   *freshly ground pepper*

Put half of the tomatoes in a blender with half of the onions and 1 garlic clove. Blend at high speed for 5 minutes and pour into a large bowl. Put the second batch in the blender—the remaining tomatoes, onion, and garlic clove, along with the basil, parsley, and oil. Blend for 5 minutes, then add it to the other batch in the bowl. Season with salt and pepper, stir well and refrigerate covered with plastic wrap (the oil will rise to the surface). The sauce will keep four or five days.

Sauce Verte
Spinach, Anchovy, and Caper Sauce

This is an unctuous but refreshing sauce, delicious with cold meat or broiled fish. You may also fill tomato or zucchini halves with it for *plateau de hors-d'oeuvre variés* (see *Oeufs et Légumes*, p. 46).

The blender is a great help for this recipe. Covered with plastic wrap, the sauce will keep two or three days in the refrigerator.

For 1 cup sauce (enough for 6 people):

> *half a 10-ounce package frozen spinach*
> 1 *thin slice bread*
> 1 *hard-boiled egg, sliced in half*
> 6 *anchovy fillets, rinsed and chopped*
> ½ *cup olive oil*
> 2 *tablespoons red wine vinegar*
> *salt*
> *freshly ground black pepper*
> 1 *tablespoon minced cornichons (see Gherkins, p. 13), or whole capers*

Blanch the spinach, let it cool, and squeeze it with your hands to remove excess moisture. Put it in the blender.

Add a little water to the bread, then squeeze it so that you have about 2 tablespoons of bread paste. Add this to the blender. Add the egg, anchovies, olive oil, and vinegar. Blend on high speed, stopping from time to time to scrape down the sides. In 3 to 4 minutes you should have a very smooth sauce.

Pour the sauce into a bowl and add salt and pepper to taste. Add the gherkins or capers and chill.

Vinaigrette
Olive Oil and Red Wine Vinegar Sauce

This is a basic sauce made in a second and with all kinds of interesting additions possible. Don't add herbs. Don't keep it in the refrigerator. The ingredients are always at hand, so only prepare what you need for the moment.

For 6 people:

> *a pinch of salt*
> 2 *tablespoons red wine vinegar*

> 6 tablespoons olive oil
> freshly ground black pepper

Dissolve salt in vinegar and beat in the oil very slowly. Add pepper and stir. Check to see if it is seasoned enough.

To this basic recipe you may add any of the following:

> 1 garlic clove, peeled and crushed
> 1 teaspoon Dijon-type mustard (mix with vinegar first and stir well)
> 2 tablespoons chives or parsley or basil or mint, finely minced with kitchen shears
> 1 onion, grated

Les Poissons

Fish

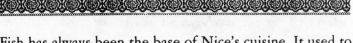

Fish has always been the base of Nice's cuisine. It used to be abundant, varied, and reasonably priced. Caught at dawn, sold early in the morning, sprinkled with herbs, and cooked over a rosemary-scented wood fire, it was a usual dish to enjoy at lunch.

The situation has changed. Although the rocky coast, cut by gulfs and bays, is still a perfect habitat for a rich variety of fish, each with its distinctive color, shape, texture and taste, problems of distribution and pollution have appeared on the Riviera. The traditional fish boats bringing loads of fresh *rascasses, loups,* and *daurades* to sleepy little harbors every morning are no longer the sole purveyors. Eighty percent of the fish sold in Nice markets now comes from the Atlantic, the English Channel, or even farther away. Lately I have seen *daurades* from Argentina, *baudroie* from Scotland, *merlan* from Denmark. As a result, the selection in Nice is becoming somewhat like that faced by most American cooks.

So it is more important than ever that the cardinal rules for buying and cooking fish be respected at all times. Learn how to choose fresh fish. Know what fish you enjoy and demand it if your fish dealer does not stock it regularly. Never overcook a fish. Enhance its flavor, but don't camouflage it. In Nice tradition has taught every cook the qualities to enhance, the shortcomings to deal with in almost any fish. A coarse, oily fish is blanched in court bouillon or boiled to get rid of its fat before herbs and spices are added. A dull fish rests in a highly flavored marinade before it is cooked.

Above all, fish is selected with the greatest care. The skin must be smooth and tight around the body, the gills very red, the whole fish straight and firm, the eyes shiny and dark, never bloodshot.

Most fish markets in the United States offer fresh catches but little choice. They tend to stock only the most easily sold items, such as lobsters, shrimp, bass, cod, and flounder. A trip to the wholesale market will show you the amazing richness available every day. So the first thing to do is to select a fish dealer who takes his business seriously, and then convince him you'll be a steady customer for any squid, belly fish, whiting, mussels, and whitebait he will sell.

All the fish I use in the following recipes are easy to find here and have the qualities required by Mediterranean cuisine.

Anchovies–*les Anchois*

The best kind to buy is the preserved variety kept in rough salt in a tin or glass jar. Niçois cooking uses this type widely in *pissaladière, salade niçoise, anchoïade, bagna cauda, mousse d'aubergines,* and more. You will need large quantities, so buy them in large cans in a Greek, Spanish, or Italian market.

Sea Bass, Striped Bass (*le Loup*)

This superb fish (sometimes called rockfish) successfully replaces *daurade* and *loup*. It is abundant all year round. Delicious in *loup farci à la niçoise* or broiled with fennel, it can also be cooked with mussels or served cold with *rouille, aïoli,* or *mayonnaise verte*. It is a staple of Niçois cuisine.

Belly Fish (*la Baudroie, la Lotte*)

This is an unimposing name for a wonderful fish. The French name is *lotte,* but in the South we call it *baudroie*. In Nice we prepare it with baked vegetables, boiled in *bouillabaisse,* or combined with mussels. It is light, delicate, firm, and virtually boneless. Most American fish markets know it, but few except those catering to Italian or Japanese customers carry it. It is about a quarter of the price of any other fish. A nationwide fast-food chain has recently discovered its virtues and is now buying it in large quantities. Try it with one of these recipes, and if you like it, ask your fish dealer to get it for you regularly—you may have to be insistent.

Dried Cod (*la Morue Sèche*)

Dried cod, which is so popular in Mediterranean countries, is available at most fish markets here. It is the base for *brandade, estockaficada, tian de morue, beignets de morue* and *morue à l'aïoli.*

It is sold in three different forms (see "Ingredients," pp. 12–13), but filleted dried cod is the most common. It should soak for at least 3 hours before it is cooked. Other kinds are salted differently. The whole fish, opened, available in Italian, Spanish, or Greek markets, is drier, requiring overnight soaking with four to five water changes, and tastier— ideal for *morue en raïto, capilotade* or *estockaficada.* Then there is a whole cod (tail, fins, skin, and bones), dried and salted until it is "wooden." The packages often indicate a Chinese company, Tai tze, but Greek and Italian markets frequently stock it as well. This type of cod is the closest thing to Nice's stockfish, superb for *estockaficada;* it requires at least three days of soaking and changing the water about 6 times.

Dried cod is very nutritious and quite inexpensive, and keeps well. It has a pungent, fresh, unique taste. Always choose a plump dried cod, the thicker the better. Stock up when you find it—it keeps well. The part near the tail is the thickest. To desalt the cod, cover it with cool water, skin side up, and change the water often. Always check to see if it has desalted enough by eating a little piece raw before cooking.

Mussels (*les Moules*)

About two hours before the mussels are to be cooked, scrub them with a strong wire brush and pull the beard off each one. Rinse them in a colander and put them in a basin of cold water. After half an hour, toss out any that are open (they aren't fresh) or any that are unusually heavy (they are full of sand). Rinse again under cold water and put back in the basin for another half hour of cold-water soaking to cleanse further and reduce saltiness. There are two kinds of mussels sold in American markets; except for *moules farcies,* where large shells are required to hold the stuffing, mussel dishes would be better with the smaller variety.

Sardines (*les Sardines*)

From September to April is the sardine season in this country. They are delicious broiled with a sprinkling of lemon juice or red wine vinegar.

Squid (*les Tautennes, les Suppions*)

There are all kinds of imaginative and delicious recipes in Nice for this delicacy. We call them poor man's lobster, but they are a rich man's delight, too. The American variety is smaller and more delicate than the Mediterranean. It is very inexpensive, readily available on request, and is sold perfectly cleaned, tender, and fresh. Americans may be startled at the thought of eating squid, but after the initial bite, prejudice dissolves. Filled with spinach and rice, cold in salads, added to fish soup or *salade de riz,* sautéed with tomatoes and white wine, simmered with tomatoes and herbs, they are a delicacy nobody can afford to ignore.

Tuna (*le Thon*)

This is not available all year round in America. From June to September you will find it where the customers are Italian, Japanese, and Spanish; or prevail upon your fish dealer to get it for you when it is in season. Fresh tuna *à la chartreuse* or cooked with tomato is a rich, wonderfully tasty dish.

Whitebait (*la Petite Friture*)

These fish are very small (about 2 inches long and ¼ inch wide). Available in September and October, they are

delicious simply floured, fried in deep fat, and eaten sprinkled with lemon juice or red wine vinegar.

Whiting (*le Merlan*)

This is a delicate, inexpensive fish, which is served in a variety of ways in Nice: baked, boiled, accompanied with mussels, or in soup. Try to buy the largest ones, for they have more flesh for the money.

Court-Bouillon
Stock for Cooking Fish

We will deal with four kinds of court bouillon here. The first one is for a fish which is somewhat bland, such as whiting, bass, belly fish, cod, or fish that has been kept on ice. The second is for fresh-water fish (trout and the like); the third is for large fish (salmon, halibut, tuna, cod, or belly fish); and the fourth is for very delicate fish, such as sole or flounder. All these versions of court bouillon can be kept frozen, so make a large amount to put in small containers and keep it ready for later use.

When you cook your fish, always make sure there is enough court bouillon to cover it. Place the fish on a rack in the fish cooker, then cover it with court bouillon. Place a few lettuce leaves on top of the fish. Bring to a boiling point, lower the flame and simmer for as long as you need to (the classic rule is 8 to 10 minutes for each pound of fish once the boiling point has been reached).

Court-Bouillon I

A court bouillon made with fish heads and bones and vegetables and wine. This fish stock will improve a dull fish or one that has been kept on ice.

For 6 people:

> 2 *pounds fish heads and backbones,*
> *roughly broken in pieces*
> 3 *onions, chopped*

Les Poissons

> 1 carrot, chopped
> the white part of 1 leek, chopped, or
>   an additional onion, chopped
> 1 teaspoon thyme
>   bouquet garni (p. 11)
> 1 cup dry white wine
> 2½ quarts water
>   salt
>   freshly ground pepper

Place the fish heads and bones in a saucepan. Add the onions, carrot, leek, thyme, bouquet garni, wine, and water. Bring to a boil and simmer for 40 minutes. Add salt and pepper before removing from heat. Pass through a sieve lined with a piece of cheesecloth, forcing through as much liquid as you can.

Court-Bouillon II

A court bouillon made with vinegar to be used with fresh-water fish such as pike, trout, and carp. The moisture of the flesh must be maintained, so do not wash the fish or remove the scales. Do not gut the fish in the usual way by slitting the belly; instead, make a small hole either in the stomach or the head and pull out the entrails, and then dry carefully with cheesecloth.

> For 6 people:
>
>   2 cups red wine vinegar
> 2½ quarts water
>   3 carrots, chopped
>   3 onions, chopped
>   bouquet garni (p. 11)
> 10 peppercorns
>   salt

Place all ingredients except peppercorns in a large pot and bring to a boil. Simmer for 1 hour. Add the peppercorns (to eliminate bitterness). Cover and remove the stock from the stove. Let it cool, then pass it through a sieve lined with cheesecloth.

Court-Bouillon III

A court bouillon made with white wine. This is for large fish—salmon, halibut, tuna, belly fish, cod. Follow the recipe for *Court-Bouillon II*, using white wine instead of vinegar.

A court bouillon made with milk. This is for very delicate fish, such as sole or flounder. Its lightness enables the fine flavor of the fish to stand out.

For 6 people:

2 cups milk
2 quarts water
3 carrots, chopped
3 onions, chopped
   bouquet garni (p. 11)
   salt
10 peppercorns

Place all ingredients except peppercorns in a large pot. Bring to a boil and simmer for 1 hour. Add the peppercorns. Cover and remove from the stove. Let it cool, then pass through a sieve lined with a piece of cheesecloth.

Brandade
Hot Dried Cod Mousse

This dish is part of the traditional "lean dinner" on Christmas Eve. The delicious, fluffy mixture is served warm in a thin puff pastry shell called *vol-au-vent* or garnished with crisp croutons and truffles; or served cold, simply stuffed in tomato halves and garnished with little black olives.

Traditionally, the cod was crushed in a marble mortar with the milk and oil to form a smooth paste, which became creamy-white when heated. I use an electric blender—a much quicker and simpler process, which *charcuteries* always favor!

Serve this mousse with a tart salad of arugula, dandelion, or watercress.

For 6 people:

1½ pounds dried cod
 2 garlic cloves
 1 potato, boiled and quartered

Les Poissons

> 1 cup milk at room temperature
> 1 cup olive oil at room temperature
>   juice of 1 lemon
> ½ to 1 teaspoon freshly grated nutmeg
>   freshly ground white pepper
>   salt (may not be needed)

Let the cod soak overnight in the sink or a large basin of cold water. Change the water four to five times. Taste a bit of cod to check if it has desalted enough.

When the cod has been adequately soaked, place it on a board. Remove the skin, bones, and all the loose pieces with your hands and a small, sharp knife. Then place the cod flesh in a pan of cold water to cover and bring to a boil. Just as the water starts to simmer, remove from the fire and let it cool. Drain.

Peel the garlic cloves and crush with a press into the blender. With your hands, flake the fish in small pieces into the blender. Add the potato and pour in ½ cup milk and ½ cup olive oil. Turn to low speed for 1 minute. Stop and stir with a long-handled wooden spoon. Blend for 2 more minutes at high speed. Put the blender on low and slowly but steadily start pouring in alternately the rest of the milk and oil, stopping from time to time to stir with the spoon. This blending should take about 8 minutes.

When all the milk and oil are incorporated, blend at high speed for 2 minutes. The paste will be fluffy and white and quite smooth. Spoon it into a pot. Add the lemon juice, nutmeg, and pepper. Taste before adding any salt. Cook over a low flame, stirring gently, for 5 minutes or until just warm.

Note: Ways to serve *brandade:* Place the *brandade* in a warm shallow dish, surround with Croutons (p. 12) and decorate with sliced truffles or black olives. Or stuff tomato halves with cold *brandade* and garnish with chopped basil. Or stuff six puff pastry shells with warm *brandade* and place in a moderate oven for 15 minutes, then sprinkle with sliced truffles or chopped olives. Or use as a filling for an omelet: Make an omelet and when the first side has set, spread some *brandade* in the center, fold the circle in half and cook for 2 minutes more; sprinkle with chopped black olives before serving.

Fish

Capilotade

Dried Cod Stewed in a Sweet Vermouth and Tomato Sauce

This is another dish traditionally served on Christmas Eve. Like the *brandade* and *estockaficada,* this should be served with a strong green salad (dandelion, arugula, watercress, or endive). Not the least of the joys of this dish is that it takes about 10 minutes to prepare.

For 6 people:

2 *pounds dried cod*
3 *tablespoons olive oil*
2 *large onions, chopped*
2 *garlic cloves, peeled and crushed*
1 *tablespoon unbleached flour*
½ *cup sweet red vermouth or* Vin Cuit
   (pp. 269–70) or good red wine
½ *cup chopped cornichons (see*
   Gherkins, p. 13) or ¼ *cup capers*
   salt (optional)
   freshly ground black pepper
¼ *cup chopped Italian parsley*

Soak the cod in a large bowl of water or in the sink for several hours or, if it is hard as wood, overnight (follow directions on the package). Change the water three or four times. Taste a piece to be sure it is not too salty; if it is, soak the fish for another hour or so. Drain and chop the cod into large pieces.

Heat 2 tablespoons of the olive oil in a large frying pan. Fry the pieces of cod for 3 minutes on each side. Remove with tongs or a slotted spoon and set aside.

Add the remaining tablespoon of olive oil and gently cook the onions over a low flame until they are soft. Stirring constantly, add the garlic and flour to the onions. Stir in the vermouth and gherkins or capers and simmer, uncovered, for 5 minutes. Put the cod back in the pot. Check for seasonings—you may want to add some salt and/or pepper and cook for a few more minutes.

Serve in a brightly colored shallow dish, sprinkled with chopped parsley.

Les Poissons

Variation:
You may omit the flour and add the pulp of 3 chopped tomatoes to
thicken the sauce.

Escargots à la Provence

Snails Simmered in Herbs and Wine

Throughout France snail hunting, *la chasse aux escargots,* is one of
the children's favorite pastimes.* Snails are gathered right after a
rainfall in wire baskets and kept there or in cages for two weeks,
and are fed only flour or chaff so that their systems are purged of
all the unpleasant slime. Before cooking they are rinsed in vinegar
or water. In Marseilles entire meals of snails, *caracolades,* are
served, and in marketplaces cooked snails are often sold as snacks
in paper cones.

In the South of France there are two kinds of escargots: *les
blanquettes,* which are whitish and plump, and *les petits gris*
(*cantareu* in Nice), which are striped gray and white and served
with *aïoli monstre* or a strong tomato and red pepper sauce.

Snails can also be the base of an omelet. Here is a Provençal
recipe that can be used for either kind of snails. For a main course,
double all the ingredients. In Provence peasants eat snails with
a straight pin. Here aluminum snail dishes and forks can be bought
to set a more elegant table.

* Since snail hunting seems to be unheard-of in America, children might
hunt for periwinkles instead. These tiny sea snails are easily found and
gathered on most rocky beaches on both the Atlantic and Pacific coasts.
Because they are so small, you will need quite a few.

As an appetizer for 6 people:

2 *tablespoons olive oil*
3 *dozen canned snails*
2 *shallots, minced*
2 *garlic cloves, peeled and crushed*
2 *tablespoons chopped Italian parsley*
  salt
  freshly ground black pepper
1 *cup dry white wine*
½ *teaspoon fennel or anise seed*
  bouquet garni (p. 11)
2 *tablespoons bread crumbs (preferably homemade)*

Heat 1 tablespoon of the olive oil in a large skillet. Add the snails but not the shells. Sauté them for 2 minutes over a medium flame, tossing with a wooden spoon. Add the shallots, 1 crushed garlic clove, 1 tablespoon parsley, and salt and pepper. Cook 2 more minutes, stirring gently. Add the wine, fennel, and bouquet garni. Cover, lower the flame, and simmer for 10 minutes. Remove snails with a slotted spoon. Reserve snails and wine sauce.

Preheat the broiler. Place the empty snail shells in a baking dish and put a snail and 1 teaspoon of wine sauce in each shell. Sprinkle on each snail some bread crumbs, crushed garlic, parsley, and olive oil. Broil for 3 minutes. Serve immediately with plenty of French bread and a dry white wine.

Variation:
Simply sauté the snails with herbs and garlic and serve as is, *comme ça*. Or serve them with hot tomato sauce or *aïoli*.

Estockaficada
Dried Cod and Vegetable Stew

This highly seasoned super fish stew made of dried cod has a place of honor in Nice: one of the most renowned culinary clubs of the city has borrowed its name. The club meets once a month to chat and taste a new interpretation of *estockaficada*.

"Stockfish" means fish that is literally "as dry as a stick." The

Les Poissons

name "stockfish" (hence the term *estockaficada*) was originally applied to the dried cod brought to Nice by Norwegian sailors (who sometimes caught the fish in New England!) in exchange for olive oil and fresh vegetables.

To buy a substitute for stockfish, try to find the hardest, driest cod available (Italian and Spanish groceries are the most likely to have it), or buy the Chinese *tai tze* in 8-ounce packages. Since it keeps forever, keep a good amount in your kitchen ready for use.

In Nice the advice is to let the stockfish sit in a running creek for two days. Depending on the dryness and saltiness of the cod you buy, the soaking time can vary from one to two days.

Estockaficada is much better reheated after the cooked fish has marinated for a few hours in its pungent sauce. It freezes successfully.

For 6 people:

    2 *pounds dried cod*
  1/2 *cup olive oil*
    5 *garlic cloves, minced*
    5 *large onions, minced*
    3 *bell peppers (green, yellow, or red)*
        seeded and sliced into 1-inch strips
    8 *tomatoes, fresh or canned, quartered*
    2 *bay leaves*
    2 *teaspoons thyme*
    2 *teaspoons savory*
     freshly ground black pepper
 1 1/2 *cups dry white wine*
    8 *potatoes, sliced 1/2 inch thick*
  1/2 *cup olives (unpitted black olives from*
       Nice or pitted oil-cured black
       olives)
    4 *tablespoons chopped parsley*
     olive oil in small cruets

If you use the very dry cod, let it soak in the sink in cold water or a large pot for two days and change the water four times. If you use the kind of cod most fishmarkets carry, one night of soaking is enough. In any case, always check with the shopkeeper on how long his particular cod needs to be soaked, and always taste before cooking it to see that it is tasty but not oversalty.

When the cod has been properly soaked, remove the tail, skin, and bones with your fingers. Shred the flesh with your fingers and

Fish

let it marinate for a few hours in a dish covered with a layer of the olive oil (save the oil for using later in this recipe).

Heat 2 tablespoons of the olive oil (or more, if necessary) from the marinade in a Doufeu or heavy-bottomed pan. Add the cod and sauté it, turning it over once with tongs or a wooden spoon, for 5 minutes. Add 1 tablespoon of the olive oil, then the garlic, onions, peppers, tomatoes, bay leaves, thyme, savory, pepper, and wine. Simmer, covered, in the pan for 1½ hours. Add the potatoes and cook, uncovered, for 20 to 30 minutes more.

Just before serving, add the olives and parsley. Check the seasoning once more (it must be highly peppered). Place the cruets of olive oil around the dinner table so that each person can crush his or her potatoes in the sauce and add a dash of olive oil to the dish.

Gigot de Mer

Fish Baked with Onion, Eggplant, Zucchini, Peppers, and White Wine

This "leg of lamb from the sea" is so called because slices of garlic are stuck into the fish the same way they would be for roast leg of lamb—*gigot d'agneau*—before the fish is baked on a bed of *ratatouille*. You may use thick slices of haddock, fresh cod, or belly fish or a whole large whiting, striped bass, or red snapper. It is a remarkably easy yet delicious dish imbued with the flavors of vegetables, garlic, and white wine. *Riz aux Herbes* (p. 225) perfectly complements the taste of *gigot de mer,* and a green tossed salad concludes the meal happily. Serve with a chilled dry white wine.

For 6 people:

- 2 *large eggplants*
  salt
- 2 *tablespoons olive oil*
- 4 *onions, chopped*
- 4 *green peppers, diced*
- 4 *zucchini or 2 cucumbers, diced*
  salt
  freshly ground white pepper
- 1 *5- to 6-pound whole fish (red snapper or*

> *whiting or bass),* or about 5 pounds*
> *fillets (haddock, cod, or belly fish),*
> *sliced 1½ inches thick*
> 2 *garlic cloves, slivered*
> 2 *bay leaves*
> 1 *teaspoon thyme*
> 4 *lettuce leaves*
> 1 *cup dry white wine or dry white ver-*
> *mouth*
> 2 *tablespoons minced basil or Italian*
> *parsley*

Peel and dice the eggplants into ½-inch pieces, toss with salt and drain in a colander for 30 minutes. Squeeze out as much moisture as possible with paper towels. Heat the olive oil in a heavy frying pan. Add about a quarter of the chopped onions and the green peppers, zucchini, and eggplant. Sprinkle with salt and pepper and simmer for 20 minutes, stirring from time to time and adding more olive oil if the mixture begins to stick to the pan. (This step can be done ahead.)

Heat the oven to 375°. If you are using whole fish, make ¼-inch slits in the skin of the fish and insert the garlic slivers as you would in a leg of lamb. For thick slices of fish, insert the garlic between the rings of muscle—two or three per slice.

Place the fish in an oiled baking dish. Sprinkle with the remaining chopped onion and the bay leaves, thyme, salt, and pepper. Cover with the lettuce leaves, pour in the wine and bake for 15 minutes.

Lift the whole fish out of the dish with two spatulas and discard the lettuce. Scrape the cooked onions into the eggplant mixture and put a part of this into the baking dish to make a bed. Lay the top half of the fish skin side down on the vegetables. Place the bottom half on top, skin side up. If you are using slices of fish, simply lay them on top of the eggplant bed. Put 2 to 3 tablespoons of the vegetables over the fish and the remainder around it. Bake for another 15 minutes, or until the fish is opaque and flakes easily. Serve immediately, sprinkled with the basil or parsley.

Note: Sprinkled with olive oil, this dish is delicious served cold the next day.

* Ask your fish dealer to remove the head and backbone but to save the bone. The dish will have a better flavor if you add the bone during the baking, placing it between the two fillets. It should be removed, of course, before serving.

Fish

Loup Farci à la Niçoise

Bass Stuffed with Tomatoes, Olives, and Mushrooms

Although this is called *loup farci*, the colorful stuffing is not cooked with the fish but added just before serving. It is a delight to the eye and an uncommon pleasure to the palate. Indigenously Niçois, it is delicious served with *Gnocchis* (p. 214–15), *Riz aux Herbes* (p. 225) or *Courgettes Râpées* (p. 183).

This recipe makes six very generous portions, but any leftovers (plus the raw fish head that has been saved) can be used for *Soupe de Pêcheurs* (pp. 37–38).

For 6 people:

Fish

- 2 tablespoons fennel or anise seed
- 2 teaspoons Dijon mustard
- 1 6-pound bass, filleted, and its backbone
  salt
- ½ teaspoon freshly ground white pepper
- 3 bay leaves
- 1 tablespoon olive oil
- 3 lettuce leaves (Boston, escarole, or iceberg)

Preheat the oven to 350°.

Mix the fennel or anise seed and mustard. Make six evenly distributed ½-inch slits in the fish and put a dab (about the size of a pea) of the mixture in each cut. Sprinkle the fillets with salt and pepper.

Place one fillet skin side down in an oiled baking dish, put the bone on it, and lay the other fillet on top, skin side up. Lay the bay leaves on the fish and sprinkle with olive oil. Cover with lettuce leaves and bake for 40 minutes.

2 tablespoons oil (half olive oil, half
    peanut oil)
½ cup finely chopped lean salt pork
3 onions, minced
1 pound mushrooms, finely chopped
3 garlic cloves, minced
1½ pounds tomatoes (fresh or canned),
    chopped
1 cup dry white wine
½ cup small black olives or pitted oil-
    cured olives
½ cup minced Italian parsley
  salt
  freshly ground white pepper

Heat the oil in a large frying pan. Add the pork, onions, mushrooms, and garlic and sauté for 5 minutes. Add the tomatoes and
wine and simmer, uncovered, for 30 minutes to reduce the liquid.
This should be a *fine* mixture. Add the olives, parsley, and salt and
pepper. Cover and keep warm.

Using two spatulas, gently place the whole fish on a warm
platter. Remove the lettuce and bay leaves. Carefully lift the top
fillet and place it skin side down next to the other fillet. Remove
the bone (save it for making soup) and pour the "stuffing" down
the middle of the fillets. If fish slices were used, simply pour the
"stuffing" over them.

Loup Grillé au Fenouil

Grilled Fish with Fennel, Lemon Juice, and Olive Oil

A grilled fish should be moist inside, crisp outside and fragrant all
over. In Nice, *loup de mer, dorades, pageots,* and *rougets* are
brushed with olive oil, stuffed with dried fennel branches, and
cooked over wood fires sprinkled with dried herbs. Often, since
they have been caught that very morning, they are neither gutted
nor scaled. This is a simple but perfect way to eat fresh fish.

Bass, porgies, and red mullet are delicious prepared with fennel
seed and a little savory and broiled, if it is not possible to have

Fish

a wood fire. You may want to place two thin slices of *Beurre d'Anchois* (p. 77–78) over each fish just before serving or to pass a bowl of *Sauce Jaune et Verte* (p. 80), *Rouille* (p. 89), *Aïoli* (p. 75), *Sauce Citronnette* (p. 78), *Sauce Dorée* (p. 80), *Sauce Tartare* (p. 90), or *Sauce Verte* (pp. 91–92), to spread on the grilled fish. Serve the fish with *Riz aux Herbes* (p. 225) *Courgettes Râpées* (p. 183), *Pommes de Terre à l'Ail* (p. 201), or *Champignons Farcis* (p. 180).

For 6 people:

6 *1-pound fish or 3 larger fish (striped bass, sea bass, porgies, red mullet), with their heads and tails left on*
6 *tablespoons fennel seed*
juice of 1 lemon
salt
freshly ground pepper
3 *tablespoons savory or oregano*
fresh fennel stalks
2 *tablespoons olive oil*
12 *to 15 vine leaves or lettuce leaves (Boston is best)*
1 *bunch parsley or watercress*
2 *lemons, sliced*

Clean and dry the fish. Cut a few slashes on the sides of each fish with a sharp knife (to allow it to cook evenly, to prevent it from curling as it cooks, and to let the flavor of the herbs penetrate it).

Sprinkle the inside with fennel seed, lemon juice, salt, pepper, and savory and rub the outside with the same ingredients. Stuff the fish with fresh or dried fennel stalks. Sprinkle olive oil over both sides of each fish and wrap loosely with vine or lettuce leaves, which will protect the fish from the heat for a few minutes and keep the flesh moist; as the fish grills they will crumble away.

If the fish are small and thin, put them on a hamburger wire grill. If you have larger fish, use the fish-shaped wire baskets, which will hold them securely and allow proper cooking.

When your wood or charcoal fire is ready (with a fine bed of embers), sprinkle on it a pinch of dried herbs, then place the wire basket over it and cook the fish for about 10 minutes on one side. Turn them over and cook the other side for 10 to 15 minutes more. The entire cooking time will vary between 20 to 30 minutes, according to the thickness of the fish. The flesh will flake easily and become opaque when cooked.

Place the fish on a warm serving platter and surround with watercress or parsley and sliced lemons.

Merlan aux Moules

Whiting, Mussels, and Vegetables Baked in a Light Curry Sauce

This is a very pretty, very light dish. The curry and lemon give a pungent flavor to the vegetable mixture. It is an easy dish to prepare, and since whiting and mussels are available all year round and are inexpensive, it is a truly reliable stand-by. Always choose the largest whiting possible, but a two- or three-pound fish will do. I like this dish served alone, but you may make it more important by serving it with *Riz aux Herbes* (p. 225), *Purée de Légumes* (pp. 201–2), or *Fenouil Braisé* (p. 186). A chilled dry white wine would be lovely with this.

For 6 people:

1 4- to 5-pound or 2 3-pound whiting
salt
freshly ground white pepper
3 pounds mussels
½ cup dry white wine
2 tablespoons olive oil
2 carrots, minced
2 onions, minced
juice of 1 lemon
2 bay leaves
6 lettuce leaves (Boston or iceberg)
1 teaspoon curry powder (or more if you prefer)
2 tablespoons chopped fresh basil or parsley

Fillet the whiting, remove the head and bones (which can be saved for making soup). Rinse and dry the fillets with paper towels and sprinkle with salt and pepper.

Scrub the mussels with a wire brush, pull out the beards with

Fish

your fingers, and place them in a large bowl of cold water for 10 minutes. Discard the mussels with open shells.

Heat the wine in a heavy-bottomed pan. Add the mussels and cook for 4 minutes, shaking the pan once. When they are cool, remove them from their shells and set aside. Pass the broth through a sieve covered with a piece of cheesecloth and reserve it.

Put 1 tablespoon of the olive oil in the skillet. Add the carrots and onions and cook for 15 minutes.

Place half of the carrots and onions in an oiled baking dish and lay the whiting on top. Salt and pepper the fish and sprinkle it with 1 tablespoon of olive oil and the lemon juice, and season with salt and pepper. Put the bay leaves on top, spread the rest of the carrots and onions on the fish and cover with the lettuce leaves.

The dish may be prepared up to this point and kept in the refrigerator until the next day, when it can be baked and finished. In that case, cover the mussels and whiting with plastic wrap and put the mussel broth in a jar.

About an hour before serving, preheat the oven to 375°. Place the dish of whiting in the oven and lower the setting to 350°. Bake for about 40 minutes.

Ten minutes before the whiting is done, boil the mussel broth in a pan for 10 minutes. Stir in the curry powder, add the mussels, and when the broth starts to boil again, cover and remove from heat.

Lift the fillets onto a warm serving platter with two spatulas. Discard the bay leaves and lettuce. Spoon the vegetables around and over the fish. Pour the mussels and the broth over the whole dish. Check the seasoning—it should be quite spicy. Sprinkle with basil or parsley and serve.

Note: You can use the leftovers from this dish for *Soupe de Pêcheurs* (pp. 37–38) or *Salade de Riz Variée* (pp. 70–71).

Merlan Magali
Whiting and Mussels in White Wine Sauce

This lovely dish shows a curious combination of influences—the egg sauce obviously comes from the North, and the oregano adds an interesting Southern touch to the delicate flavor of the whiting.

Serve with boiled new potatoes or *Riz aux Herbes* (p. 225) and an endive salad or *Salade Mesclun* p. 73).

The recipe calls for a large whiting, which may seem a bit excessive, but you can make *Salade de Riz Variée* (pp.70–71) with the leftovers.

For 6 people:

    1 *4- to 5-pound whiting*
    4 *pounds mussels*
    ½ *cup dry white wine (California Chablis
        is acceptable)*
    1 *onion, minced*
    1 *carrot, minced*
    1 *tablespoon olive oil*
      bouquet garni (p. 11)
      salt
      freshly ground white pepper
    2 *egg yolks*
      juice of 1 lemon
    1 *tablespoon flour*
    1 *tablespoon butter*
    1 *teaspoon oregano*
    ¼ *cup chopped Italian parsley, plus 2
        sprigs*

Scrub the mussels with a metal or strong nylon brush and remove the beards. Set them in cold water for 10 minutes. Discard any opened mussels.

Heat the wine in an earthenware dish or a Doufeu. Add the mussels, cover, and cook for 5 minutes, tossing gently with a spoon. Cool. Take out the mussels and discard the shells. Strain the broth through a piece of cheesecloth spread over a sieve and reserve.

Preheat oven to 375°.

Spread the oñion and carrot in a deep baking dish and add the oil and bouquet garni. Lay the fish on top, season with salt and pepper, and bake for 25 to 30 minutes. Peel off the fish skin with a knife and discard it.

Blend the egg yolks and lemon juice in a small bowl. In a heavy-bottomed pan, blend the flour and butter over low heat. Add the mussel broth while stirring gently with a wooden spoon over a low flame. Remove from heat and add the oregano and egg-lemon mixture. Heat the sauce for 1 minute, adding the mussels. Cover and remove from heat.

Place the whiting on a warm serving platter and pour the mussels and sauce over it. Before serving, sprinkle with chopped parsley and put a sprig of parsley at each end of the dish.

Moules de Pêcheurs

Steamed Mussels with Mayonnaise, Mustard, Served Cold

This is a tart and invigorating dish. It can be done ahead of time, and is dressy enough to be either the first course of an elegant dinner or the main attraction of a brunch. Serve with a crisp white wine.

For 6 people:

5 *pounds mussels (there should be about*
    12 mussels in a pound)
2 *large onions, chopped*
5 *tablespoons water*
    about 1 teaspoon salt
2 *garlic cloves, chopped*
    freshly ground black pepper
1 *egg yolk*
¾ *cup oil (half olive oil, half peanut oil)*
1 *tablespoon Dijon mustard*
    juice of half a lemon
½ *cup minced Italian parsley*

Scrub the mussels under cold water with a stiff brush and remove the beards. Let the mussels stand for 10 minutes in cold water and discard the mussels that either have opened shells or are very heavy.

Put the onions in a large frying pan with the water, salt, garlic, and pepper. Boil, covered, for 10 minutes. Add the mussels and cook, covered, for 4 minutes, stirring occasionally. Remove the mussels with a slotted spoon and discard the shells. Strain the liquid through a piece of cheesecloth spread over a sieve.

Prepare the sauce with the egg yolk, oil, mustard, and lemon juice (for instructions, see *Mayonnaise,* pp. 81–82). Add the parsley, then slowly stir in 2 to 3 tablespoons of the mussel broth. Pour the sauce over the mussels, sprinkle with parsley, and chill.

Moules aux Épinards

Baked Mussels Filled with Spinach and Mushrooms

Delicious and quite dressy as a first course. If it is your main course, double the proportions.

For 6 people:

- 2 *pounds (about 24) mussels*
- 1/2 *cup dry white wine or water*
- 1 *teaspoon thyme*
- 2 *tablespoons olive oil*
- 1 *large onion, chopped*
- 12 *mushrooms, chopped*
- 1 *teaspoon freshly grated nutmeg*
- 2 *tablespoons chopped parsley*
  salt
  freshly ground black pepper
- 1 *10-ounce box frozen spinach, cooked, drained, and chopped*
- 2 *tablespoons bread crumbs (preferably homemade)*
  lemon juice

Scrub the mussels and remove the beards. Soak them in cold water for 10 minutes, then discard all those that are opened or too heavy. Place the mussels in a large pan with the wine or water and thyme. Cover and cook for 5 minutes, or until the shells have opened. Cool.

Preheat oven to 375°.

Discard half of the shell of each mussel. Heat 1 tablespoon of the oil in a heavy-bottomed pan. Add the onion and mushrooms. Cook for 5 minutes, add the nutmeg, parsley, and salt and pepper, and cook for 5 more minutes. Check to see if the seasoning is right. Add the spinach and remove from heat.

If the mussels are unusually large, cut them into two or three pieces with kitchen shears. Put a mussel or a piece of mussel in

Fish

117

each shell and spoon the spinach stuffing over it, then smooth the top with your fingers. Sprinkle bread crumbs and a little olive oil on each. Arrange the stuffed mussel shells on a large baking dish with ½ cup of water at the bottom (to prevent sticking), and bake for 15 minutes. Sprinkle with lemon juice just before serving.

Note: Some people add 2 eggs to the stuffing to bind it, but I prefer the looser version given here.

Morue et Légumes Cuits sur Braise
Dried Cod and Vegetable Barbecue

This is associated with an old Provençal custom. On Sunday nights fathers were responsible for dinner, and this was one of their treats. They would light a fire with the help of all the children, then the whole family would sit around the fireplace and chat while the cod and the vegetables sizzled on the grill.

The dish was sometimes prepared with unsoaked dried cod, but cooked that way it is too salty for my taste. This is the version I have chosen.

> For 6 people:
>
> 2 *pounds dried cod*
> 12 *small potatoes, unpeeled and washed*
> 6 *small white onions, peeled*
> 6 *garlic cloves,* unpeeled
> 1 *bottle good olive oil*
> 1 *bottle red wine vinegar*
> *salt*
> *peppercorns in a pepper mill*

Soak the cod for several hours or overnight in cold water, changing the water according to the instructions on the package. Drain the cod and cut the fillets in half.

Light a fire and wait until the flames are out and the wood or charcoal is glowing. Place the potatoes and the onions on a fine-meshed grill. Add the cod and the garlic cloves. After 15 minutes turn the potatoes over with tongs (do not turn the cod—it might fall apart) and cook until all the ingredients are tender—it will take from 20 to 30 minutes.

Place all the ingredients on a warm platter and pass it around with the cruets of oil and of vinegar, the salt shaker, and the pepper mill. Each person will peel his or her potato and garlic clove, and the seasoning will be done individually.

Serve with a cool rosé and a *Salade Mesclun* (p. 73) or *Salade Amère* (p. 59).

Nu et Cru

Sliced Raw Fish with Lemon and Parsley

This fascinating dish is one of the quickest and simplest to prepare. It can be served as an hors d'oeuvre, but if you double the proportions it can be the main part of a summer meal followed by a vegetable dish and a light dessert. Prepare it the day before, then chill it. It needs no last-minute preparation and will be ready to serve when you need it.

For 6 people:

1 2-pound whiting, filleted
salt
juice of 2 lemons
3 tablespoons chopped parsley
2 tablespoons chopped chives
freshly ground white pepper
2 tablespoons olive oil
2 tablespoons chopped capers

Skin the fillets and dry them with a paper towel. With a sharp knife, cut them into ¼-inch strips. Put them on a plate and cover with salt. Cover and refrigerate overnight. The next day, taste a little of the fish and if it is too salty, rinse it under cold water. Dry with paper towels and place on a plate. Sprinkle with lemon juice, parsley, chives, pepper, and olive oil. Cover with plastic wrap and chill for about 4 hours.

Check the seasoning. Add pepper if needed, and sprinkle with capers.

Fish

Omelette de Moules

Mussel Omelet

One of the lightest and tastiest luncheon dishes, it is also one of the easiest to prepare. Served with a tossed salad and followed by a light dessert, it makes for a lively and inexpensive meal you can prepare all year round.

For 6 people:

2 pounds mussels (there will be about 24
good mussels left after the bad ones
have been sorted out)
8 eggs
2 tablespoons chopped parsley
salt
freshly ground pepper
2 tablespoons olive oil

Scrub the mussels and remove the beards with your fingers. Place them in a bowl of cold water for 10 minutes. Discard all the mussels that have opened and place the rest in a heavy-bottomed pan. Cover and cook for about 5 minutes, tossing once. Remove from heat and let cool. Discard the shells and place the mussels in a bowl. With a pair of kitchen shears, cut each mussel into two or three pieces.

Beat the eggs in a large bowl. Add the mussels, parsley, and salt and pepper.

Heat the olive oil in a frying pan. Add the omelet mixture and cook for a few minutes, shaking gently. Slide the omelet onto a warm dish and sprinkle with a little olive oil.

Poisson au Court-Bouillon

Cold Poached Fish

Les Poissons

This is served throughout the South of France in the summertime. It makes a superb buffet dish surrounded by colorful vegetables and a variety of cold sauces. The best fish for this dish are the large, firm kinds, such as red snapper, striped or sea bass, whiting, and salmon.

For 6 people:

Court-Bouillon (*pp. 100–2*)
1 *5-pound fish (people tend to eat more when it's cold)*
white wine or water if needed
salt
freshly ground white pepper
2 *hard-boiled eggs, sliced lengthwise*
10 *cherry tomatoes*
8 *sprigs arugula or watercress or basil*
2 *small bunches Italian parsley*
2 *lemons, sliced*
8 *black olives*
2 *tablespoons capers*
1 *bowl of each sauce:* Rouille (*p. 89*), Aïoli (*p. 75*), Pistou (*p. 86*), Sauce Verte (*pp. 91–92*)

Prepare the court bouillon (this takes at least 2 hours).

Clean the fish and lay it on the cheesecloth in a pan with sides as high as the fish is thick. Be sure the cloth hangs over the sides so you can pick up the fish when it's ready. Cover the fish with court bouillon (if there isn't enough, add white wine or water). Fold the edges of the cloth over the fish. Simmer on top of the stove for 45 minutes. (A rule of thumb is 10 minutes per inch of the measurement across the widest part of the fish.)

Let the liquid cool. Gently remove the fish with two spatulas, using the cloth to hold it together and let it drain on a platter. Remove the cloth and peel off the visible skin. Blot the fish with a kitchen towel and sprinkle with salt and pepper.

Arrange the eggs, tomatoes, and arugula or watercress or basil to surround the fish. Decorate the head with bunches of parsley on each side and place lemon slices, olives, and capers on top of the fish.

Serve at room temperature or chilled. Offer a variety of sauces; the fish will seem to be several different dishes.

Fish

Poisson à la Chartreuse

Baked Fish and Vegetables in White Wine

This is a delicious way to cook a strong fishy fish (such as fresh tuna or cod)—a variation on a recipe created by the monks of La Grande Chartreuse. Fresh red tuna is not always easy to find, but swordfish, cod, or halibut are available most of the year and lend themselves to this preparation. Serve this with a light tossed salad and a dry white wine.

For 6 people:

3 *pounds fresh red tuna (or halibut, cod, or swordfish), cut in a thick slice as for a fish steak*
  boiling water to cover
  salt
1 *lemon, cut in half*
12 *anchovy fillets, cut in half*
3 *tablespoons olive oil*
2 *carrots, sliced thin*
2 *onions, sliced thin*
  salt
  freshly ground black pepper
3 *garlic cloves, minced*
½ *teaspoon fennel seed*
1 *cup sorrel leaves, chopped (optional)*
4 *leaves Boston or romaine lettuce, blanched and cut in strips*
1 *cup dry white wine*

Blanch the slice of tuna in a pot of boiling water with salt and the lemon halves for 5 minutes and drain it. Because the fish has been cut crosswise, the flesh will have concentric rings—insert the anchovies between these rings by first making small cuts with a knife.

You can prepare this much ahead of time. Cover with plastic wrap and refrigerate until ready to cook. (The carrots, onions, and blanched lettuce can also be cut and kept covered and refrigerated.)

Heat the olive oil in a heavy-bottomed pan and add the carrots and onions. Lay the fish on them, sprinkle with salt and pepper,

Les Poissons

and cook over a medium flame for 10 minutes. Gently turn the fish over with two spatulas. Add the garlic and fennel seed. Cover with the sorrel and lettuce leaves and simmer for 10 minutes more. Add the wine and cook over a low flame for 20 to 30 minutes. Check the seasoning.

Place the fish in the center of a warm platter. Pile the carrots and onions at one end of the dish, the sorrel at the other end, and lettuce along the sides. Pour the juices over the fish and vegetables and season again with a little salt and pepper.

Poisson aux Champignons
Baked Fish with Mushrooms in White Wine

This delectable, light dish is very easy to prepare. The delicate, subtly flavored sauce is thickened only by the cooked onions, so make sure you mince or grate them very fine.

I like to serve this dish by itself, followed by a green tossed salad. But if you want a more substantial meal, *Courgettes Râpées* (p. 183) or *Riz aux Herbes* (p. 225) are good accompaniments.

Choose a large, firm fillet of bass, red snapper, fresh cod, haddock, or belly fish. This dish is highly seasoned but not rich, and the lettuce or sorrel infuses the fish with moisture and flavor.

For 6 people:

4 pounds fish fillets or trimmed slices
freshly ground white pepper
1 teaspoon savory
3 tablespoons oil (half olive and half pea-
nut oil)
1 tablespoon cognac (optional)
1 pound white or yellow onions, grated or
finely minced
2 pounds fresh mushrooms, sliced 1/4 inch
thick
salt
1 cup dry white wine
3 lettuce leaves (Boston, escarole, or ice-
*berg) or 1 cup chopped sorrel leaves**

Fish

* If you have neither of these on hand, you may use aluminum foil instead.

Dry the fillets with paper towels. Sprinkle with pepper and savory and set aside. Heat 2 tablespoons of the olive oil in a baking dish that covers two burners on the stove.* Add the fish and sauté for 2 minutes. Turn over gently with two spatulas and cook for 5 minutes. Remove from the stove. Add cognac, if you have it on hand, and light it. Set aside.

Heat 1 tablespoon of the olive oil in a heavy-bottomed skillet. Add the onions and mushrooms and sauté for 10 minutes. When the vegetables are limp, add salt, pepper, and the wine and continue cooking. Gently lift the fish onto a platter. Add its juices and salt and pepper to the onion-mushroom mixture. Wash and oil the baking dish and place half of the mixture in it. Gently lay the fish on this bed and cover with the rest of the mixture. Spread the lettuce leaves (or the sorrel sautéed in 1 tablespoon olive oil) on top and cook over low heat for 40 minutes. (When you can easily prick a needle through to the bone, it is done.) Remove the lettuce leaves.

Sprinkle the fish with salt and pepper and serve surrounded with sprigs of parsley on a large warm platter.

Poisson en Papillotte

Baked Fish with Shallots

You may use any large, firm fish for this dish: red snapper, bass, whiting, or cod. The lettuce leaves will keep it moist during the baking. You may serve this with *Céleri Paysanne* (p. 179), *Févettes à la Verdure* (p. 188), *Riz aux Herbes* (p. 225), or *Pommes de Terre aux Herbes* (pp. 202–3).

For 6 people:

> 2 *tablespoons white or red wine vinegar*
> 1 *cup minced shallots*
> 1 *5-pound bass*
> *salt*
> *freshly ground black pepper*
> 2 *teaspoons thyme*
> 1 *tablespoon olive oil*
> 1 *bay leaf, cut in half*

Les Poissons

* If you use a very delicate fish, you may prefer to bake it in a 375° oven for about 40 minutes instead of cooking it on top of the stove.

> 4 lettuce leaves (Boston, escarole, or ice-
> berg)
> 1/4 cup chopped Italian parsley

Heat the vinegar in a frying pan and cook the shallots gently for 5 minutes, or until soft.

Preheat oven to 350°.

Clean and dry the fish. Sprinkle salt, pepper, and thyme inside and outside. Spread the shallots and vinegar inside the fish and rub the outside with olive oil. Place the bay leaf on top and cover with lettuce leaves. Wrap in aluminum foil and seal the folded edges. Put in a large baking dish and bake for 40 minutes. Remove the foil and lettuce, sprinkle the parsley on top, and serve.

Poisson Mariné

Cold Broiled Fish Marinated with Vegetables

This is a delectable way to serve fish in summer—perfect for a buffet or a luncheon followed by a tossed lettuce salad and a dessert. This needs to marinate for five days but is otherwise very easy to prepare and none of the ingredients are exotic. Offer a cool crisp white wine with this.

> For 6 people:
>
> 6 small fish (sardines, bass or whiting) or
>   1 large 5-pound fish (striped bass,
>   whiting, red snapper)
>   salt
> 1 quart wine vinegar
> 1 large onion, chopped
> 1 carrot, chopped
> 2 shallots or 2 small white onions
> 1 celery stalk, chopped
> 5 tablespoons minced parsley
> 1 whole clove
> 1 teaspoon thyme
> 3 bay leaves
>   freshly ground pepper
> 4 tablespoons olive oil
> 2 lemons, sliced

Fish

Fillet the fish and rinse and dry them. Sprinkle heavily with salt and cover with plastic wrap. Refrigerate for 3 hours.

Meanwhile, prepare the marinade. Heat the vinegar in a heavy-bottomed pan and add the onion, carrot, shallots or onions, celery stalk, 3 tablespoons of the parsley, clove, thyme, bay leaves, and pepper. Bring to a boil and simmer for 30 minutes. Remove from heat and let it cool.

Preheat the oven to 400°. Rub the fillets with a paper towel to remove the excess salt. Place under the broiler for 3 minutes on each side. Remove the skin with a sharp knife and place the fillets side by side in a shallow dish. Pour the cold marinade over them, cover with plastic wrap, and refrigerate.

After three days, discard the marinade and cover the fillets with olive oil. Leave them, covered with plastic wrap, two days longer in the refrigerator.

Using two spatulas, place the fish on a platter. Sprinkle 2 tablespoons of parsley on top and garnish with slices of lemon before serving.

Poisson en Raïto

Fish Stewed in a Vegetable and Red Wine Sauce

The preparation *en raïto* means the fish is first fried in a little olive oil, then slowly cooked in a sauce consisting of red wine (or red vermouth), tomatoes, and herbs. You can use a variety of fish for this, but make sure all skin is removed and the fillets are trimmed and completely boneless when you add them to the sauce. Since *raïto* is thick and will camouflage whatever bones that are in it, you don't want any unpleasant surprises as you bite into the fish.

You can serve this substantial dish with *Fenouil Braisé* (p. 186), *Gnocchis* (pp. 214–15), *Tout-Nus* (p. 227), or *Riz aux Herbes* (p. 225), along with a watercress or endive salad and a full-bodied red wine.

For 6 people:

> 6 *medium-sized whiting or mullet,*
>   *filleted, or 1 3-pound piece of hali-*
>   *but, fresh cod, or haddock, cut in a*
>   *slice 1½ inches thick*

2 teaspoons thyme
4 tablespoons olive oil
3 large onions, chopped
2 cups red wine
4 tomatoes, peeled and quartered, or 1⅓
    cups canned, quartered
6 garlic cloves, peeled and crushed
3 bay leaves
2 teaspoons savory
  salt
  freshly ground black pepper
12 little black Niçois olives, unpitted, or 6
    black oil-cured olives
½ cup capers
2 tablespoons chopped parsley

Sprinkle the fish fillets or slices with 1 teaspoon of the thyme. Heat 3 tablespoons of the olive oil in a frying pan and cook the fish 3 minutes on each side,* turning delicately with a spatula. Let it cool and then carefully remove the skin with a sharp knife.

Heat 2 tablespoons of the olive oil in a heavy-bottomed pan, add onions, and stir for 2 minutes. Add the wine and simmer for 10 minutes, then stir in the tomatoes, garlic, bay leaves, 1 teaspoon of the thyme, savory, and salt and pepper. Cook, uncovered, for 30 minutes.

Purée the mixture through a Mouli mill into a bowl. Put half of the purée in a wide pan or baking dish. Place the fish on it, sprinkle with salt and pepper, and cover with the rest of the purée. Cook, uncovered, on top of the stove for 20 minutes.

Add the olives and capers, check the seasoning, and cook for 5 minutes. Transfer to a warm serving dish and sprinkle with parsley.

* Instead of frying, you can bake the fish in a 350° oven for 30 minutes.

Poulpes Provençale
Octopus Cooked in a Tomato and White Wine Sauce

There is an unfortunate prejudice in the United States against serving squid and octopus. Along the Mediterranean coast and in the

Orient they are considered delicacies. It would surprise many to know that much of the canned "lobster" sold in France is rumored to be octopus. In any case, *le homard du pauvre* is simply delicious. It should be served with a robust dry white wine.

For 6 people:

2 *pounds fresh octopus*
3 *quarts water*
3 *tablespoons olive oil*
⅓ *cup cognac*
2 *medium-sized onions, chopped*
5 *large tomatoes, chopped*
  bouquet garni (p. 11)
  a pinch of Spanish saffron (not the powdered kind) or curry
2 *garlic cloves, crushed*
1 *teaspoon thyme*
1 *cup dry white wine*
  salt
  freshly ground black pepper
2 *tablespoons chopped parsley*
1 *garlic clove, minced*

Wash the octopus under running water. Make sure the fish dealer has removed the ends of the tentacles, eyes, ink bag, and intestines. Soak the octopus for 3 hours in cold water, changing the water twice.

Bring the water to a boil in a large pot and scald the octopus in it three times, counting to three each time. Then cut the octopus into 1½-inch cubes with a large knife or kitchen shears and dry thoroughly.

Heat 2 tablespoons of the olive oil in a heavy skillet, add the octopus, and toss for a few minutes. Reduce the heat, cover, and simmer slowly for 30 minutes. Put the octopus in a bowl.

Pour the cognac into the skillet, swishing it around, and scrape the bottom of the pan. Pour this liquid over the octopus in the bowl. Add 1 tablespoon of the olive oil to the skillet and gently cook the onions and tomatoes for 15 minutes. Add the octopus with its juice, the bouquet garni, saffron (or curry), crushed garlic, thyme, wine, and salt and pepper. Simmer, covered, for 1 hour, or until tender. Remove the octopus from the sauce.

Sprinkle the octopus with parsley and minced garlic and put it in the center of a crown of rice. Serve the sauce separately in a bowl.

Sardines Grillées

Grilled Fresh Sardines with Parsley and Garlic

Fresh sardines are available in the fall. This is an incredibly easy way to prepare them, and to my taste one of the best. It will take about 10 minutes from start to finish. If you cannot grill them over an open fire, a broiler will do. Serve this alone as an hors d'oeuvre or with *Salade Mesclun* (p. 73) or *Salade Amère* (p. 59) and *Riz au Safran* (p. 226).

For 6 people:

24 *small sardines, cleaned but left whole*
    with their heads
  salt
 2 *tablespoons flour*
  juice of 2 lemons
  freshly ground pepper
 3 *tablespoons minced parsley*
 3 *garlic cloves, finely chopped*
 1 *tablespoon olive oil*

Preheat the broiler. Rinse and dry the sardines between paper towels and sprinkle them with salt and flour. Place them in a shallow baking dish and put them 2 inches from the broiler flame for 2 minutes. Using two spatulas, turn them over on the other side. If you feel they are too small and fragile to turn over, let them cook 2 minutes longer on the same side.

Carefully take the sardines out of the broiler with two spatulas and place them on a warm platter. Sprinkle them with lemon juice, salt, pepper, parsley, garlic, and olive oil and serve.

Note: If the sardines are large, you may want to treat them more elaborately. Stuff them with chopped cooked spinach and lay them on a gratin dish. Sprinkle with bread crumbs and a little oil and broil for 5 minutes. Sprinkle with lemon juice before serving.

Fish

Suppions aux Légumes
Squid with Mushrooms and Peppers

Cooked squid is light and tender. It acquires an entirely new flavor when simmered with vegetables and white wine. Served with lettuce, bread, and cheese, this dish makes a rich meal. It reheats beautifully.

For 6 people:

2 *pounds squid*
2 *tablespoons olive oil*
4 *medium-sized onions, chopped*
1 *pound mushrooms, thinly sliced*
2 *yellow or red bell peppers, seeded and*
   cut into 1/2-inch-thick strips
3 *garlic cloves, peeled and crushed*
1 *bay leaf*
1 *teaspoon thyme*
1 *to 2 cups dry white wine*
salt
freshly ground black pepper
1/4 *cup chopped Italian parsley*

Wash and dry the squid. Cut it into 1/2-inch slices with heavy kitchen shears. Heat the olive oil in a large frying pan. Sauté the onions, mushrooms, and peppers, and add the garlic, bay leaf, thyme, wine, and salt and pepper. Simmer, uncovered, for 40 minutes, adding more wine if the vegetable mixture becomes too thick. Remove the bay leaf. Sprinkle with parsley and serve.

Suppions Farcis
Squid Stuffed with Spinach and Cheese and Simmered in Wine

Americans should really overcome their prejudice against squid because it can be so delicious. Filled with a delicate mixture of spinach, cheese, and herbs and simmered in a tomato and wine sauce, squid makes not only a light and tasty dish but an inexpensive one as well.

Don't choose the smallest squid, as they would take too long to fill. Serve with *Riz aux Herbes* (p. 225), a green tossed salad and a dry white wine.

For 6 people:
Squid and Stuffing

 3 *pounds rather large squid, cleaned*
 2 *tablespoons olive oil*
 2 *medium-sized onions, chopped*
 1 *teaspoon savory*
 1 *teaspoon freshly grated nutmeg*
   salt
   freshly ground pepper
 2 *egg yolks*
 ½ *cup grated Swiss or Parmesan cheese*
 2 *10-ounce packages frozen spinach,
     cooked, drained, and chopped*

Wash the squid and drain on paper towels. Cut off the tentacles (reserve the bodies) and chop them with kitchen shears. Put them in a skillet, add the olive oil, onions, savory, nutmeg, and salt and pepper, and cook slowly for 10 minutes. In a large bowl, beat the egg yolks, and add the cheese, spinach, tentacles, and onions. Check the seasoning and set aside.

Put some stuffing on each squid and close with a toothpick or tie with string. (Toothpicks are easier to remove than string, but choose whichever you find more convenient.) The squid will shrink as they cook, so they must not be too full.

You can prepare this much ahead of time. Cover with plastic wrap and set aside in the refrigerator until ready to use.

Sauce

2 tablespoons olive oil
3 medium-sized onions, chopped
4 fresh tomatoes, or 1⅔ cups canned,
    chopped
1 cup dry white wine
2 bay leaves
2 teaspoons savory
1 teaspoon thyme
½ teaspoon Spanish saffron, crumbled
    about 1 teaspoon salt
    freshly ground pepper
3 tablespoons chopped parsley

Heat the olive oil in a Doufeu or a large cast-iron pan, then add the stuffed squid. Cook for 5 minutes over a medium flame, reduce the heat and turn the squid over with a pair of tongs. Add the onions, tomatoes, wine, bay leaves, savory, thyme, saffron, and salt and pepper. Simmer, covered, for 20 minutes, then remove the cover and cook, uncovered, for 35 minutes. Check the seasonings (this dish must be highly seasoned). Add more saffron and salt and pepper, if necessary. Remove the bay leaves.

Serve in a warm shallow dish. Protect your hand with a kitchen towel or an oven mitt and remove the toothpicks. Sprinkle with parsley. If some of the stuffing escapes into the sauce, put the sauce through a sieve before pouring over the squid.

Note: Rice is sometimes added to the filling for a more substantial dish.

If you have leftover filling, you can use it for *Tout-Nus* (p. 227) or *Tian d'Épinards* (pp. 207–8), or for *Caillettes de Nice* (p. 143) by replacing the chicken liver with the leftover squid filling.

Suppions à la Niçoise
Squid Simmered in Tomatoes and White Wine

Squid are readily available in most fish markets, and since they are not very popular in America, they are usually quite inexpensive.

They come cleaned and are easy to slice with kitchen shears. They are excellent served with *Riz au Safran* (p. 226), *Pâtes aux Oeufs* (p. 216), *Pâtes à la Verdure* (pp. 219–20) or as a hot first course with French bread and a green tossed salad.

This dish is also good served cold as a first course or as part of a buffet, and can be successfully reheated by adding a tablespoon of olive oil before serving.

For 6 people:

2 *pounds squid (the smaller the better)*
3 *tablespoons olive oil*
2 *large onions, minced*
3 *tomatoes (fresh or canned), quartered*
2 *garlic cloves, peeled and crushed*
1 *cup dry white wine*
bouquet garni (p. 11)
1 *bay leaf*
salt
freshly ground black pepper
1 *teaspoon Spanish saffron (do not use the powdered kind)*
½ *cup small black olives or oil-cured large*
¼ *cup chopped Italian parsley*

Rinse the squid in cold water and pat dry. Cut them into ½-inch slices with kitchen shears.

Heat 2 tablespoons of the olive oil in a large skillet and sauté the pieces of squid for 5 minutes, turning them frequently. Remove them with a slotted spoon and set aside in a bowl. Add 1 tablespoon of the olive oil and cook the onions and tomatoes slowly for 10 minutes. Put the squid back in and cook for another 5 minutes. Add the garlic, wine, bouquet garni, bay leaf, salt, pepper, and saffron (crush it between your fingers as you sprinkle it on). Cover and simmer over a low flame for 40 to 45 minutes. Add the olives and cook, uncovered, for 10 to 15 minutes. Check the seasoning and discard the bay leaf. The squid should be tender and moist.

Place the squid on a warm dish and sprinkle with parsley before serving.

Fish

Thon Provençale
Fresh Red Tuna Cooked with Vegetables and White Wine

In this hearty dish the tuna is first marinated in vinegar, then simmered with wine and vegetables until it has absorbed all their flavor. Tuna is available only from early summer to early fall, but you can substitute swordfish or halibut for this recipe. Serve with *Riz aux Herbes* (p. 225) or, if you want some green vegetables with it, with *Épinards aux Pignons* (pp. 183–84) or *Courgettes Râpées* (p. 183).

For 6 people:

  1 *3-pound piece fresh red tuna, cut 1½ inches thick and skinned*
  ½ *cup red wine vinegar*
  2 *tablespoons olive oil*
  2 *garlic cloves, peeled and crushed*
  2 *large onions, sliced*
  3 *carrots, sliced*
  2 *tomatoes, quartered, or ⅔ cup canned, drained*
    salt
    freshly ground pepper
  3 *bay leaves*
  1 *lemon, sliced*
  ¾ *cup dry white wine (add more if necessary)*
  ½ *cup finely chopped Italian parsley or basil*

Marinate the fish in the vinegar for 2 hours, adding enough cold water to cover it.

Put the olive oil in a large shallow baking dish. Add the garlic, onions, carrots, and tomatoes and lay the tuna on top. Sprinkle with salt and pepper and arrange the bay leaves and lemon slices on top of the fish. Add the wine.

Place the baking dish over two burners on top of the stove and simmer, uncovered, over low heat for 40 minutes (30 minutes for swordfish and halibut) or in a 350° oven for 40 minutes.

Turn the slices of fish over with two spatulas. Cover and simmer for another 20 to 30 minutes (swordfish and halibut require less time, so start checking after the first 10 minutes). If the tuna absorbs all the liquid before the end of the cooking time, add more wine at any point to keep it from going dry.

Remove the bay leaves and lemon slices. Purée the vegetables through a Mouli food mill. Place the fish on a warm serving platter and spread the vegetable purée over it. Sprinkle with parsley or basil and serve.

Les Viandes

Meats

Some Northerners find Nice's cooking to have "not enough meat and too many bones," but the frugality of this cuisine is balanced by the imagination with which it deals with inexpensive cuts of meat. Since meat was never plentiful in the South, every part of the animal is treated with respect.

Choose your meat carefully: beef should be bright red, lamb dark pink. Trim it well and use seasonings with care. The heady *boeuf à la niçoise,* the vigorous *gardiane,* the pungent *poulet en saupiquet* rely on inexpensive materials —but God is in the details.

Most of the meat recipes here are better the next day. Many freeze well and leftover dishes are the basis for delicious preparations like *boeuf mironton, tians, salade de riz variée, farcis, ravioli niçoise, capoun.* So be generous with your proportions.

Beef (*le Boeuf*)

In Provence in the past, beef was a rare commodity because the land was better suited to raising goats and sheep— these animals could climb the steep hills and manage on any grass they could find. So even today beef is seldom eaten rare in large hunks; the broiled steaks covered with herbs and barbecued are newcomers to the repertory of Southern French cooking.

Beef is mostly prepared *mijoté,* carefully simmered with onions, carrots, orange rind, and herbs and moistened with wine. American beef is as good as the French kind, if not better, but it often has a large amount of fat, so trim it carefully.

Chicken (*le Poulet*)

We usually sauté chicken in olive oil, deglaze it with white wine or tomato sauce, then simmer it with herbs or vegetables and garlic. But most chicken in the United States is so tender that it cannot cook in a sauce long enough to absorb its taste without disintegrating. After I have rinsed and dried the chicken, I let it marinate in oil and herbs so the flavor can penetrate the meat before it is cooked.

Lamb (*l'Agneau*)

This meat is widely used simmered with thyme, rosemary, garlic, and white wine. The leg or shoulder is usually roasted with slivers of garlic or anchovies inserted in it and sprinkled with olive oil. Or it may be stuffed with red tuna, hard-boiled eggs, and herbs and served with a purée of garlic.

Since American lamb is generally more mature and fatter than Provençal lamb, it should be trimmed well and simmered long enough for the herbs and wine to flavor and tenderize the meat.

Pork (*le Porc*)

Like all the other meats, American pork is fatter than French pork. Because it is also less flavorful, it will benefit from the Provençal use of sage, fennel and anise seed, white wine, and vinegar. Trim it carefully so you can start with a reasonably lean meat.

Agneau à la Niçoise
Lamb and Vegetables Simmered in White Wine and Herbs

Curiously enough, garlic—often used with lamb—is not an ingredient in this delicate stew. The turnips enhance the flavor of the lamb and the fresh baby lima beans add a substantial texture.

Meats

Serve with a chilled dry white wine. You may like this with *Polente* (p. 222), *Gnocchis* (pp. 214–15), *Riz aux Herbes* (p. 225), or a *Purée de Légumes* (pp. 201–2), but it is a very complete dish in itself.

For 6 people:

- 4 *pounds lamb shoulder or leg, cut into 1½-inch cubes*
- 1 *teaspoon rosemary*
- 1 *teaspoon thyme*
- 2 *teaspoons salt*
  freshly ground black pepper
- 3 *cups baby lima beans (fresh or frozen)*
- 2 *tablespoons olive oil*
- ½ *cup chopped lean salt pork*
- 2 *onions, sliced*
- 2 *carrots, sliced*
- 3 *turnips, quartered*
- 2 *tomatoes, chopped, or ⅔ cup canned tomatoes*
- 3 *celery stalks, chopped*
- 2 *bay leaves*
- 2 *cups dry white wine*
- ¼ *cup finely chopped fresh parsley or mint*

Dry the lamb with a paper towel and sprinkle with rosemary, thyme, and salt and pepper. (If you add a few bones to the pot, the dish will be less elegant but even tastier.) Blanch fresh or frozen lima beans for 5 minutes and drain. Set aside.

Heat the oil in a Doufeu or cast-iron pan and add the salt pork. Lower the flame and add the lamb. Sauté for a few minutes until the lamb is browned on all sides, then add the onions, carrots, turnips, tomatoes, celery, and bay leaves. Cook, stirring well, for 5 minutes. Add the wine, cover, and cook over a low flame for 1 hour, or until the lamb is tender. Add the lima beans and cook, uncovered, for 5 minutes more.

Sprinkle with the parsley or mint and serve in a preheated shallow dish.

Boeuf Mironton*

Boiled Beef Baked in Vinegar and Caper Sauce

This crisp, golden gratin is one of the favorite Niçois ways to use leftover beef. In Provence they use what is left of their *pot-au-feu*.

Serve with a chilled dry white wine or a rosé, since the dish is not as strong as its ingredients may suggest.

For 6 people:

2 tablespoons olive oil
2 onions, minced
2 tomatoes, chopped, or ⅔ cup canned, drained
2 tablespoons beef broth or water
1 teaspoon red wine vinegar
1 garlic clove, peeled and crushed
1 bay leaf
½ to 1 teaspoon freshly grated nutmeg
⅓ cup chopped parsley
  salt
  freshly ground black pepper
6 to 8 slices or 3 cups chopped cooked beef
2 teaspoons capers
⅓ cup bread crumbs, preferably home-made

Preheat the oven to 375°. Oil a baking dish.

Gently heat 1 tablespoon of the olive oil in a cast-iron skillet and cook the onions over a low flame for about 5 minutes. Add the tomatoes and cook 5 minutes more. With a wooden spoon, stir in the beef broth and vinegar to make a smooth sauce. Add the garlic, bay leaf, nutmeg, parsley, and salt and pepper. Simmer, uncovered, for 10 minutes.

Remove the bay leaf and pour half of the sauce into the oiled baking dish. Put the slices of beef and the capers on the sauce and

* The word *mironton* is thought to have originated in the eighteenth century and the more commonly used variant *miroton* is a corruption.

pour the rest of it over them. Sprinkle with bread crumbs and the remaining olive oil. Bake 30 minutes.

Note: If you have any of this dish left over, you can prepare *croquettes de boeuf ménagère.* Add 3 potatoes, boiled and mashed, and 1 egg to 1 cup of the beef mixture. Mix well with your hands, check the seasoning, and make little balls the size of an egg. Roll the balls in flour and fry in oil. Serve with *Coulis* (p. 79).

Boeuf à la Niçoise

Marinated Beef Simmered with Tomatoes, Wine, and Spices

Although this takes two days to prepare, it is well worth the effort. This Niçois version of the classic *boeuf bourguignon* is superb. The orange rind, herbs, garlic, and olives give it a fresh and distinctive flavor. Be generous with your proportions because this dish is not only delicious the day after but its leftovers are the basis for *Ravioli Niçoise* (pp. 222–25).

Serve this with *Pâtes aux Oeufs* (p. 216), *Gnocchis* (pp. 214–15), or plain boiled potatoes—nothing too emphatic. If it is served cold, a perfect accompaniment would be *Salade Verte* (pp. 91–92).

For 6 people:

1 *3- to 4-pound boneless rump or round
    of beef*
salt
4 *tablespoons olive oil*
3 *large onions, chopped*
1 *carrot, sliced*
1 *celery stalk, chopped*
3 *cups red wine*
1 *garlic clove, peeled*
    bouquet garni (p. 11)
    freshly ground black pepper
1 *tablespoon olive oil*
½ *cup diced lean salt pork*
2 *garlic cloves, peeled and crushed*
6 *small white onions*

2 *tomatoes, chopped*
1 *small piece pork rind*
2 *teaspoons thyme*
1 *whole clove*
  rind of 1 small orange (or 4 2-inch
    pieces of rind)
6 *carrots, sliced*
½ *cup small Niçois black olives or pitted*
    oil-cured olives
2 *tablespoons finely chopped parsley*
1 *cup freshly grated Parmesan or Swiss*
    cheese

Trim the beef to remove fat and gristle and cut into 2-inch cubes. Rub the beef with 1 teaspoon of salt and set aside in a large bowl.

Heat 3 tablespoons of the olive oil in a large cast-iron skillet. Add the chopped onions, carrot, and celery and sauté gently for 5 minutes. Stir in the wine, garlic clove, bouquet garni, salt, and pepper and cook for 20 minutes. Let the liquid cool before pouring it over the meat. Cover the marinade and refrigerate overnight.

The next day, remove the meat from the marinade with a slotted spoon and dry with paper towels.

Heat 1 tablespoon of the olive oil in a Doufeu or cast-iron pan. Sauté the salt pork gently for 5 minutes, add the beef cubes and cook for 10 minutes, using tongs to turn them so that they brown evenly on all sides. Add the crushed garlic and cook for 10 minutes. Add the peeled white onions, tomatoes, pork rind, thyme, clove, orange rind, salt and pepper, and the marinade. Scrape the bottom of the pan with a spoon, lower the flame and simmer, covered, for 2 hours. Then add the carrots and cook for 30 minutes (do not overcook—the carrots should be firm).

Refrigerate for 24 hours and then remove the fat, which will look like a sheet of wax. Discard the bouquet garni and the pork and orange rinds. Add the black olives and sprinkle with parsley and cheese. Serve with a red Burgundy.

Meats

Brochettes de Nice

Lamb Heart and Kidney Skewered with Vegetables

Lamb kidneys are not difficult to find, but hearts may have to be specially ordered at your butcher's. Both kidney and heart freeze well. This recipe also works well with shoulder of lamb but it won't be as interesting.

Serve with *Pommes de Terre à l'Ail* (p. 201), *Riz aux Herbes* (p. 225), *Tomates Provençale* (p. 204), and a green tossed salad.

For 6 people:

- 6 *lamb kidneys, cut in 2-inch cubes*
- 3 *lamb hearts, cut in 2-inch cubes*
- ½ *cup lean salt pork, cut in 1-inch rectangles*
- 6 *tiny white onions, peeled and cut in half*
- 24 *mushroom caps, unpeeled (save the stems for other use)*
- 6 *very firm tomatoes, quartered*
- 3 *large green bell peppers, cut in 2-inch cubes*
- 3 *teaspoons rosemary*
- 2 *teaspoons thyme*
- *salt*
- *freshly ground black pepper*
- 3 *tablespoons olive oil*
- 12 *sprigs fresh rosemary (if available)*

Place the kidneys, hearts, salt pork, and vegetables in a large bowl and sprinkle with rosemary, thyme, salt, pepper, and olive oil. Marinate for at least 1 hour. If kept for several hours, cover with plastic wrap and refrigerate until ready to cook.

Preheat the broiler.

Using *flat* skewers (two for each brochette, to make sure the ingredients are securely held), string the brochettes, alternating meat and vegetables and placing sprigs of fresh rosemary in between if you have some. Preferably start and end with an onion half or a piece of green pepper. Place brochettes over a deep pan and broil for 5 minutes. Baste, turn on the other side, and broil for 15 minutes. Check the tenderness of the heart and kidney by piercing them with a fork, and cook for 5 minutes more if necessary.

Remove the brochettes from the broiler. Pour the wine into the pan and scrape up the coagulated juices with a spoon. Pour into a saucepan and heat on top of the stove for 2 minutes. Put the brochettes on a bed of watercress or parsley or on a bed of *Riz aux Herbes* (p. 225) and pour the juices over them. Sprinkle with salt and pepper just before serving.

Caillettes de Nice
Crisp Spinach, Chicken Liver, and Rice Balls

Caillette means little quail, and that is what these plump balls look like. The crispy *caillettes* are usually served warm at Christmas time and cold as an hors d'oeuvre in summer. They are wrapped with caul, the veil-like membrane taken from the pig's abdomen. If caul is unavailable, use very thin strips of salt pork or slices of bacon. *Caillettes* are especially popular with children and are perfect for a buffet.

For 6 people:

- 1½ *pounds chicken livers*
- *salt*
- *freshly ground black pepper*
- 2 *tablespoons unbleached flour*
- 3 *tablespoons olive oil*
- 1 *onion, chopped*
- 1½ *pounds lean fresh pork, chopped*
- 1 *cup cooked rice*
- ½ *cup chopped parsley*
- 2 *10-ounce boxes frozen spinach, cooked and chopped*
- 2 *garlic cloves, peeled and crushed*
- 1 *teaspoon thyme*
- 2 *eggs, slightly beaten*
- 12 *3 x 3-inch pieces of caul (or slices of bacon or salt pork)*
- 6 *leaves fresh sage*

Meats

Sprinkle the livers with salt, pepper, and flour and set aside. Heat 1 tablespoon of the olive oil in a large skillet and cook the onion for 10 minutes, or until it is transparent. Remove with a slotted spoon and put into a bowl. Add 1 tablespoon of olive oil to the skillet and sauté the chicken livers for 5 minutes, tossing with a wooden spoon. Remove from the pan, and when cool enough to handle, chop them with kitchen shears and add to the onion. Sauté the chopped pork in the same skillet and add this to the bowl of sautéed onions.

Preheat the oven to 400°.

Mix the rice, liver, onion, parsley, pork, spinach, garlic, thyme, eggs, salt, and pepper in a large bowl. Shape balls about 1½ inches in diameter of this mixture with your hands (the balls will shrink a little when they cook). Wrap each ball in caul (or bacon or salt pork) and place in an oiled baking dish. (You can keep the balls up to two days in the refrigerator.) Stick a sage leaf on top of each ball, sprinkle with 1 tablespoon of olive oil and bake for 30 minutes. Serve hot or cold.

Variations:

Instead of shaping into balls, the mixture itself can be baked in a terrine for 45 minutes. As it cools, cover the entire surface with a piece of foil-covered wood or cardboard, put something heavy on top, and weight it down for 3 hours to squeeze out the fat. Refrigerate. Slice the terrine holding a chopping board against the end so it can be cut without crumbling.

Another version of this dish, very popular near Grasse, is made with an equal amount of sliced pork liver and sliced pork lung, sprinkled with sage, chopped parsley, and salt and pepper. Tight rolls are made of the liver and lung, then tied with string, and cooked slowly in dry white wine. They are served warm or kept throughout the winter in a large jar covered with lard to be eaten cold as an hors d'oeuvre.

Canard comme à Nice

Stuffed Duck Roasted with Tomato, White Wine, and Olives

This is a wonderful way to give zest to the otherwise rather dull Long Island duck. Serve with *Céleri Paysanne* (p. 179), *Tian de*

Navets Rosés (pp. 208–9), *Papeton d'Aubergines* (p. 199), or a *Purée de Légumes* (pp. 201–2).

For 6 to 8 people:

Stuffing

1	10-ounce box frozen spinach, blanched, drained, and chopped
½	cup cooked rice
½	cup finely chopped parsley
2	garlic cloves, peeled and crushed
⅓	cup chopped chicken livers
2	duck livers, chopped
2	eggs, beaten
1	teaspoon savory
1	teaspoon thyme
2	bay leaves
	salt
	freshly ground black pepper

Combine all ingredients and set aside.

Duck and Sauce

2	4-pound ducks
	salt
	freshly ground black pepper
2	tablespoons olive oil
2	onions, minced
3	garlic cloves, peeled
4	tomatoes (fresh or canned), quartered
1	cup dry white wine
2	teaspoons thyme
3	bay leaves
½	cup olives
6	to 8 sprigs parsley

Preheat oven to 450°. Pull out the loose fat inside the ducks. Dry them carefully and season both inside and out with salt and pepper. Fill them with the stuffing and sew or skewer the skin over the opening. Truss the legs and wings, place in a roasting pan, and with a sharp fork prick them all over to allow the fat to escape. Place the pan, uncovered, in the middle of the oven and cook for 30 minutes. Remove and discard all the fat. Lower the heat to 375°.

Meats

Meanwhile, heat the olive oil in a heavy-bottomed pan, add the onions and cook for 5 minutes. Add the tomatoes, ½ cup of the wine, the garlic cloves, thyme, bay leaves, salt, and pepper. Cook, covered, for 20 minutes over a low flame. Add the olives and set the sauce aside.

Again discard the fat in the pan and turn the ducks over on the other side. Pour the sauce over them and lower the heat to 350°. Cook for 50 minutes. (The entire cooking time is about 1¾ hours to 2 hours.)

Place the ducks on a warm platter. Add the remaining wine to the sauce in the pan and scrape up the bottom of the pan while cooking 2 minutes over high heat.

To serve, scoop out the stuffing and mound it in the center of a warm serving platter. Carve the ducks, arrange the pieces around the stuffing, and spoon the sauce over them. (There will be very little sauce, as the duck will have absorbed most of it while cooking.) Garnish with parsley.

Note: The ducks can be prepared in a slightly different way, which may be more convenient for you. Sprinkle them with salt and pepper, prick them all over with a fork, and cook in a 375° oven for 1½ hours. After they are roasted, stuff them and refrigerate them, and the following day reheat with the sauce. The ducks will be drier but equally tasty.

Daube d'Avignon

Lamb, Vegetable, and Herb Stew

This hearty dish does not need an expensive cut of lamb or rare fresh vegetables, yet it is very special. It must marinate overnight before cooking. It freezes well and reheats beautifully, so make a generous amount. Serve with a fresh mixed green salad and a robust white wine.

For 6 people:

1 4-pound lamb shoulder, cut into 2-inch
  cubes
3 carrots, thickly sliced

        3 onions, chopped
        5 tablespoons olive oil
        1 tablespoon rosemary
        2 teaspoons thyme
        2 bay leaves
        3 2-inch pieces orange rind
        1 teaspoon salt
          freshly ground black pepper
     1/3 cup chopped lean salt pork
        3 garlic cloves, chopped
        2 cups dry white wine
        1 cup white (Great Northern) beans,
          dried
        2 tablespoons chopped parsley

Place the lamb (and bones if you have them—they will give additional flavor), carrots, onions, and the olive oil in a large bowl. Sprinkle with the rosemary, thyme, bay leaves, orange rind, and salt and pepper and refrigerate overnight. Also soak the beans overnight in 3 cups of water.

The next day, cook the beans (see instructions on the package for cooking time) until tender. Heat 3 tablespoons of the marinade oil in a heavy-bottomed pan (preferably a Doufeu). Add the salt pork, half of the carrots and onions from the marinade, the garlic, and the lamb. Sprinkle again with salt and pepper and cover with the rest of the carrots and onions. Add the wine. Lower the flame and simmer, covered, for 2 hours, or until very tender. Remove the bay leaves and orange rind. Add the beans and check the seasoning. Simmer for 5 minutes.

Serve in a warm shallow dish sprinkled with parsley.

Estouffade
Lamb and Beef Stew

This is a simple, delicious stew. It can be made *à la fortune du pot*, so meat proportions can vary according to what you have on hand. *Estouffade* means that all meats are smothered with herbs and tomatoes in a covered Doufeu. In this unexpected combination all the ingredients complement each other. Marinate the meats overnight before cooking.

Meats

You can prepare this dish a day or so ahead, since it always seems to taste better when reheated. It also freezes superbly. Serve with *Pâtes aux Oeufs* (p. 216), *Pâtes à la Verdure* (pp. 219–20), *Gnocchis* (pp. 214–15), *Févettes à la Verdure* (p. 188), or *Céleri Paysanne* (p. 179), along with a green salad (Boston lettuce, watercress, endive, or arugula) and a hearty red wine.

For 6 people:

1½ pounds chuck or bottom round of
    beef, cut into 2-inch cubes, plus
    bones
1½ pounds neck or shoulder of lamb, cut
    into 2-inch cubes
  1 onion, quartered
 ½ cup dry white wine
  1 tablespoon olive oil
  2 bay leaves
  2 tablespoons unbleached flour
  2 tablespoons peanut oil
  3 onions, minced
 ½ cup chopped lean salt pork
  1 teaspoon savory
    bouquet garni (p. 11)
  3 2-inch pieces orange rind
  2 garlic cloves, minced
  1 cup broth, water, or white wine
    salt
    freshly ground black pepper
  3 tomatoes, chopped, or 1 cup canned
 ½ cup small black olives from Nice or
    pitted oil-cured olives
  2 tablespoons finely chopped parsley

Put the beef and lamb in a large bowl, add the quartered onion, wine, olive oil, and bay leaves. Marinate overnight.

Drain the beef and lamb and spread them out on paper towels to dry. Sprinkle with flour.

Heat 2 tablespoons of the peanut oil in a Doufeu or heavy-bottomed pan. Add the minced onions, cook gently for 5 minutes, and remove with a slotted spoon. In the same pan, brown the meat on all sides, turning with tongs, and add the sautéed onions, salt pork, savory, bouquet garni, orange rind, garlic, and the marinade liquid. While stirring, scrape the bottom of the pan. Add broth or water or wine, salt and pepper, and bring to a boil. Lower the flame and cook, covered, for 1½ hours, or until the meat is tender. Add the tomatoes and cook, covered, for 1 hour. Skim off as much fat as possible (or refrigerate overnight and lift off the hardened fat). Discard the bouquet garni and orange rind. Add the olives, sprinkle with parsley and serve.

Fausses Grives

Pork Liver Filled with Juniper and Garlic

This is delicious served with *Pommes de Terre aux Herbes* (pp. 202–3), or *Purées de Légumes* (pp. 201–2).

For 6 people:

6 *slices pork liver, cut ⅓ inch thick*
2 *teaspoons juniper berries, crushed*
  salt
  freshly ground pepper
6 *pieces of caul or thinly sliced bacon*
2 *tablespoons mixture of peanut and*
  olive oil
6 *garlic cloves, peeled*
½ *cup dry white vermouth*

Dry the liver with paper towels and sprinkle with juniper berries, salt, and pepper. Roll up each slice, wrap with caul or bacon, and secure it with half a toothpick or tie with a piece of string.

Heat the oil in a heavy-bottomed pan. Add the liver rolls and garlic cloves and sauté for 2 minutes. Turn the rolls with tongs and lower the flame. Sprinkle with salt and pepper, add the vermouth and cook, uncovered, for 30 minutes. Serve on a warm platter.

Gardiane

Lamb and Potatoes Stewed with Garlic and Orange Rind

Orange rind, garlic, and white wine enliven the flavor of this very simple stew. You can use a variety of cuts, but I find lamb shoulder the best. Serve with *Céleri Paysanne* (p. 179), *Fenouil Braisé* (p. 186), or a plain *Salade Amère* (p. 59) and a dry white wine, well chilled.

For 6 people:

3 pounds lamb shoulder
1 tablespoon thyme
salt
freshly ground black pepper
4 tablespoons olive oil
1 cup dry white wine
4 onions, thinly sliced
8 potatoes, cut in half lengthwise and
*   then into slices 1/2 inch thick*
4 garlic cloves, peeled and quartered
2 2-inch pieces orange rind
2 bay leaves
1/2 cup little black olives
2 tablespoons finely chopped parsley or
*   fennel leaves*

Trim the lamb of all fat, bone, and gristle. Cut into 2-inch cubes and sprinkle with thyme, salt, and pepper.

Heat 2 tablespoons of the olive oil in a heavy-bottomed pan. Add the lamb and sauté for 5 minutes. Sprinkle with salt and pepper, cook for 15 minutes, and set aside in a bowl. Put the wine in the pan, scrape up the bottom, and pour into the bowl of lamb. (You can prepare this much ahead of time and cover with plastic wrap until ready to use. Or you can prepare the whole dish ahead, and at serving time, reheat over a low flame for 10 minutes.)

Heat 2 tablespoons of the olive oil in the skillet. Add the onions, potatoes, garlic, orange rind, and bay leaves, and cook for 5 minutes. Add the lamb and the liquid. Cook, covered, for 40 minutes or until the lamb is tender (add more wine if necessary). Check the seasoning.

Remove the bay leaf and orange rind. Five minutes before serving add the olives. Garnish with parsley or fennel and serve.

Les Viandes

Gigot d'Agneau à l'Aillade

Leg of Lamb with Garlic Sauce

This recipe embodies all the flavors of Provence. It can be served with Great Northern beans, red beans, *Pâtes aux Oeufs* (p. 216), *Gnocchis* (pp. 214–15), *Tomates Provençale* (p. 204), *Céleri Paysanne* (p. 179), *Févettes à l'Ail* (p. 187), *Fenouil Braisé* (p. 186), *Carottes Paysanne* (p. 178), *Épinards aux Pignons* (pp. 183–84), *Pommes de Terre aux Herbes* (pp. 202–3), or a crisp green tossed salad. It is traditionally served at Easter with a green salad garnished with hard-boiled eggs and followed by little "pâtés" of marrow of beef.

For 6 people:

- 1 5-pound leg of lamb
- 6 garlic cloves, slivered
- 12 anchovy fillets, chopped
- 3 tablespoons olive oil
- 1 teaspoon rosemary
- 1 teaspoon thyme
- salt
- freshly ground black pepper
- 12 garlic cloves, peeled
- ½ cup dry white wine
- 2 tablespoons chopped parsley or mint

Make slits in the lamb and insert a sliver of garlic and a piece of anchovy in each incision. Rub the lamb with 2 tablespoons of the olive oil, rosemary, thyme, salt, and pepper. Let it stand for 1 to 2 hours.

Preheat the oven to 425°. Place the meat on a rack in a roasting pan and cook, uncovered, for 20 minutes. Reduce the heat to 350° and cook for 40 to 45 minutes for medium-rare lamb.

Heat 1 tablespoon of the olive oil in an iron skillet and cook the garlic cloves slowly for about 10 minutes, or until they are soft (do not let the edges become crisp). Set aside in a small bowl.

Remove the lamb from the pan. Pour the wine into the pan, scrape the bottom well and cook down the wine over a high flame to reduce it. Add the reduced liquid to the garlic cloves. Mash well with a fork and add salt and pepper to taste.

Meats

Slice the lamb and sprinkle with pepper. Spoon the sauce over it and sprinkle with parsley or mint.

Note: Leftover lamb can be used to make Nice's shepherd's pie. Finely chop it, along with some parsley and garlic; cover with mashed potatoes, then sprinkle with Parmesan cheese and olive oil and bake for 15 minutes.

Pietsch (Poche de Veau Farcie)
Breast of Veal Stuffed with Vegetables and Simmered in White Wine

This is a spectacular dish whether it is served hot or cold. The long simmering in wine and vegetables enlivens the delicate flavor of the veal, and the stuffing which consists of spinach, lima beans, and peas is light, fresh, and very pretty.

For 6 to 8 people:

Meat and Filling

1 *large breast (about 7 pounds) of veal*
  or 2 small (2 to 4 pounds) breasts
  sewn together
½ *cup finely chopped lean salt pork*
1 *pound peas (fresh or frozen), cooked*
1 *pound frozen lima beans, cooked*
1 *cup cooked rice (⅓ cup raw)*
3 *10-ounce frozen packages of chopped*
  spinach, cooked and drained
3 *garlic cloves, minced*
½ *cup grated Parmesan or Romano*
  cheese
½ *cup finely chopped parsley*
4 *eggs, beaten*
1 *teaspoon thyme*
½ *tablespoon freshly grated nutmeg*
  salt
  freshly ground pepper
3 *tablespoons olive oil*
2 *carrots, chopped*

> 2 onions, *chopped*
> 1 leek, *chopped*
> 2 celery stalks, *chopped*
> 2 tomatoes (*fresh or canned*), *chopped*
> 2 to 3 cups dry white wine
> 2 bay leaves
> 3 tablespoons chopped parsley

Ask the butcher to prepare the breast for stuffing by making a pocket. Check to see that all the little rib bones have been removed. Reserve the bones.

In a large bowl, mix the salt pork, peas, lima beans, rice, spinach, garlic, cheese, parsley, eggs, thyme, nutmeg, salt, and pepper. Check the seasoning and stuff the breast or breasts with the mixture (do not overstuff). Use a needle and thread to sew up the opening. (The stuffed breast will look like a plump cushion.) Set aside.

Heat 2 tablespoons of the olive oil in a large heavy-bottomed pan or a large baking dish that you can place over two burners on top of the stove. Add the carrots, onions, leek, celery, tomatoes, and the breast bones (soup bones may be substituted). Sauté for 5 minutes, then remove with a slotted spoon. Add 1 tablespoon of the olive oil and put the veal in the pan. Cook over a high flame for 15 minutes to brown on both sides.

Make a layer of half the vegetable mixture. Lay the veal on top and cover with the remaining vegetables. Add the wine and bay leaves. Cover and cook on top of the stove for 2 hours or in a 375° oven for 2½ hours. Baste twice. During the first half hour, check to be sure there is enough liquid (if too dry, add some wine). Uncover the pan for the last 1½ hours of cooking.

When the veal is cooked, place it on a chopping board, but leave the vegetables and liquid in the pan in the oven or over a low flame. Pull out the thread from the veal. With the help of a plate, or better, a wooden board with a handle (*planche à hacher*—see Techniques and Tools, p. 20), keep the stuffing together while you cut the veal in ½-inch slices. Arrange the slices on a warm platter and sprinkle with salt and pepper. Cover and keep warm in the oven.

Skim the fat from the liquid. Pass it through a Mouli food mill, along with the vegetables, into a bowl. Correct the seasoning. Pour over the sliced veal and sprinkle with parsley before serving.

Note: If you serve the veal cold, slice it when it is cold—it will be easier. Serve with a bowl of *Sauce Piquante* (p. 84).

Meats

Porc à la Sauge et aux Câpres

Pork with Sage, Capers, and White Vermouth

Sage is a wonderful accompaniment for pork; it is not only savory, but is thought to help the digestion.

This dish is delicious served with *Gnocchis* (pp. 214–15), *Céleri Paysanne* (p. 179), *Pâtes aux Oeufs* (p. 216), or *Fenouil Braisé* (p. 186) and a rosé or dry white wine. Try to use fresh or recently dried sage leaves.

For 6 people:

3 *pounds pork loin or shoulder*
2 *teaspoons salt*
freshly ground black pepper
4 *tablespoons olive oil*
2 *onions, chopped*
4 *teaspoons sage*
2 *bay leaves*
1/3 *cup finely chopped Italian parsley or*
  fennel leaves
2 *teaspoons thyme*
1/2 *cup dry white wine*
1/2 *cup dry white vermouth*
1/2 *cup capers*
sprigs of parsley or fennel leaves

Trim the fat and bones from the pork and cut it into 2-inch pieces 1-inch thick. (You may use the bones to add flavor.) Sprinkle the pork with salt and pepper.

Heat the olive oil in a Doufeu or a heavy-bottomed pan. Sauté the pork on all sides for 5 minutes. Lower the flame and add the onions, sage, bay leaves, parsley, thyme, and more salt. Add wine. Cover and cook very slowly for 1½ hours, checking to be sure the pork is not dry (add a little water if necessary). Remove the meat and set aside in a warm, covered dish. Add the vermouth to the pan juices while scraping the bottom of the pan. Add the capers, put the pork back in, and reheat for 5 minutes. Remove the bay leaves and serve on a warm platter garnished with parsley or fennel leaves.

Les Viandes

Tian de Boeuf aux Légumes

Baked Beef with Onions, Mushrooms, and Garlic

This is a lovely dish in its own right, and nobody will ever guess it is based on leftovers.

For 6 people:

> 1 *pound mushrooms, sliced*
> 6 *garlic cloves, minced*
> 6 *shallots or 3 scallions, minced*
> ½ *cup bread crumbs (preferably home-made)*
> ½ *cup chopped parsley*
> *salt*
> *freshly ground black pepper*
> 8 *to 10 slices beef, or 3 cups chopped (use what you have—exact proportions are not essential)*
> ½ *cup dry white wine*
> 1 *tablespoon olive oil*

In a large bowl, mix the mushrooms, garlic, shallots or scallions, half of the bread crumbs, parsley, salt, and pepper.

Preheat the oven to 375°. Oil a large baking dish and spread half of the vegetable mixture in it, spread the meat on it, and cover with the rest of the vegetables. Add the wine. Sprinkle with the rest of the bread crumbs and the olive oil and bake for 30 minutes.

Pot-au-Feu Provencale

Boiled Beef, Lamb, and Vegetables

The Provençal version of *pot-au-feu* requires lamb, garlic, and chickpeas. It may even include chicken feet to thicken the broth a bit. The rich broth should always be prepared a day in advance so that the fat will congeal on top and can be removed completely. Leftover *pot-au-feu* provides the base for several other dishes:

Meats

Boeuf Mironton (p. 139), *Tian de Boeuf aux Légumes* (p. 155), *Capoun* (pp. 176–78), and *Salade de Riz Variée* (pp. 70–71), so be generous with your proportions. Serve with a hearty red wine.

It is said that one must be at least thirty years old to enjoy fully this simple dish.

For 6 to 8 people:

- 10 *carrots*
- 1 *large yellow onion*
- 2 *garlic cloves, peeled*
- 4 *leeks*
- 1 *bunch celery*
- 2 *pounds short ribs or flanken, tied with string to stay intact while cooking*
- 2 *pounds beef shank*
- 2 *pounds lamb (shoulder, shank, or left-over leg)*
- 1 *veal knuckle*
- 2 *chicken feet (optional)*
  salt
  bouquet garni (p. 000)
- 10 *juniper berries*
- 10 *peppercorns*
- 8 *small white onions*
- 3 *pink turnips*
- 6 *small potatoes*
- 1 *large beef marrow bone (or 4 to 5 small ones)*
  freshly ground black pepper
- ⅓ *cup chopped parsley*
- 6 *slices firm white bread for making tri-angular* Croutons *(p. 12)*
- ½ *cup* Vinaigrette *(pp. 92–93)*
- 1 *1-pound 4-ounce can chickpeas*
- 2 *tablespoons kosher salt*
- 2 *tablespoons* Cornichons *(p. 13)*

Peel 1 carrot (save the others for a later step), yellow onion, and garlic cloves and leave them whole. Stick 2 cloves in the onion. Trim the leeks and celery stalks (reserve the heart).

Bring a pot of water to a boil. Add the three pieces of meat, the veal knuckle, and chicken feet (if you have them). Boil, skim off the surface fat, add salt and skim again. Add the clove-studded onion, carrot, celery stalks, leeks, garlic cloves, bouquet garni, juniper berries, peppercorns, and salt. Lower the flame and simmer for 2 hours. Cool and refrigerate overnight.

The next day, remove the layer of fat from the broth (and discard the chicken feet if they were added). Remove the celery, bouquet garni, and clove-studded onion. Bring the broth to a boil. Peel the white onions, turnips, carrots, and potatoes and leave them whole. Add to the broth the celery heart, turnips, and carrots. Lower the flame and simmer for 10 minutes. Add the onions and potatoes and simmer for about 15 minutes. (Cooking time will depend on the size of the vegetables; check frequently to see if they are tender.)

Prepare the croutons and Vinaigrette.

Put the meat on a platter, untie the string and slice it. Arrange the meat slices attractively and surround with the vegetables. Cover with foil and keep warm in a turned-off oven.

Add the marrow bone to the broth and cook for 10 minutes, then remove it. Use a slender knife to scrape the marrow out of the bone, chop it and sprinkle with kosher salt.

Strain the broth and reheat to serve as the first course. Line individual soup bowls with the croutons and place a piece of marrow on top of each crouton.

For the main course, remove the platter of meat and vegetables from the oven, sprinkle with salt, pepper, and parsley, and pour a ladleful of hot broth over it. Pass around small bowls of chickpeas (heated in a separate pan), *cornichons,* kosher salt, Dijon mustard, and vinaigrette.

Note: You can use the leftover lamb for *Farcis à la Niçoise* (pp. 184–85). Serve the leftover beef with *Aïoli* (p. 75), in a *tian* or in a cold salad with potato or rice.

The leftover vegetables can be a lovely first course: Slice and serve chilled or lukewarm with a vinaigrette and chopped *cornichons.*

Poulet aux Artichauts
Chicken Sautéed with Artichokes and White Wine

The artichokes give this very simple dish a rich, pungent flavor—but they must be very fresh and young. This is delicious served with

Courgettes Râpées (p. 183), *Pommes de Terre à l'Ail* (p. 201), *Tomates Provençale* (p. 204), *Févettes à l'Ail* (p. 187), or *Carottes Paysanne* (p. 178).

Wine goes very poorly with artichokes, but a dry white wine may be acceptable if it is well chilled.

For 6 people:

6 *young artichokes*
  juice of 1 lemon
4 *tablespoons olive oil*
  salt
  freshly ground black pepper
6 *chicken breasts, boned and split*
2 *teaspoons thyme*
1 *cup dry white wine*

Cut the artichokes in half lengthwise, remove the tough outer leaves and the choke, and cut off the stems. Soak them in water and lemon juice for 30 minutes.

Heat the olive oil in a heavy skillet. Drain the artichokes and fry them over a medium flame for 30 minutes. Sprinkle with salt and pepper. Remove from heat and set aside in a covered dish.

Sprinkle the chicken breasts with thyme. Reheat the oil in which the artichokes were cooked and brown the chicken on all sides. Lower the flame and cook for 10 minutes. Add the artichokes and cook for 5 minutes.

Arrange the chicken in the center of a warm platter and surround it with the artichokes. Add the wine to the pan juices while scraping the bottom with a spatula, and cook over high heat for 1 minute. Pour this over the chicken and serve immediately.

Poulet en Gelée

Jellied Chicken

This is a delicious dish, perfect for a summer meal or a buffet. The vegetables, white wine, lemon juice, and herbs impart a subtle flavor to the chicken, and the jellied mound looks inviting garnished with crisp greens. Though never perfect aesthetically (the jelly will be cloudy), this dish is delectable when properly seasoned.

For 6 people:

> 3 tablespoons oil (*half peanut, half olive*)
> 3 carrots, sliced
> 2 celery stalks, sliced
> 2 onions, chopped
> 5 garlic cloves, minced
> ½ cup white vinegar
> 1 cup dry white wine or dry vermouth juice of 3 lemons
> 1 cup water or stock (*made with wings, neck, gizzard, bay leaves, salt, and water*)
> 2 teaspoons thyme
> 2 bay leaves
> salt
> freshly ground pepper
> 1 5-pound roasting chicken, cut into serving pieces
> 2 egg whites, beaten stiff
> 2 tablespoons sherry
> 1 bunch watercress or several lettuce leaves
> 3 lemons, cut in wedges
> 2 tablespoons chopped parsley or chives

Heat the oil in a heavy-bottomed pan and add the carrots, celery, onions, and garlic. Lower the heat and cook for 15 minutes. Add the vinegar, wine or vermouth, lemon juice, water or stock, 1 teaspoon of the thyme, bay leaves, salt, and pepper and simmer for 15 minutes. Correct the seasoning (the broth should not be bland).

Place half of the pieces of chicken in a large pan and sprinkle with salt and pepper. Lay the vegetables on them, put the rest of the chicken on top and sprinkle with 1 teaspoon of the thyme, salt, and pepper. Pour the broth over the chicken and vegetables so that they are barely covered. Bring to a boil, cover, and simmer slowly for 2 to 3 hours. Cool.

Remove the chicken from the pan. Bone and skin carefully with a sharp knife and cut into 1-inch cubes. (If the wings, neck, and gizzard were used, discard them or use for soup.)

Boil the broth, uncovered, over high heat for 15 minutes, or until it has thickened. Add the egg whites. Lower the flame and simmer for a few minutes so the egg whites will rise to the surface along with the scum. Remove the froth. Strain the broth through a sieve lined with cheesecloth and let it cool. Remove as much fat as possible and discard all vegetables except the carrots and bay leaves. Check the seasoning and add the sherry.

Oil a shallow bowl and arrange the carrots and the bay leaves in the center. Place the chicken on and around the carrots and pour the cool broth on them. Refrigerate for several hours until the broth has jelled.

When ready to serve, run a knife around the rim of the bowl, then turn it upside down on a platter. Place watercress or lettuce leaves all around the mound of jelled chicken and garnish with lemon wedges. Sprinkle with parsley or chives.

To serve, scoop out portions with a large serving spoon and put a lemon wedge, to be squeezed on the chicken, on each plate.

Poulet à la Niçoise

Chicken Cooked with Onion, Tomato, Olives, and White Wine

This is an uncomplicated dish that is light and refreshing. It can be made ahead of time and reheated, so that all the flavors are absorbed by the chicken. Serve it with *Fenouil Braisé* (p. 186), *Courgettes Râpées* (p. 183), *Févettes à la Verdure* (p. 188) or *Épinards aux Pignons* (pp. 183–84).

For 6 people:

1 4-pound chicken, cut into serving
    pieces
juice of 1 lemon
2 teaspoons thyme
salt
freshly ground black pepper
5 tablespoons olive oil
½ cup chopped lean salt pork
4 onions, minced
2 garlic cloves, peeled

Les Viandes

5 tomatoes, quartered, or 1⅔ cups
    canned
2 bay leaves
½ cup dry white wine
½ cup black olives (Nice's unpitted olives
    or pitted oil-cured olives)
½ cup chopped parsley or basil

Dry the pieces of chicken thoroughly and sprinkle with lemon juice, thyme, salt, and pepper. Set aside.

Heat the olive oil in a large heavy-bottomed pan. Add the salt pork and chicken. Sauté for 15 minutes, turning the pieces on all sides with tongs. Remove the pork and chicken from the pan with a slotted spoon and add onions, adding more oil if necessary. Cook over a low flame for 10 minutes. Add the garlic cloves, tomatoes, bay leaves, and wine and cook for 10 minutes. Return the salt pork and chicken to the pan and cook slowly, uncovered, for 35 to 40 minutes, basting frequently. Check the seasoning.

Five minutes before serving, remove the bay leaves and garlic cloves and add the olives. Sprinkle with the parsley or basil and serve at once.

Poulet en Saupiquet

Marinated Chicken Cooked in an Anchovy and Garlic Wine Sauce

I love the traditional *lapin en saupiquet,* but since fresh rabbits are hard to find in America, I decided to create a variation using chicken. This is a rich, wonderful dish. I use only the breasts and thighs of the chicken. Since most American chickens are so tender that they cannot cook in a sauce without disintegrating, I marinate the pieces overnight to allow various flavors to penetrate the meat before it is cooked. The sauce is cooked separately and then added to the chicken so that it retains its own full flavor.

This is a superb dish—strong in flavor, yet not heavy. Serve it with *Pâtes à la Verdure* (pp. 219–20) or *Gnocchis* (pp. 214–15) and perhaps *Courgettes Râpées* (p. 183) or *Épinards aux Pignons* (pp. 183–84), accompanied by a dry white wine.

Meats

161

For 6 people:

3 3- to 4-pound chickens (use only 3
    breasts and 6 thighs), cut into serving
    pieces
5 tablespoons olive oil
1 teaspoon rosemary
5 garlic cloves
2 bay leaves
3 teaspoons thyme
3 onions, chopped
10 peppercorns
2 cups dry white wine
4 chicken livers
  flour for dredging
8 anchovy fillets, chopped
2 tablespoons finely chopped parsley
2 tablespoons capers
1/2 cup black olives (Nice's unpitted olives or
    pitted oil-cured olives)
4 slices bread for making triangular Crou-
    tons (p. 12)
2 tablespoons chopped parsley

Put the chicken in a bowl, sprinkle with 3 tablespoons of the olive oil and rosemary. Peel and crush 2 garlic cloves and spread on the chicken. Add bay leaves, cover, and leave overnight in the refrigerator.

The next day remove the chicken from the marinade and sprinkle with 1 teaspoon of the thyme. Heat the marinade in a heavy-bottomed pan, add the chicken and sauté on all sides for 10 minutes. Remove from the pan and set aside.

Add the onions to the pan and sauté for 5 minutes. Return the chicken to the pan, add 2 teaspoons of the thyme, peppercorns, and wine. Simmer uncovered, for 30 minutes, or until the chicken is tender and there is only about 1 cup of juice left in the pan. Remove the skin from the chicken and discard it. Put the chicken and juices aside in a bowl.

Dredge the chicken livers lightly with flour. Heat 2 tablespoons of the olive oil in the pan, add the livers and sauté for 3 minutes. Purée the livers, anchovies, and 3 peeled garlic cloves in a blender for 2 minutes, adding some of the cooking juice to make the blending easier. Stir in the parsley, capers, and olives. (This should be a rather thick purée.) At this point the dish is fully cooked. It can rest for a few hours before serving.

When ready to serve, place the pieces of chicken in the pan. Combine the liver purée and the chicken juices, stir carefully, and check the seasoning. Pour over the chicken and heat, uncovered, for 20 minutes. Meanwhile prepare the croutons.

To serve, spread the croutons along the sides of a warm platter and put the chicken in the center. Pour the sauce over the chicken and garnish with the parsley.

Rôti de Porc Provençale

Roast Pork with Fennel

There are few imaginative ways to enhance the taste of pork, but to my mind this combination of sage and fennel is the most successful. This must be prepared a day in advance and is especially good with *Fenouil Braisé* (p. 186), *Pois Gourmands Paysanne* (p. 200), *Papeton d'Aubergines* (p. 199), or *Carottes Paysanne* (p. 178).

> For 6 people:
>
> *2 fennel bulbs*
> *1 3-pound pork loin roast, boned*
> *2 teaspoons dried fennel or anise seed*
> *2 teaspoons sage*
> *salt*
> *freshly ground black pepper*
> *1 cup dry white wine*
> *2 tablespoons peanut oil*
> *1 teaspoon anise extract or Pernod*
> *2 tablespoons chopped fresh fennel leaves*

Slice the fennel bulbs into 1 x 1½-inch strips. Make slits over the whole surface of the roast and insert a strip of fennel and a little of the fennel or anise seed into each cut. Rub the roast with 1 teaspoon of the sage, salt, and pepper. Place it in a bowl and add the wine. Let it stand overnight, turning it over once.

The next day, remove the roast from the marinade and rub it with more salt and pepper, 1 teaspoon of the sage, and the remaining fennel or anise seed. Bind it securely with a string.

Meats

Preheat the oven to 400°. Oil a roasting pan and add the peanut oil. Place the pork in the pan and roast for 15 minutes. Reduce the temperature to 375° and cook for 1½ hours. Transfer the roast to a warm platter and let it stand for 5 minutes. Remove the string and slice it.

Pour the marinade into the pan and cook for 2 minutes over high heat, scraping the bottom with a fork. Add anise extract or Pernod and pour over the carved slices of pork. Sprinkle with fennel leaves and serve.

Roustissouns

Pork Sautéed with Herbs and Red Wine Vinegar

This is a light and zesty dish. Serve it with *Pâtes à la Verdure* (pp. 219–20) or *Gnocchis* (pp. 214–15), and if you want a lighter meal, with *Céleri Paysanne* (p. 179), *Fenouil Braisé* (p. 186), or *Courgettes Râpées* (p. 183).

For 6 people:

3 *pounds lean pork (loin or other cut care-*
fully trimmed of fat)
2 *teaspoons thyme*
2 *teaspoons sage*
1 *tablespoon peanut oil*
salt
freshly ground black pepper
3 *to 5 tablespoons red wine vinegar*
2 *tablespoons chopped parsley, basil, or*
fennel

Cut the pork into 2-inch cubes and sprinkle with the thyme and sage. Let it stand for 1 hour.

Heat the oil in a heavy-bottomed frying pan and add the pork. Sprinkle with salt and pepper and cook for about 30 minutes, browning evenly on all sides. Add the vinegar and scrape the bottom of the pan. Cover tightly and cook for 30 to 40 minutes, or until tender, checking to be sure there is enough liquid in the pan. Add a few tablespoons of water if necessary.

Check the seasoning, sprinkle with parsley, fresh fennel, or basil and serve.

Les Viandes

Les Légumes

Vegetables

Vegetables are the core of Niçois and Provençal cooking. Gastronomy in the South of France begins with vegetables instead of meat. They are very often the main dish, and a variety are served with dips (*bagna cauda* is an outstanding example) instead of potato chips or crackers. Soups and sauces are thickened with vegetables instead of cream or egg yolks.

Some Niçois claim they know more than seventy ways to cook vegetables. Often three or four of them are demonstrated in a single meal; there may be a vegetable dip, salad, soup, stew, and gratin. Vegetables are always treated with the utmost respect and imagination. The following recipes are designed to enhance their natural flavor, never to overpower it.

Most Niçois vegetables are easily found in the United States, and because of sunny weather in places like California most are available all year round. Unfortunately, in the East they often lose in freshness what they gain in availability. The crispness of the raw material is essential to the success of all these dishes. So select vegetables carefully, and if possible, cook them the same day you buy them. I never use frozen vegetables except spinach, which is wonderful for stuffing (as in *ravioli, tout-nus, poche de veau, tourte de blettes*), and baby lima beans, since fresh baby limas are so rare and the frozen are crisp and rather tasty.

Most of Nice's vegetables are cooked in the Chinese and Indian way—quickly sautéed in oil that seals in the flavor as well as vitamins. The vegetables retain their taste, texture, and nutritional qualities. When a vegetable is to be boiled, it is cooked in a large pot of boiling salted water and it will be a little undercooked—*al dente*.

Vegetable dishes are garnished with a mixture of fresh herbs—mint, basil, chives, Italian parsley—either shredded with a *hachoir* or with kitchen shears or pounded in a mortar.

The following are the vegetables most commonly used in the South of France.

Artichokes (*les Artichauts*)

There are mainly two varieties in the United States. The globe artichoke (the most common and mainly grown in California) is delicious in *artichauts à la barigoule*. The small, tender purple kind is eaten raw or just blanched, and is used in *omelette aux artichauts, salade niçoise, poulet aux artichauts*. It can be found in Italian and Spanish markets. Artichokes must be firm, unspotted, and evenly colored, and squeak when you squeeze them. Never serve anything but cool water (or perhaps cold beer) with artichokes—wine tastes awful with them.

Asparagus (*les Asperges*)

The little thin asparagus found wild in olive groves and woods in the South of France are superb in omelets. The large ones are served warm with vinaigrette or are eaten dipped in a soft-boiled egg. Always choose asparagus with closed tips and firm stalks and peel the stalk up to about 2 inches from the tip (a vegetable peeler is handy for this chore).

Beans—String Beans (*les Haricots*)

The flattish green beans are good for *soupe au pistou;* the round plump ones are delicious warm with vinaigrette; all the green and yellow beans are good with *aïoli* or in a marinade. They must always be fresh enough to snap between your fingers when you break them and be served crisp, not overcooked. Put them in a large amount of salted boiling water; bring to a second boil, then uncover and simmer

Les Légumes

until just tender; drain at once and rinse in cold water. This process seals in the color and the flavor.

Cauliflower (*le Chou-fleur*)

This goes perfectly with *aïoli*. It can be eaten warm with vinaigrette or raw dipped in *bagna cauda*. Cauliflower must have a firm, heavy head and a creamy color. Before cooking, break it into florets or cut off the stem and leave it whole.

Celery (*le Céleri*)

At Christmas time we eat celery raw in salad; in the summer we dip the stalks in *bagna cauda* or *aïoli*. We cook it in *soupe au pistou* and in marinades, or serve it braised.

In America I have found it hard to find the celeriac (knob celery) we use in salad, so no recipe for it is included.

Eggplant (*l'Aubergine*)

The little dark-purple eggplants of Nice are cooked unpeeled, but the very large, lighter *aubergine americaine* available here should generally be peeled, salted, and drained. It is a wonderfully versatile vegetable that can be used for fried *beignets,* sautéed and stuffed *farcis,* puréed *caviar provençale,* simmered *ratatouille,* and baked *tians.* The fleshier variety commonly found in supermarkets is less fragrant than the small dark kind, but this staple of Nice's treats will be delicious as long as it is shiny and smooth-skinned.

Fennel (*le Fenouil*)

There are two kinds: the sweet fennel with a fleshy bulb and the wild fennel with seeds and stalks. The light licorice-flavored bulb with its feathery green leaves is wonderful braised with pork or cooked with fish. It is fresh and lovely raw—dipped in *bagna cauda* or minced in salads. Large supermarkets carry it twice a year. The dried stalks of wild fennel are harder to find in America. In Nice we add its special flavor to fish by using it for stuffing or as a bed for broiling or by simmering it in *bouillabaisse.* It can be replaced by minced fresh fennel or fennel or anise seed.

Vegetables

Garlic (*l'Ail*)

Since ancient times, when the Chinese, the Egyptians and the Hebrews discovered it, garlic has been used in both cooking and medicine. This potent, healthful vegetable is a staple of Provençal cuisine and, to a lesser degree, of Niçois cooking. It is the base for *aïoli, rouille,* and fish dishes (*brandade, gigot de mer*), soups (*aïgo bouido*), meats (*gigot d'agneau à l'aillade*), *champignons provençale,* and *caviar provençale*).

Choose large, plump garlic bulbs. Red garlic comes from Mexico and is tastier, stronger, and keeps better. The white variety generally sold in supermarkets is milder, but as long as it is firm and fresh it is acceptable. Never use a clove of garlic that is soft, yellow, or dark and has a green sprout in the center. Wreaths of two hundred bulbs are sold in Italian and Spanish markets; if you use garlic in quantity, hang a wreath in a dry place in your kitchen.

Cooked garlic is very different from raw. Cooked slowly, it tastes sweet and nutty; sautéed whole, it is light and delicate. Raw garlic, minced or crushed, is potent enough to revive or enliven any dish. For guests fussy about their breath, offer mint or parsley leaves to chew after dinner.

Mushrooms (*les Champignons*)

In Nice there is a rich variety of edible mushrooms. The most common are *mousserolles, girolles, sanguins, cêpes,* and each variety is prepared in all ways imaginable. White caps are abundant around Nice and are always eaten unpeeled, either raw with *bagna cauda, citronnette,* or *aïoli,* or sautéed with parsley and garlic, marinated, stuffed, or added to various salads. Cultivated mushrooms sold in American supermarkets should have plump, smooth, creamy-colored caps.

Olives (*les Olives*)

There are three hundred varieties in Provence and almost as many ways to eat them. In the United States there are only the unpitted little black olives imported from Nice and sold in gourmet shops or black olives packed in oil or in brine with herbs found in some supermarkets and in Italian, Greek, and Spanish markets. There are also the olives canned in water, but these are tasteless and should not be used for the recipes in this book.

In Niçois cooking, olives are used raw with hors d'oeuvres and salads, cooked with meats (*poulet en saupiquet, boeuf niçoise*) or with fish (*estockaficada, daube d' Avignon*).

Onions (*les Oignons*)
The small white onions (about 1½ inches in diameter, and also called pearl onions) are used in omelets or with fresh peas in spring. The larger yellow ones are for *pissaladière*, stews, soups, or *farcis*. The red Spanish onions are for court bouillon and marinades. When you make a sauce, grate or finely chop the onion so it cooks quickly into a smooth purée and thickens the juices of the sauce.

Peppers (*les Poivrons*)
The little narrow Italian green peppers are delicious raw in salads. Plump red, green, and yellow bell peppers are for *estockaficada, salade rouge, farcis*. Choose peppers that are firm and shiny. Before you peel a pepper, set it 2 inches below the broiler for 5 to 10 minutes, turning it once with tongs. Peel under running water with a sharp knife, and seed.

Scallions (*les Cébettes*)
Delicious with *bagna cauda, salade niçoise,* in omelets, with *pâtes verdure,* and *gnocchis verts,* and with lima beans in *févettes à la laitue.*

Spinach (*les Épinards*)
Frozen spinach is perfect mixed with ham or rice. Use 3 10-ounce boxes for 6 people.

Squash (*la Courge*)
Widely used in Niçois cooking in *soupe de courges, tians,*

Vegetables

and *tarte de courges*. Pumpkin and acorn or butternut squash need lots of salt, so double-check the seasoning.

Swiss Chard (*la Blette*)

The white ribs are eaten blanched or braised, and the green leaves are prepared like spinach. A staple in Niçois cooking, it is rather difficult to find here, but it can be successfully replaced by spinach. It is used in *pietsch, ravioli, tian, caillettes,* and omelets, and is also part of a curious mixture of sweets and nuts for *épinards aux pignons* and *tourte de blettes*.

Tomatoes (*les Tomates*)

To peel them, submerge each tomato in a pot of boiling water for 5 seconds, then slip off the loose skin with a sharp knife. Select firm tomatoes for *salade niçoise* and *farcis* and very ripe ones for all other dishes.

Zucchini (*les Courgettes*)

Zucchini are in season all year round in America. Never buy limp zucchini; they must be shiny, smooth, and firm. Cook in soups, *farcis,* and omelets, or grate them raw for *beignets*. Zucchini should always be thoroughly scrubbed and left unpeeled.

Artichauts à la Barigoule I

Artichokes Stuffed with Herbs, Carrots, and Ham and Simmered in Wine and Vegetables

In America, artichokes are seldom served without either melted butter or hollandaise sauce, but in the South of France they are served in several different ways: stuffed *au gratin, à la vinaigrette,* or simply seasoned.

In this version of *artichauts à la barigoule* (or *farigoule,* which is the Provençal word for thyme), small amounts of cooked vegetables and ham are wedged between the artichoke leaves, then the

Les Légumes

artichokes are simmered in white wine, vegetables, and herbs. It is a savory and delicate dish, perfect for a luncheon's main dish.

For 6 people:

  6 *artichokes**
    juice of half a lemon
  5 *tablespoons olive oil*
  3 *onions, chopped*
½ *cup chopped parsley*
  1 *cup chopped prosciutto, country ham,*
     or lean salt pork
    salt
    freshly ground black pepper
  1 *teaspoon thyme*
  2 *garlic cloves, crushed*
  2 *carrots, chopped*
    bouquet garni (p. 11)
½ *cup dry white wine*
½ *cup water*

Wash the artichokes, cut off the stems, and remove the outer leaves. Cut off the hard tips of the leaves with kitchen shears. Scald the artichokes in a large pot of salted boiling water, to which the lemon juice has been added, for 5 minutes. Set aside.

Remove the fuzzy choke with a spoon or knife or a melon scoop by forcing open the inner leaves and scooping it out. Scrape the bottom to clean it out as much as possible.

To make the stuffing, heat 2 tablespoons of the olive oil in a large frying pan and gently cook a third of the chopped onions until tender, adding a little salt so they won't stick to the pan. Turn off the heat and add the parsley, ham, salt, pepper, thyme, and garlic. Stir well and check the seasoning.

When the artichokes have cooled, put them upside down and press to force the leaves to open. Push the stuffing between the layers of leaves, forcing it down as deeply as you can. (The distribution need not be precise, but be sure to use all of the filling if possible.) Sprinkle the artichokes with a little olive oil, pepper, and salt (omit this if you used salt pork), and place in a heavy-bottomed casserole or Doufeu.

---

* Instead of the globe, use 12 small purple artichokes if you can find them. They are easier to prepare because their tenderness makes it unnecessary to blanch them.

Vegetables

Sprinkle the carrots, the remaining onions, and 3 tablespoons of the olive oil around the stuffed artichokes in the casserole. Add the bouquet garni and cook over a moderate flame until the vegetables just begin to turn brown. Add the wine and let it come to a boil. Simmer, uncovered, for 3 to 5 minutes, then add the water. Cover and cook gently for 45 minutes (you may need to add more wine or water if the sauce becomes too thick).

Place the artichokes in a covered shallow dish to keep warm. Force the carrots and onions through a sieve with a large spoon or pestle. Put the purée back into the wine broth, simmer for 5 minutes and pour over the artichokes.

Artichauts à la Barigoule II
Artichokes Stuffed with Herbs and Garlic

This cruder version of the *barigoule* is designed only for small purple artichokes. It is a lovely first course.

For 6 people:

> *12 small purple artichokes*
> *½ cup finely chopped parsley*
> *1 teaspoon thyme*
> *3 garlic cloves, 1 crushed and 2 left*
>   *whole and unpeeled*
> *salt*
> *freshly ground black pepper*
> *2 tablespoons olive oil*
> *2 onions, chopped*
> *1 bay leaf*

Trim the artichokes of their tough outer leaves and tips and cut off the stems. Press each one upside down so that the leaves are forced apart. Combine the parsley, thyme, crushed garlic, salt, and pepper and stuff the mixture between the leaves of each artichoke.

Place the artichokes in the olive oil in a cast-iron frying pan or Doufeu. Scatter the onions around the artichokes in the pan with the 2 *unpeeled* garlic cloves. Heat slowly over a low flame for 5 minutes. Add about 1 inch of warm water and a bay leaf and simmer, covered, for 1½ hours.

Les Légumes

174

Beignets de Légumes

Vegetable Fritters

These are the Niçois tempura. Always choose the smallest vegetables possible and serve them like hot bread in a basket lined with a bright napkin. I have selected the vegetables traditionally used for this dish. You can, of course, add anything you wish: asparagus tips, green beans, carrots, celery, snow peas, bell peppers.

For 6 people:

- 2 egg yolks
- 2 tablespoons olive oil
- ¾ cup beer
- 1 cup flour, unbleached
  salt
  freshly ground pepper
- 3 small unpeeled zucchini, sliced into ¼-inch strips
- 1 small narrow eggplant, peeled and sliced lengthwise into ¼-inch strips
- 1 fennel bulb, cut into strips
- 12 firm mushrooms
- ½ head cauliflower, broken into florets and cooked
- 1 tablespoon thyme
- 2 tablespoons olive oil
- 8 zucchini flowers (if available)
  peanut oil for deep-frying
- 2 egg whites
- ½ cup chopped parsley
  Coulis (p. 79)

Prepare the batter. With a wire whisk, beat the egg yolks, then very slowly add the oil, beer, and flour, beating constantly to prevent lumps. Season with salt (½ teaspoon) and pepper and set aside, covered, for 1 hour in a warm place.

Blanch the zucchini, eggplant, fennel bulb, and mushrooms* for

* Mushrooms can be blanched for 4 minutes in ½ cup of dry white wine and the juice of half a lemon instead of water. But if they are very fresh, do not blanch them at all.

Vegetables

3 minutes in salted boiling water and drain. Blanch the cauliflower florets for at least 5 minutes and drain. Dry them all and marinate in salt, pepper, thyme, and olive oil for 1 hour or until ready to cook. Remove the stems of the zucchini flowers, rinse and drain them carefully.

Preheat the oven to 300°. Beat the egg whites until stiff but not dry, and fold them gently into the batter. Add the parsley and marinated vegetables.

Heat the peanut oil in a large frying pan. Test the oil with a drop of batter—if it sizzles it is ready. Using tongs, pick the vegetables out of the batter, one at a time, shaking off excess batter. Dip the zucchini flowers in the batter one by one. Drop into the oil and fry about five pieces of vegetable at a time, turning them once gently with the tongs after 1 or 2 minutes. (Do not cook too many fritters at one time because the temperature will drop and the fritters will stick together. Each fritter should have room to puff and roll over easily.) Fry for 4 to 5 minutes, or until the fritters are golden brown. Drain them on layers of paper towels placed on a cookie sheet and cover them with another layer of towels.

When all the fritters are made, place them on a large serving dish or in a basket lined with a folded napkin. Sprinkle with salt and pepper. Serve as soon as possible, as they will lose their crispness if they wait. Serve with a warm *coulis* sauce in a separate bowl.

Capoun

Cabbage Stuffed with Ham, Rice, Vegetables, and Herbs and Simmered in White Wine

This is a hearty cold-weather dish and a good way to use leftover ham, beef, rice, or vegetables. The stuffed cabbage is baked slowly on a bed of vegetables in a wine and herb broth. When served, the cabbage is sliced like a melon and looks most appetizing, with the green leaves surrounding the colorful stuffing. This is a meal in itself.

For 6 to 8 people:

    1 *large head green cabbage*
    ½ *teaspoon cumin*
      salt
      freshly ground pepper
    2 *onions, finely minced*
    6 *tablespoons olive oil*
    3 *garlic cloves, peeled and crushed*
    1½ *cups finely minced parsley*
    2 *eggs, beaten*
    1 *cup cooked rice*
    1 *cup cooked peas (fresh or frozen)*
    ½ *cup diced lean salt pork*
    1½ *cups chopped cooked ham, boiled*
      beef, or pork
    1 *or 2 thick slices of country ham, Vir-*
      ginia ham, or prosciutto, diced
    ½ *teaspoon Spanish saffron*
    3 *carrots, sliced*
    2 *onions, sliced*
    1 *garlic clove, peeled*
    ¾ *cup dry white wine*
    ¾ *cup water or beef broth*
      bouquet garni (p. 11)

Remove the tough outer leaves of the cabbage. Wash and shred them. Wash and cook the head of cabbage for 10 minutes in a large pot of salted boiling water. Drain in a colander, and when cool enough, gently peel off the leaves and spread each one on a paper towel. Sprinkle with cumin, salt, and pepper.

Sauté the onions in 4 tablespoons of the olive oil for 5 minutes and put them into a large bowl. Add to the bowl the crushed garlic, parsley, eggs, rice, peas, all the meats, and shredded cabbage leaves. Add the saffron, salt, and pepper and mix thoroughly with your hands. Taste to see if it is well seasoned.

Take a large piece of cheesecloth and place four or five of the biggest leaves in a circle in the center of the cloth. Place all the stuffing in the center of the leaves, and cover with the rest of the leaves. Pull up the corners of the cheesecloth and tie tightly with a piece of string so that you have a firm, melon-shaped ball.

Preheat the oven to 350°. Sauté the carrots, onions, and the whole peeled garlic clove in a deep roasting pan for 5 minutes.

Vegetables

177

Add the wine, the water or broth, and the bouquet garni, and place the stuffed cabbage on top of the vegetables. Cover with aluminum foil and cover the pan. Bake for 3 to 4 hours, checking now and then to see that there is enough liquid. When a knife slides through the cabbage ball easily it is done. Remove the bouquet garni. Skim off the fat and remove the string and the cloth from the cabbage.

Place the cabbage ball on a warm shallow serving dish. Slice it in large wedges as you would a melon. Pour a little of the cooking juices over each slice and sprinkle with salt and pepper.

Note: Cutting the *capoun* will be easy if you use the kind of chopping board described in Techniques and Tools (p. 20).

Carottes Paysanne

Carrots Sautéed with Parsley and Garlic

In every province in France except Provence, carrots are sautéed in butter. In Provence, olive oil, parsley, and garlic are added to contrast with instead of to enhance the natural sweetness of the carrots.

For 6 people:

3 pounds small carrots
5 tablespoons olive oil
2 garlic cloves, peeled and crushed
1 cup water
2 teaspoons sugar
salt
freshly ground black pepper
2 tablespoons minced parsley

Wash and peel the carrots and slice them on the bias into ½-inch slices. Heat the olive oil in a frying pan and add the carrots. Sprinkle with salt. Cover, and cook over a low flame for 10 minutes, shaking the pan from time to time. Add the garlic, water, sugar, salt, and pepper and cook for 20 minutes. Add the parsley and toss gently. Check the seasoning before serving.

Céleri Paysanne

Celery Braised in White Wine

The fresh flavor and the lightness of this dish make it one of my favorites. Served in individual dishes and sprinkled with cheese, it is a lovely first course, and as an accompaniment to lamb, pork, or chicken, it gives spirit to the meat. Make sure the celery you buy is as crisp as possible.

For 6 people:

3 pounds celery (about 3 bunches)—do
    not use the tough outer stalks
3 quarts salted water
    salt
    freshly ground black pepper
2 tablespoons olive oil
⅔ cup diced lean salt pork
1 garlic clove, peeled
2 onions, chopped
4 carrots, chopped
3 bay leaves
1 cup dry white wine
    juice of 1 lemon (optional)

Wash the celery, remove as many strings as possible, and cut into 1-inch pieces. Drop them into boiling water, add salt, and cook for 15 minutes. Drain and sprinkle with salt and pepper.

Heat the olive oil in a large cast-iron skillet. Add the salt pork, garlic, onions, and carrots and cook gently for 10 minutes, or until tender but not browned. Add the celery,* bay leaves, wine, salt, and pepper. Simmer, covered, for 40 minutes, and then, uncovered, for about 5 minutes, or until the liquid has thickened. Remove the bay leaves and garlic and check the seasoning. You may wish to sprinkle the juice of a lemon on top of the celery before serving.

---

* If you want the dish to have a thicker consistency, you may put the coarser celery stalks through a Mouli food mill and stir the purée into the cooked vegetables.

Vegetables

Note: This dish can be reheated quite successfully. If this is to be a first course, use individual china or copper bowls, slightly oiled. Add 1 heaping tablespoon of celery purée to each bowl and stir. Sprinkle with a little grated cheese and heat in a 375° oven for 15 minutes. The dish can be prepared in advance, of course, and baked at the last minute.

Champignons Farcis
Stuffed Mushrooms

In Nice, mushrooms are cooked in innumerable ways. This recipe is a wonderful first course, served piping hot. Select firm, cream-colored mushrooms for this dish.

For 6 people:

1 *pound mushrooms (about 2 inches in diameter)*
salt
2 *tablespoons olive oil*
2 *thin slices bread*
2 *tablespoons milk*
2 *tablespoons minced parsley*
2 *garlic cloves, peeled and crushed*
1 *egg, beaten*
1/4 *cup minced ham*
freshly ground black pepper
1 *tablespoon bread crumbs (preferably homemade)*

Rinse the mushrooms, dry them well and remove the stems. Rub the caps of the 12 largest with salt and 1 tablespoon of the olive oil so that they are thoroughly coated. Mince the rest of the mushrooms along with the stems.

Dip the slices of bread (with crusts removed) in the milk, then squeeze out the excess moisture.

Heat 1 tablespoon of the olive oil in a large frying pan, add the minced mushrooms, and cook gently for 5 minutes. Remove the pan from heat and add the parsley, garlic, bread paste, egg, ham, salt and pepper, and blend well. Check the seasoning.

Les Légumes

Preheat the oven to 350°. Fill the mushroom caps with the mixture. Sprinkle with bread crumbs and 1 tablespoon of the olive oil and place them in an oiled baking dish. Bake for 20 minutes, then set the pan under the broiler for 3 minutes to brown the top.

Champignons Provencale

Mushrooms Sautéed with Parsley and Garlic

This dish can be served with almost any meat, fish, or fowl and is a good substitute for potatoes and other starches. All ingredients must be superfresh.

For 6 people:

> 2 pounds mushrooms
> ½ cup oil (half olive, half peanut)
> 1 teaspoon butter
> ½ cup finely chopped parsley (preferably Italian)
> ½ cup bread crumbs (preferably homemade)
> salt
> freshly ground black pepper
> 2 garlic cloves, peeled and crushed
> juice of 1 lemon

Rinse the mushrooms and dry them thoroughly. Mince the stems (with ends cut off), and slice the caps or quarter them if they are small. Heat the oil and butter in a skillet and add the mushrooms. Cook, stirring occasionally, for 5 minutes, or until browned. Lower the flame and add the parsley, bread crumbs, salt, and pepper to the pan and cook for about 3 minutes.

Put the mushrooms on a warm platter and sprinkle with garlic and lemon juice.

Chou-fleur Rouge

Cauliflower, Potatoes, and Onions Simmered with Tomatoes and Saffron

With its subtle counterpoint of flavors, this is one of the most interesting of vegetable stews. The cauliflower should remain crisp and the potato slices firm. The vegetables are delicious as a hot first course or as an accompaniment for plain broiled fish or meat.

For 6 people:

- 2 tablespoons olive oil
- 6 small white onions, minced, or scallions cut into 1/2-inch pieces
- 2 garlic cloves, peeled and cut in half
- 5 tomatoes (canned or fresh), chopped
- 2 heads cauliflower, separated into florets
- 2 teaspoons salt
  a pinch of freshly ground white pepper
- 1/2 teaspoon Spanish saffron
- 4 large or 6 medium-sized potatoes, sliced

Heat the olive oil in a heavy-bottomed pan and sauté the onions and garlic for 3 minutes. Add the tomatoes and cook over high heat until they begin to bubble. Add the cauliflower and lower the flame. Add salt, pepper, and saffron (crush between your fingers and sprinkle). Cook, uncovered, over low heat for about 10 minutes. Add about 1/2 cup water if the dish becomes dry. Add the potatoes and cook, uncovered, for 25 minutes, adding more water if necessary, until the potatoes are just cooked. Check the seasoning and serve.

Courgettes Râpées

Grated Zucchini Sautéed in Olive Oil

This is a quick, delicious dish. Make sure the zucchini are firm, smooth, and glossy.

For 6 people:

8 *small zucchini*
3 *tablespoons olive oil*
½ *cup minced parsley or basil*
salt
freshly ground white pepper

Scrub and dry the zucchini. Slice off the stems and tips but do not peel them. Grate them coarsely and sprinkle with salt. Drain them on a kitchen towel for 30 minutes, then fold the towel over and squeeze out as much water as possible, or take handfuls of the zucchini and squeeze.

Heat the oil and add the zucchini and parsley. Sauté over a medium flame for 15 to 20 minutes, tossing gently with a wooden spoon. Add salt and pepper to taste.

This dish can be prepared ahead and quickly reheated before serving.

Épinards aux Pignons

Spinach Cooked with Pine Nuts and Orange Blossom Water

The combining of greens and sweet ingredients in this way is known to be indigenously Niçois, though it would be difficult to trace its origin through the complex layers of Nice's history. The famous *tourte de blettes,* a thin pastry filled with Swiss chard, raisins, eggs, sugar, pine nuts, and orange blossom water, is another example of this treatment.

Here is an intriguing dish, a perfect complement to almost any meat or fish.

Vegetables

For 6 people:

2 *pounds fresh spinach, or 2 10-ounce*
boxes frozen
3 *tablespoons olive oil*
½ *cup pine nuts*
2 *tablespoons orange blossom water*
1 *teaspoon salt*
freshly ground black pepper

Cook the spinach until tender. Squeeze out as much water as possible and chop it (it should be quite dry). Put it in a pan and toss with the other ingredients. Cook, uncovered, only until the spinach is heated through and serve at once.

Farcis à la Niçoise

Lightly Stuffed Vegetables

Like the *crudités et bagna cauda* and *salade niçoise*, *farcis* are a summer staple in Nice. On Sundays and festive days, housewives and children carry large trays of freshly stuffed vegetables to the village baker's oven, returning at noon to pick up their crisp, golden *farcis*.

Served at most picnics or buffets, *farcis* are usually prepared in large quantities, since they are delicious warm or cold. Be sure to choose small vegetables and not to overstuff them.

For 6 people:

3 *tablespoons olive oil*
3 *medium-sized or 6 small eggplants,*
with stems removed and cut in half
lengthwise
6 *green bell peppers, with the bottom*
end cut off and seeded
6 *onions, peeled*
6 *small cucumbers, peeled*
6 *small zucchini, with stems removed*
6 *medium-sized tomatoes*
1 *onion, chopped*
2 *cups chopped beef, lamb, or ham*

Les Légumes

½ cup chopped lean salt pork
3 cups cooked rice
1 cup finely chopped Italian parsley
2 teaspoons thyme
2 garlic cloves, peeled and crushed
salt
freshly ground black pepper
2 eggs, lightly beaten
½ cup freshly grated Parmesan or Swiss cheese
½ cup bread crumbs (preferably home-made)

Preheat the oven to 350°. Lightly oil the eggplants and peppers with 1 tablespoon of the olive oil and place on an oiled baking dish (you may need two). Bake for 10 minutes. Scoop out the pulp from the eggplants and set aside in a large bowl.

Heat a large pot of salted water. Blanch the whole onions, cucumbers, and zucchini for 10 to 15 minutes. Remove them with a slotted spoon.

Prepare the vegetable shells, which should be about ½ inch thick so that they are firm enough to hold the filling. Cut the onions in half crosswise and remove the centers, leaving about 3 layers of skin. Cut the zucchini and cucumbers in half and scoop out the pulp. Cut the tomatoes in half lengthwise, sprinkle with salt, and leave them upside down to drain for 10 minutes; gently squeeze out excess juice and scoop out the pulp. Add the onion centers and the pulp of the zucchini, cucumbers, and tomatoes to the eggplant pulp in the bowl, and set aside.

Preheat the oven to 375°. Heat 2 tablespoons of the olive oil in a large frying pan and add the chopped onion. Cook gently for 5 minutes, or until tender. Stir in the pulp of all the vegetables and then the meat, salt pork, rice, parsley, thyme, garlic, salt, and pepper. (Taste before adding salt because it may not be needed with salt pork and ham.) Cook over a low flame, stirring occasionally, for 15 minutes. Turn off the flame and add the eggs. (The stuffing should be fairly solid, but if you think it is too dry, add a chopped tomato.)

Place the vegetable shells on one or two oiled baking dishes. Fill them with the stuffing and sprinkle with cheese. Sprinkle bread crumbs only on the tomatoes and onions. Dribble olive oil over all the vegetables and bake for 30 minutes. Serve hot (preferably) or cold.

Vegetables

Note: I have added the cucumbers to this otherwise traditional recipe because cucumbers are fresher and more available in winter than zucchini.

Fenouil Braisé
Braised Fennel

This anise-scented vegetable is available in Italian and Greek markets, but you can also find it in most supermarkets in the fall, winter, and early spring. Fennel will brighten your winter meals.

This dish can be reheated easily and it complements both lamb and fish. Here are two versions.

For 6 people:

Fenouil Braisé I

6 *large fennel bulbs*
4 *quarts salted water*
   bouquet garni (p. 11)
1 *tablespoon olive oil*
1 *tablespoon freshly grated Parmesan cheese*
   salt
   freshly ground black pepper
   fresh fennel leaves, minced

Cut off the stems of the fennel bulbs, remove the outer stalks and wash them well.

Preheat the oven to 375°. Bring the water to a boil in a large pot. Add the bouquet garni and the bulbs and cook, uncovered, for 25 to 30 minutes, or until tender but still crisp. Drain, cool, and squeeze the bulbs gently to remove the excess water. Cut the bulbs in half lengthwise and arrange them on a baking dish. Sprinkle with the olive oil, cheese, salt, and pepper. Bake for 10 minutes.

Before serving, garnish with the fennel leaves, cut finely over the dish with scissors.

6 *fennel bulbs*
2 *tablespoons olive oil*
salt
4 *tablespoons water or, preferably, stock*
   (which improves the flavor and glazes
   the fennel)
freshly ground black pepper
fresh fennel leaves, minced

Remove the outer stalks of the fennel bulbs and wash and dry the bulbs. Heat the olive oil in a frying pan. Add the bulbs, sprinkle with salt, and simmer for 30 minutes. Add water and bring to a boil. Cover and simmer for 1 to 1½ hours, or until the bulbs are tender to the touch.

Slice each bulb in half lengthwise, add salt and pepper to taste, and serve hot sprinkled with the fennel leaves.

Févettes à l'Ail

Baby Lima Beans Sautéed with Garlic

A delicious dish made with newly picked baby lima beans. Since fresh limas are hard to find here and the frozen ones are available all year round, this is a modified but still interesting version of the Niçois recipe.

For 6 people:

2 *10-ounce boxes frozen lima beans**
5 *tablespoons oil (half olive, half pea-*
   nut)
6 *garlic cloves, peeled and sliced in half*
½ *cup bread crumbs (preferably home-*
   made)
salt
freshly ground black pepper

Blanch the beans according to package instructions and drain them.

* Fresh string beans, cut into 1-inch pieces, may be substituted.

Heat the oil in a large frying pan and sauté the garlic until it is golden. Add the beans, bread crumbs, and salt and pepper. Stir and cook, stirring constantly, for 3 minutes, or until the beans are coated with oil and crumbs. The lima beans should remain slightly crisp. Serve at once in a warm bowl.

Févettes à la Verdure

Baby Lima Beans Simmered with Lettuce, Scallions, and Thyme

Ideally, the lima beans used in this recipe should be fresh ones, but because they are generally unavailable, I use the frozen kind. Cooked with lettuce, scallions, and herbs, even frozen lima beans make one of the most refreshing of all vegetable dishes.

For 6 people:

2 10-ounce boxes frozen lima beans
1 cup water
2 large heads lettuce (Boston, escarole, or iceberg), shredded
4 scallions, finely chopped, or ½ cup chopped chives
1 teaspoon thyme
salt
freshly ground black pepper
1 tablespoon olive oil
2 tablespoons chopped basil and/or mint

Take the lima beans out of the freezer 1 hour in advance. Boil the water in a pot and add the lima beans, lettuce, scallions or chives, thyme, salt, and pepper. Cover and bring to a boil. Cook, uncovered, for 20 to 30 minutes over a moderate flame. Check the salt and pepper.

Place the beans in a serving bowl. (There should not be any liquid left, but if there is, just leave it in the pot.) Add the olive oil and the basil and/or mint and serve.

Note: The leftovers can be used in *Capoun* (pp. 176–78) or *Pietsch* (pp. 152–53).

Mélange Printanier

Small Artichokes with Fresh Peas

This is a dish to be served in the spring—both the artichokes and peas must be very young, crisp, and sweet. It is glorious sprinkled with fresh mint leaves and served as a first course.

For 6 people:

        1½ pounds fresh peas
         6 small artichokes
         2 heads Boston lettuce, shredded
         1 teaspoon sugar
         1 teaspoon salt
         3 tablespoons olive oil
         2 small onions, chopped
        ½ cup chopped lean salt pork
         2 tablespoons chopped mint or parsley

Shell the peas and keep about half of the empty pods. Pull off the transparent lining of the pods. Remove the outer leaves of the artichokes and the stems. Split them lengthwise and remove the chokes.

In a pot of boiling water, cook the peas, empty pods, and lettuce with sugar and salt for 20 minutes, or until they are tender.

Meanwhile, in a deep frying pan, heat the olive oil and add the artichokes, onions, and salt pork. Cook for 20 minutes over a medium flame until the artichokes are tender, then add the drained peas, pods, and lettuce and cook for 5 minutes.

Sprinkle with mint or parsley. Serve as a separate course accompanied by good, fresh bread.

Ratatouille

Vegetable Mélange Simmered with Herbs

Ratatouille is an eminently versatile dish—you can serve it warm or cold, as the center of a meal, or as an hors d'oeuvre or accompaniment. You may want to prepare this a day or two ahead, since it is even better reheated. Some cooks feel strongly that the vegetables in a *ratatouille* should be puréed; I prefer it when the vegetables retain their shape because the flavor seems better.

For 6 people:

2 *large eggplants or 6 small ones*
salt
3 *yellow or red peppers*
6 *zucchini*
6 *tomatoes*
8 *tablespoons oil (half peanut, half olive)*
3 *onions, minced*
4 *garlic cloves, peeled and crushed*
2 *bay leaves*
2 *teaspoons thyme*
freshly ground black pepper
1/2 *cup dry white wine*
1 *cup chopped fresh basil (or parsley)*
juice of 1 lemon

Peel the large eggplants; leave the small ones unpeeled. Remove the stem ends and cut the large eggplants in 1-inch cubes; slice the small ones into 1-inch slices and cut each slice in half. Put them in a colander with salt and leave them to drain for 30 minutes. Press them down and blot with paper towels. Reserve.

Slice the peppers in half vertically. Remove the seeds and stems and cut into 1-inch strips. Cut off the stem ends of the zucchini and cut them into 1-inch slices. Quarter the tomatoes and squeeze them gently to extract the excess water and seeds.

Heat 1 tablespoon of the oil in a heavy-bottomed skillet. Add the onions, tomatoes, garlic cloves, 1 bay leaf, 1 teaspoon of thyme, salt, and pepper. Cook for 10 minutes, or until the sauce thickens a bit. Pour the sauce into a bowl.

Clean the skillet with a paper towel and heat 3 tablespoons of the oil in it. Add the eggplant and cook for 5 minutes. Add salt and pepper, remove from the skillet, and put in the bowl with the tomato-onion sauce.

Clean the skillet and heat 2 tablespoons more oil in it. Add the peppers, salt, and pepper and cook for 5 minutes. Put them in the bowl with the eggplant. Clean the skillet again and heat 2 tablespoons more oil. Add the zucchini and cook until tender—about 10 minutes. Pour the entire bowl of vegetables on top of the cooked zucchini and sprinkle with 1 teaspoon of thyme. Add the wine, 1 bay leaf, salt, and pepper to taste and stir well with a wooden spoon. Simmer, uncovered, for 1 hour, or cover and cook in a 350° oven for about 45 minutes.

Before serving, remove the bay leaves, carefully pour off the excess oil, check the seasoning and add more pepper and salt if necessary. Serve sprinkled heavily with basil—it will keep the dish fresh.

If you serve the *ratatouille* cold, add about 1 tablespoon of olive oil and the juice of a lemon just before serving.

Note: If you keep this dish in the refrigerator, allow the excess oil to stay floating on the surface. The oil will protect it and keep it fresh.

Omelettes Jardinières
A Variety of Vegetable and Herb Omelets

The following nine recipes are for vegetable omelets that can be eaten cold or warm. They are Nice's omelets—fresher, lighter, tastier than their northern French counterparts. Wonderful for picnics or buffets, they can also be served warm for lunch. They look like plump pancakes—green, red, or yellow, depending on whether you choose spinach (*troucha*), tomatoes, (*crespeou*), or potatoes (*crique*). For any of these *omelettes jardinières*, the process of cooking them is the same.

Basic Omelet-Making Procedure
Heat the olive oil (sometimes with a little butter). Pour the egg-vegetable mixture into the pan and lower the flame. After a few minutes the omelet will start to coagulate. Shake the pan gently. Put a large plate over the frying pan (of course, the plate must be wider than the pan), then, holding the plate firmly against the pan, turn the omelet upside down on the plate. Add a little oil to the pan, then slide the omelet back into the pan with the raw side

down, and let it cook over a medium flame for about 5 minutes. Do not fold the omelet over—it should remain round so that it can be cut in wedges for serving.

The process may sound complicated, but once you have tried it you will see how simple it is. If the omelet sticks to the pan, lift it with a large spatula and add a little oil.

Never wash the oiled frying pan that you use for making omelets; rub it with kosher salt and wipe clean with paper towels.

Omelette aux Artichauts
Artichoke Omelet

Use only the fresh small purple artichokes for this omelet. Avoid canned artichokes. Frozen artichoke hearts are acceptable if they are rinsed with cold water, sprinkled with salt, pepper, and olive oil and set aside for 10 minutes before cooking.

For 6 people:

5 *small purple artichokes*
2 *tablespoons oil*
8 *eggs, beaten with a fork*
  salt
  pepper
1 *tablespoon Parmesan cheese (optional)*

Rinse the artichokes in cold water and quarter them. Cut off the tips of the leaves and remove the "beard" in the center. Cut off any wilted or very tough leaves. Heat 1 tablespoon of the olive oil in a skillet and gently sauté the artichokes for 10 minutes. Season the eggs with salt and pepper and pour over the artichokes. Cook for 4 minutes, then turn on the other side (see Basic Omelet-Making Procedure, p. 191) and cook for 2 minutes more. If you like, you may sprinkle Parmesan cheese on top of the omelet before serving.

Note: Wild asparagus makes a delicious omelet. Following this recipe, you may use it, trimmed and chopped, instead of the artichokes.

Les Légumes

Omelette aux Courgettes

Zucchini Omelet

This is the simplest, quickest dish to make. The main point to keep in mind is to pick very firm, fresh zucchini.

For 6 people:

4 tablespoons oil (3 tablespoons olive, 1
    tablespoon peanut)
7 small zucchini, unpeeled and sliced ¼
    inch thick
salt
freshly ground black pepper
1 garlic clove, minced
8 eggs, beaten with a fork
1 tablespoon butter
a pinch of chopped parsley

In a skillet, heat 2 tablespoons of the mixed olive and peanut oil and sauté the zucchini slices over a medium flame for 10 minutes, or until they are soft. Remove with a slotted spoon and drain on paper towels.

Place the zucchini in a large bowl, add salt, pepper, and garlic and add the eggs.

Heat the remaining 2 tablespoons of the mixed oil with the butter in the skillet and pour in the egg and vegetable mixture. When the bottom is firm, turn the omelette over (see Basic Omelet-Making Procedure, pp. 191–92) and cook for 2 minutes. Sprinkle with parsley and a little olive oil before serving.

Crespeou

Tomato Omelet

For 6 people:

> 4 tablespoons olive oil
> 1 onion, finely chopped or grated
> 4 ripe tomatoes, peeled, quartered, and
>   squeezed dry
> 1 garlic clove, peeled and crushed
> 2 teaspoons flour
>   salt
>   freshly ground black pepper
> 1/3 cup chopped parsley or basil
> 6 eggs, beaten with a fork

Heat 2 tablespoons of the olive oil in a skillet, add the onion and cook gently for 5 minutes. Add the tomatoes and garlic, sprinkle with flour, salt, and pepper. Stir in half of the parsley or basil and cook over a low flame for 10 to 15 minutes, or until the mixture has become a little dry. Add the mixture to the beaten eggs.

Heat 2 tablespoons of the olive oil in a skillet, pour in the tomato mixture, and cook for about 5 minutes before turning (see Basic Omelet-Making Procedure, pp. 191–92). Cook on the other side for 2 to 3 minutes.

Variation:
Slice the tomatoes 1/2 inch thick, mix them with beaten eggs, salt, and pepper and cook. The tomatoes remain very firm, making this one of the most refreshing of summer omelets.

Crique

Potato and Onion Omelet

Les Légumes

This is a substantial omelet, quick to prepare, with the commonest of ingredients. Freshly grated potatoes give it its creamy substance.

For 6 people:

    3 medium-sized onions
    3 medium-sized potatoes
    4 tablespoons olive oil
    6 eggs, beaten with a fork
    3 tablespoons chopped parsley
    salt
    freshly ground pepper

Peel the onions and potatoes and grate them into a bowl. Place them in a kitchen towel and squeeze dry.

Heat 2 tablespoons of the olive oil in a heavy-bottomed frying pan, add the potatoes and onions and sauté them, covered, for 10 minutes, stirring from time to time.

Add to the beaten eggs the potatoes, onions, parsley, salt, and pepper.

Heat 2 tablespoons of the olive oil in a skillet, pour in the egg-vegetable mixture and cook slowly for 5 minutes (see Basic Omelet-Making Procedure, pp. 191–92). Then turn on the other side and cook for about 1 minute. Sprinkle with olive oil before serving.

Omelette Moissonière

Onion and Clove Omelet

This omelet is called *moissonière* because it was eaten cold under the trees after the harvest (*la moisson*). It can also be served warm.

For 6 people:

    3 or 4 large onions
    3 or 4 cloves
    1 tablespoon red wine vinegar
    3 tablespoons olive oil
    8 eggs, beaten with a fork
    salt
    pepper

Peel the onions. With a sharp knife make an incision in each and put in a clove. Place the onions in a bowl of water, add the vinegar, and marinate them for half a day. Then dip them in boiling water for a few minutes and drain. Remove the cloves and slice the onions into thin slices.

Vegetables

Heat 1 tablespoon of the olive oil in a heavy frying pan. Add the onions and sauté them for about 5 minutes, or until they are tender. Meanwhile, beat the eggs in a bowl and add salt and pepper. Add a little olive oil to the onions. Season the beaten eggs with salt and pepper and pour over the onions. Cook for a few minutes until firm underneath (see Basic Omelet-Making Procedure, pp. 191–92), then cook the other side for 1 or 2 minutes. Sprinkle with a little olive oil.

Omelette aux Oignons
Onion Omelet

This can be served either cold or warm.

For 6 people:

2 tablespoons olive oil
1 pound (about 10 to 12) small white
   onions, finely minced
8 eggs, beaten with a fork
   salt
   pepper

Heat 1 tablespoon of the olive oil in a frying pan, add the onions, cover, and cook over a low flame for 30 to 40 minutes. The onions must remain pale, yet be very soft. To the eggs in a bowl, add salt and pepper and the onions.

Heat 1 tablespoon oil in the frying pan and pour in the onion-egg mixture. Cook for 6 to 8 minutes over a low flame (see Basic Omelet-Making Procedure, pp. 191–92). Then turn on the other side and cook for about 1 minute. Sprinkle with 1 tablespoon olive oil and serve.

Omelette Panachée
Mixed Vegetable Omelet

Les Légumes

This is a typically Niçois omelet. Best in springtime and eaten warm.

For 6 people:

4 *artichokes (use only the hearts)*
2 *tablespoons olive oil*
¼ *cup blanched and drained chopped*
   spinach (fresh or frozen)
8 *eggs, beaten with a fork*
  salt
  pepper
¼ *cup cooked peas (fresh or frozen)*
2 *tablespoons chopped parsley or basil*

Prepare the artichoke hearts: Remove and discard the leaves and the fuzzy choke, and cut the hearts into ¼-inch slices.

Heat the olive oil in the frying pan and add the artichoke hearts and the spinach. Add to the eggs in a bowl the salt, pepper, and peas. Pour the egg-peas mixture over the artichoke hearts and spinach. Cook for about 5 minutes (see Basic Omelet-Making Procedure, pp. 191–92), turn it over and cook for about 3 minutes. Sprinkle with a little olive oil and basil or parsley before serving.

Omelette aux Pommes de Terre

Potato Omelet

For 6 people:

2 *tablespoons olive oil*
½ *cup finely chopped lean salt pork*
3 *potatoes, diced*
1 *onion, grated or thinly minced*
½ *cup chopped parsley or chives*
  freshly ground black pepper
5 *eggs, beaten with a fork*

Heat the olive oil and add the salt pork, potatoes, and onion. Cook, stirring gently from time to time and scraping the bottom with a spatula, for about 20 minutes, or until the potatoes are crispy and lightly browned. Add half of the parsley or chives and the pepper (no salt is needed because of the salt pork), and pour in the beaten eggs. Cook until the underside is firm (see Basic Omelet-Making Procedure, pp. 191–92), then cook the other side for about 2 minutes.

Vegetables

Troucha

Spinach Omelet

This is the buffet and picnic dish par excellence because it is delicious cold.

For 6 people:

> 2 tablespoons olive oil
> ½ cup chopped lean salt pork
> ½ onion, grated
> 5 eggs, beaten with a fork
> 4 10-ounce packages frozen spinach,
>   cooked and squeezed dry
> ½ cup freshly grated Swiss or Parmesan
>   cheese
> 1½ cups chopped parsley or basil
> ½ teaspoon nutmeg
>   salt
>   freshly ground black pepper

Heat the olive oil in a large frying pan and sauté the salt pork for a few minutes. Add the onion and cook for 5 minutes. In a bowl, mix together the beaten eggs, spinach, cheese, parsley, nutmeg, and salt and pepper. Pour the mixture on top of the onions and salt pork. Cook over a medium flame for 4 or 5 minutes, or until the underside is firm (see Basic Omelet-Making Procedure, pp. 191–92), then cook the other side for 2 minutes.

Papeton d'Aubergines

Eggplant Mousse

This recipe was created in the fourteenth century by the French papal chef in Avignon. It was his response to the Italian pope's criticism of French cuisine. It is a delicate, unique way to serve eggplant—light and delicious. Be sure to select eggplants that are firm, shiny, and smooth.

For 6 people:

    3 large eggplants, unpeeled and
        coarsely chopped
    about 3 tablespoons salt
    3 tablespoons olive oil
    2 tablespoons peanut oil
    3 onions, minced
    6 eggs, beaten
 1⅓ cups minced parsley
    2 garlic cloves, peeled and crushed
    ½ teaspoon freshly grated nutmeg
    1 teaspoon thyme
        freshly ground black pepper
    3 tablespoons freshly grated Parmesan
        or Swiss cheese
    2 tablespoons chopped basil or parsley
        Coulis (p. 79)—optional*

Put the chopped eggplant in a colander or large bowl and toss with 1 tablespoon of salt. Let stand for 30 minutes to draw out the bitter juice. Rinse well under cold water and squeeze out as much moisture as possible with your hands.

Heat the oils in a large frying pan. When they begin to smoke, add the onions and eggplant and lower the flame. Cook slowly, uncovered, stirring occasionally, for 30 minutes, or until the eggplant is translucent and tender. Pass it through a Mouli food mill† into

---

* This sauce is sometimes served with the dish, but I think the delicate *papeton* is overwhelmed by it.

† Instead of using the Mouli food mill, you can use a blender, set at high speed, to purée the eggplant, along with the eggs, garlic, onions, parsley, nutmeg, thyme, salt and pepper.

Vegetables

a large bowl and discard the seeds. The purée will be smooth and thick.

Preheat the oven to 350°. Oil a soufflé dish.

Stir the eggs, parsley, and garlic into the eggplant purée. Add the nutmeg, thyme, and salt (about 2 tablespoons) and pepper to taste. Pour the mixture into the oiled soufflé dish and set it in a pan of hot water 1½ inches deep. Bake for 40 minutes, or until a knife inserted comes out clean. Sprinkle the cheese on top and bake for 5 minutes more. Garnish with basil or parsley and serve.

Pois Gourmands à la Paysanne
Snow Peas Sautéed with Lean Salt Pork and Chives

One of the quickest and freshest vegetable dishes. Make sure the snow peas are fresh and crisp, and don't overcook them.

For 6 to 8 people:

2 pounds fresh snow peas
3 tablespoons olive oil
⅓ cup diced lean salt pork
2 garlic cloves, peeled and cut into 3 slices apiece
4 tablespoons finely chopped chives
salt
freshly ground pepper

Break off the ends of the snow peas and pull off the strings. Wash and drain them.

Heat the olive oil in a heavy-bottomed pan and add the salt pork, garlic, and chives. Lower the flame and cook, tossing well, for 3 to 5 minutes. Add the snow peas, salt, and pepper and toss again. Cover and cook for 4 to 6 minutes, stirring occasionally. (The snow peas should retain their bright color and crispness.) Check the seasoning and serve.

Pommes de Terre a l'Ail

Sautéed Potatoes with Garlic

An easy way to infuse potatoes with the spirit of Nice.

For 6 people:

6 *garlic cloves, unpeeled and cut in half*
3 *tablespoons olive oil*
3 *tablespoons peanut oil*
12 *to 18 medium-sized potatoes, diced*
salt
freshly ground black pepper
½ *cup chopped fresh basil or parsley*

Crush the garlic cloves on a board with your closed fist or the broad wooden end of a heavy knife.

Heat the oils in a heavy-bottomed pan, add the garlic and sauté for 2 minutes. Add the potatoes, salt, and pepper. Lower the flame, cover, and cook, turning often with a spatula, for 20 minutes, or until tender.

Remove the garlic cloves and drain off the excess oil. Put the potatoes in a serving dish and add the basil or parsley. Toss gently and serve.

Purées de Légumes

Vegetable Purées

Cook any of the following vegetables: potatoes, turnips, zucchini, chickpeas, Great Northern beans, cauliflower, celery, carrots. Drain them and use your Mouli food mill to purée them. They will turn light and fluffy and have an interesting texture (whereas a blender would turn them into a sticky paste). Add a little broth, salt, freshly ground pepper, and olive oil to taste. Add, if you wish, a little crushed garlic or finely minced onion. Serve surrounded with Croutons (p. 12) as an accompaniment to any fish or meat dish.

Vegetables

If you have some leftover vegetable purée, you can prepare these simple but delicious little *"boulettes."*

For 6 people:

Vegetable Balls

1 onion
½ cup finely chopped chives, mint, basil, or parsley
4 cups vegetable purée (of any one vegetable or a mixture of two or more) *
2 eggs, beaten
salt
freshly ground pepper
½ cup bread crumbs (preferably home-made)
peanut and olive oil for frying

Grate the onion into a bowl and add to it the chives, mint, basil, or parsley.

Whip the vegetable purée with a fork so it is smooth but not runny. Add it, along with the eggs, to the bowl, and beat for a few minutes. Add salt and pepper. Form little balls the size of small plums with your hands and roll them in bread crumbs.

Heat a little oil in a frying pan and fry the balls, leaving enough space so you can turn them easily. Keep them warm as you fry successive batches. Serve as accompaniments for a leg of lamb, a broiled fish, or by themselves as an hors d'oeuvre with a bowl of warm *Coulis* (p. 79).

* Cooked zucchini put through the Mouli and mixed with an egg will not be firm enough to be made into a ball. The same would be true for cauliflower or celery, both of which are too watery and will need firming up with some potato or bean purée.

Pommes de Terre aux Herbes
Sliced Potatoes Baked with Herbs and Olive Oil

Les Légumes

This is a lovely, golden dish; some of the potato slices will be crunchy, some tender—all will taste delicious. It is one of my favorite accompaniments for *gigot d'agneau à l'aillade,* broiled fish, or plain broiled lamb chops.

For 6 people:

8 *medium potatoes, very thinly sliced*
½ to ⅔ *cup oil (half olive, half peanut)*
½ *tablespoon thyme*
½ *tablespoon savory*
2 *teaspoons salt*
1 *teaspoon freshly ground black pepper*

Preheat the oven to 425°.

Dry the potato slices on paper towels and place them in a large bowl. Add the oil, thyme, savory, and salt and pepper and mix thoroughly with your hands to be sure each slice of potato is coated.

Spread the slices in two or three layers on a flat baking dish or cookie sheet and bake 35 to 40 minutes, or until crisp and golden. Remove from the dish with a spatula. Check the seasoning and serve.

Tian d'Artichauts

Baked Artichoke Hearts

This dish is common throughout Provence and is especially good with roast lamb or baked fish.

For 6 people:

2 *onions, chopped*
½ *cup chopped parsley*
2 *garlic cloves, peeled and crushed*
4 *slices bread, soaked in a little milk and
   squeezed into a paste*
6 *large globe artichoke hearts*
1 *tablespoon olive oil*
   salt
   freshly ground black pepper
½ *cup freshly grated Parmesan cheese*

Vegetables

Put the onions and parsley in a bowl. Add the garlic and the bread paste and toss gently.

Preheat the oven to 375°

Cut off the stem of each artichoke at the base and cut in half lengthwise with a large, heavy knife, using a mallet to bang it if necessary. Pull off all the hard outer leaves of each half and then slice off the remaining inner leaves. Discard the leaves. With a little knife or spoon, scrape out the choke. Cut each heart in half again and sprinkle with a little olive oil and salt and pepper.

Line an oiled baking dish with half of the bread paste. Arrange the pieces of artichoke heart on this layer and cover them with the rest of the bread paste. Sprinkle with cheese, olive oil, and pepper and bake for 1½ hours.

Tomates Provencale

Baked Tomatoes with Parsley and Garlic

Most *tomates provençale* served in American restaurants are burnt on the outside and watery and soggy on the inside. In Provence they are prepared quite differently. In the traditional recipe the tomatoes are cooked on top of the stove *before being baked*, so that all their excess water is cooked away and they look transparent—like candied fruit. In Provence, they say they must look like a *vitrail* (stained-glass window). This dish is sometimes eaten cold in Nice, but I prefer it warm.

For 6 people:

6 *firm tomatoes, cut in half*
3 *tablespoons olive oil*
salt
freshly ground black pepper
½ *cup bread crumbs (preferably home-made)*
3 *garlic cloves, minced*
½ *cup minced parsley*

Preheat the oven to 375°.

Put the tomato halves upside down on paper towels and drain the excess juice.

Heat 1½ tablespoons of the olive oil in a large frying pan. Add the tomato halves and cook them—six halves at a time—cut side down for 5 minutes over a medium flame. Sprinkle with salt and pepper and carefully turn them over with a spatula. Cook for 3 minutes, then delicately remove the tomatoes with a spatula and put into an oiled baking dish. This can be done in advance to this point.

Just before serving, sprinkle the tomatoes with bread crumbs, salt, pepper, and 1½ tablespoons of the olive oil and bake for 10 minutes. Sprinkle with garlic and parsley and serve immediately.

Tian d'Aubergines

Eggplant and Meat Gratin

In rural Provence this dish is prepared from leftover meat and fish and is often eaten at the end of the day for a light meal. It can be reheated in a 350° oven.

For 6 people:

- 3 *large eggplants, peeled and diced into*
  ½-inch cubes
  salt
- ½ *cup olive oil*
- 1 *onion, chopped*
- 1 *to 2 cups chopped cooked meat or fish*
- 2 *tomatoes, chopped, or ⅔ cup canned*
- ½ *cup minced parsley*
- 1 *garlic clove, peeled and crushed*
- ½ *cup freshly grated Parmesan or Swiss*
  cheese
- 2 *tablespoons bread crumbs*
- 2 *tablespoons chopped basil or parsley*
  Coulis (*p. 79*)

Sprinkle the diced eggplant with salt and let it stand in a bowl for 10 minutes to draw out the bitterness. Rinse under cold water, drain and pat dry.

Preheat oven to 375°

Vegetables

Heat ¼ cup of the olive oil in a large cast-iron frying pan. Sauté the eggplant over a low flame, adding more oil as you need it, for about 20 minutes, or until tender and golden. (If the pan is not large enough, you may have to do this in two batches.) Drain the eggplant on paper towels and put them in an oiled baking dish. Put 2 tablespoons of the olive oil in the frying pan and cook the onion slowly until transparent. Add the meat, tomatoes, and parsley and cook for 5 minutes. Turn off the heat. Add the garlic and stir well. Spoon the mixture over the eggplant and sprinkle with cheese, bread crumbs, and the remaining olive oil. Bake for 30 minutes.

Serve sprinkled with basil or parsley and with a bowl of warm *coulis* sauce.

Tian de Courges

Baked Zucchini, Pumpkin, or Squash with Rice and Cheese

According to the season, this dish can be made with any of the three vegetables: zucchini, squash, or pumpkin. Serve as a separate course or with a roast leg of lamb. It is a light, delicate dish which deserves your good homemade bread crumbs on top.

For 6 people:

6 *zucchini, unpeeled, or 2 pounds pumpkin* or squash, peeled*
3 *tablespoons olive oil*
1 *onion, minced*
⅔ *cup cooked rice*
½ *cup freshly grated Swiss or Parmesan cheese*
½ *cup chopped parsley*
1 *egg, beaten*
salt
freshly ground black pepper
2 *tablespoons bread crumbs*

Les Légumes

* Pumpkin is very sweet and bland, so it requires a fair amount of salt. Taste to be sure it is seasoned enough.

Chop the zucchini or pumpkin or squash. Preheat the oven to 375°.

Heat the olive oil in a large frying pan and gently cook the onion until tender. Add the zucchini or pumpkin or squash and cook for 10 minutes over a low flame, stirring from time to time. Remove from heat and cool a little.

Blend the rice, cheese, parsley, egg, salt, and pepper and combine with the zucchini and onion. Spread the mixture in an oiled shallow baking dish. Sprinkle with the bread crumbs and 1 tablespoon of the olive oil and bake for 20 minutes.

Variations:
Before baking, cover the dish with 4 tomatoes, cut in half and gently squeeze to remove excess water and seeds; omit the bread crumbs and sprinkle ½ cup chopped parsley, salt, pepper, and a little olive oil all over the top.

If you want to make a finer, more delicate version of this dish, pass the vegetables through a Mouli food mill before covering with the bread crumbs and olive oil. Bake for only 15 minutes at 375°.

Tian d'Épinards et de Morue
Spinach and Dried Cod Gratin

This is a very fresh preparation, high in flavor because the spinach is cooked in olive oil. You may use frozen chopped spinach for this. A delicious luncheon dish.

For 6 people:

½ pound dried cod (double this amount if you like a strong flavor)
4 10-ounce packages of frozen spinach
4 tablespoons olive oil
1 large onion, grated
3 garlic cloves, minched
salt
freshly ground pepper
½ cup chopped parsley
3 tablespoons bread crumbs

Vegetables

Soak the cod in water for several hours or overnight, according to the instructions on the package. When adequately soaked, shred the cod with your hands. Thaw the spinach at room temperature, then squeeze out all excess water.

Preheat the oven to 350°. Heat 2 tablespoons of the olive oil in a heavy-bottomed pan and add the onion, spinach, garlic, salt, and pepper. Cook, stirring with a wooden spoon, for 10 minutes. Remove from heat and add the parsley. Put half of the spinach into an oiled shallow baking dish. Add the cod and cover with the rest of the spinach. Sprinkle the bread crumbs and 2 tablespoons of the olive oil on top and heat in the oven for 1 hour.

Note: For a more substantial dish, you may add ½ cup of cooked rice to the spinach before baking it.

Tian de Navets Rosés

Pink Turnip Gratin

Little pink turnips have a lovely subtle flavor. This *tian* is light and tasty and can be served with pork, lamb, or fish, or as the main course.

> For 6 people:
>
> 3 *pounds small pink turnips (about 2 dozen; 2 inches in diameter)*
> 2 *onions*
> 2 *garlic cloves*
>   *salt*
>   *freshly ground black pepper*
> ⅓ *cup water (or more if needed)*
> 3 *tablespoons freshly grated Swiss or Parmesan cheese*

Peel and slice the turnips and onions as thinly as possible and put them in a large bowl.

Preheat the oven to 375°. Oil a china, Pyrex, or earthenware baking dish.

Peel and crush the garlic into the bowl. Add salt and pepper and the vegetables and mix together. Spread them in the baking dish

Les Légumes

and pour the water over them. Bake, covered, for 1 hour. Uncover and cook for 30 minutes more. Stir once with a spatula during the baking so that the vegetables on top are moved to the bottom of the dish. When the turnips are uniformly tender, sprinkle the cheese on top and bake for 5 minutes.

Note: This can be fully baked (except for the very last step) ahead of time and kept for a few hours at room temperature. When ready to serve, sprinkle the cheese on top and bake for a few minutes until it melts.

Farineux

Pasta and Grain Dishes

Ever since Marco Polo brought back pasta from China we have tried to improve on it. Italians serve it with cream and butter sauces; Americans now eat it warm or cold with a wide variety of sauces and dressings.

In Nice, pasta is always homemade and offered with a light sauce so that the fresh taste of the dough is never smothered by its accompaniment. And pasta is often served as a main course as a good alternative to meat or fish.

When I was a child we used to make pasta once a month. It was quite a production. The kitchen, the pantry, and the entire guest room would be strung with sheets of drying noodles. They were draped from beds, tables, chairs, and brooms propped up like clotheslines. The air would be misty with flour and rich with the smell of the fresh dough.

Making pasta has now become a weekly routine in my American kitchen. With the aid of an Italian pasta machine (available at gourmet stores and department stores and through mail orders), the arduous production has become a simple production. Like baking bread, pasta-making is time-consuming, but its rewards quickly compensate for the labor involved. And it is addictive: after you have made your own, all processed pasta will seem a poor substitute.

Pasta is the basis for many delicious and economical meals, particularly for large groups of people. It takes about 2 ½ hours to prepare: 15 minutes to mix and knead the dough; 1 hour to let it rest; 15 minutes to roll it through the machine; 30 minutes to let it rest; 15 minutes to cut it to the desired width; and 5 minutes to cook it.

Always remember to boil the pasta with a tablespoon of oil, to prevent it from sticking, and salt to add flavor. When the pasta has boiled for 3 or 4 minutes, start testing to be sure they will be served *al dente*.

Drain and pour the pasta in a warm bowl and add a little olive oil, toss quickly with two forks, and then add whatever sauce you choose: *pistou, coulis,* walnut, *saussoun, tapenade,* or plain grated Parmesan or Swiss cheese.

Barba Jouan

Pastry Filled with Cheese, Ham, Rice, Herbs, and Pumpkin

These delicious little turnovers can be served with drinks or as a first course, or as a main course warm or cold. Why they are called *Barba Jouan* (Uncle John, in the Niçois dialect) is truly a mystery.

It will be best to use a pasta machine for the pastry.

Makes 6 turnovers and a *tourte,* or pie (to serve 6 people):

Pastry

2 *cups unbleached flour*
4 *tablespoons olive oil*
4 *to 5 tablespoons warm water*
1 *egg, beaten*
  salt

Place the flour in a large bowl. Make a well in the center, add the olive oil, water, egg, and salt, and mix well with a fork. Flour your hands and knead until the dough becomes smooth (this will take about 5 minutes). Form a ball and let it rest in the bowl for 1 hour under a clean towel. Meanwhile, prepare the filling.

Filling

8 cups raw pumpkin (*cooked and
    drained, it will yield about 2 cups*),
    or 2 cups canned unseasoned pump-
    kin purée
1 *tablespoon olive oil*
2 *large onions, chopped*
5 *garlic cloves, chopped*
  salt
2 *teaspoons savory, oregano, or thyme*
2 *cups grated Parmesan cheese* (*Roque-*
    fort or blue cheese or any strong
    Italian or Greek cheese may be used
    instead)
1 *egg, beaten*
¾ *cup cooked rice* (¼ *cup raw*)
⅓ *cup finely diced prosciutto, country*
    ham, or very lean salt pork
  freshly ground black pepper

Using a heavy knife, cut the pumpkin into several pieces and scrape out the seeds. Peel each piece and cut into 2-inch cubes. Heat 1 tablespoon of olive oil in a heavy-bottomed pan, put in the onions and garlic, and sauté for 1 minute. Add the pumpkin and sprinkle with salt and the savory, oregano, or thyme. Cover and cook slowly for 1 hour, stirring from time to time. When the pumpkin is soft (this will take between 45 minutes to 1 hour), put it through a Mouli food mill and then into a sieve and let it drain for 10 minutes over a bowl. Press it to help it drain. Put the pumpkin purée into a bowl and add the cheese, egg, rice, and ham. Add salt and pepper to taste.

Put your pasta machine on a table or a counter. Place one small ball of dough, the size of an orange, in the machine. Pass it through Nos. 1, 3, 5, and 6. Let this thin sheet (about 4 inches wide) rest on a floured tray or counter and repeat the process until all the dough is used up. Set aside half of the sheets for making the pie. Cut the other half in large circles (about 4 inches in diameter) or into 4-inch squares with a pastry wheel or a knife and use for making the turnovers.

To Make the Turnovers

Preheat the oven to 375°. Put a square or circle of dough in your left hand and place a teaspoon of the pumpkin-rice-ham mixture in the center. Fold the dough over and seal the edges with fingers dipped in water. Pinch the edges to make a thick, curly edge. Continue to do this until all the pastry is used. Place the turnovers on an oiled baking sheet. Dip your fingers in olive oil and brush their surface. Bake in the oven for 20 minutes, or until they are golden.

To Make the Pie
Preheat the oven to 375°. Oil a cookie sheet and place on it the reserved half of the thin sheets of dough side by side and spread the pumpkin filling evenly on them. Cover with the rest of the sheets of dough and seal by pressing the two layers together with wet fingers. With a fork, prick the top of the pie so the steam can escape. Brush with olive oil. Bake for 45 minutes, or until the pie looks golden and crisp. This is better warm but it is often eaten cold at picnics or buffets.

Fada Riquet
Rice, Spinach, and Cheese

A truly delicious dish adored by children and appreciated by all. It is often made with leftovers and can be reheated many times. If any amount is left over, it can be used for *Tout-Nus* (p. 227), *Capoun* (pp. 176–78), or *Suppions Farcis* (pp. 130–31).

For 6 people:

3 10-ounce packages frozen spinach
½ cup raw rice
½ cup milk
4 tablespoons freshly grated Parmesan
   or Swiss cheese
2 eggs, beaten
½ teaspoon freshly grated nutmeg
   salt
freshly ground pepper
2 tablespoons olive oil

Take the spinach out of the freezer for at least 1 hour before cooking. Bring a pot of salted water to a boil. Add the rice and cook for 15 minutes. Add the spinach and cook for 10 minutes more. Drain the rice and the spinach in a colander, pressing out as much liquid as possible. They should not be overcooked.

Pasta and
Grain Dishes

Place the spinach and rice in a heavy-bottomed pan and add the milk. Cook over low heat and, stirring rapidly, add the cheese and eggs. Add the nutmeg, salt, and pepper. After 4 or 5 minutes, add the olive oil and blend well. Serve with a bowl of grated cheese on the side.

Note: To make this dish out of leftovers, you will need 1½ cups of cooked rice and 2 cups of cooked spinach. Chop the spinach and combine with the rice and milk in a heavy-bottomed pan, and follow the remaining steps of the recipe.

Gnocchis

Potato Gnocchi

This is a favorite with children, and is also a succulent, delicate accompaniment to any meat or fish dish which most adults will love. It can be very elegant as a first course served in individual dishes and sprinkled with freshly grated cheese.

For 6 people:

5 *medium-sized potatoes (about 2
    pounds), as mealy as possible*
2 *egg yolks*
¼ *cup butter*
½ *to 1 teaspoon freshly grated nutmeg*
2 *teaspoons salt (or more)
    freshly ground white pepper*
1½ *cups flour*
1 *tablespoon peanut oil*
3 *tablespoons olive oil
    one of these sauces:* Pistou *(p. 86) ;*
    Sauce aux Noix *(p. 84) ;* Coulis
    *(p. 79) ; juices from a roast de-
    glazed with white wine
    freshly grated Parmesan or Swiss
    cheese*
3 *tablespoons finely minced chives,
    mint, or basil*

Scrub the potatoes and cook them in boiling salted water until they are tender. Protect your hands by using a kitchen towel or an oven mitt and peel them while they are still hot. Immediately put them through a Mouli food mill (do not use a blender because it would turn them into a sticky paste).

Slowly beat in the egg yolks, butter, nutmeg, salt, and pepper. Add the flour gradually, beat with a wooden spoon or an electric mixer. The finished dough should be soft and smooth but not too sticky. Add more flour if it is too moist. Dust your hands with flour and divide the dough into balls the size of small apples. Roll each one out to a cylindrical shape about 1/2 inch in diameter, then cut it into pieces about 1/2 inch long.

The dish can be prepared in advance up to this point; cover the *gnocchis* with a towel and keep in the refrigerator or at room temperature for a few hours.

Bring a large kettle of salted water to a boil. Put in the gnocchis and the peanut oil. Cook the squares of dough for 7 to 10 minutes, or until all have floated to the surface. They should be elastic to the touch. Drain well and place in a warm shallow dish. Sprinkle with the olive oil and stir gently, then add your favorite sauce and cheese. Sprinkle with the chives, mint, or basil just before serving.

Variation:
The *gnocchis* can be made to resemble shells—they not only will look prettier but will absorb the sauce better. To make the shells, put each of the square pieces of dough on the topside tines of a fork and press down. Cook the shells for only about 3 or 4 minutes.

Panisses
Chickpea "French Fries"

This is one of Nice's oldest recipes. Each morning, pasta and ravioli shops sell *panisses* freshly made and displayed on dozens of unmatched saucers. Every family saves a precious collection of chipped saucers for the *panisse* preparation. These chickpea sticks are the children's favorite lunch, favorite snack, and, when sprinkled with sugar, favorite dessert. Fried *panisses* seasoned with freshly ground pepper are delicious with broiled chicken, leg of lamb, or plain hamburgers.

Pasta and
Grain Dishes

For 6 people:

1½ *cups chickpea flour*
3 *cups cold water*
salt
freshly ground white pepper
1½ *tablespoons olive oil*
peanut oil for frying

Oil 6 to 8 saucers or 2 dinner plates. Put the chickpea flour in a large bowl and stir in the cold water, beat with an eggbeater or wire whisk for 1 or 2 minutes, or until you have a smooth paste. Stir in the salt, pepper, and olive oil.

Pour into a heavy-bottomed saucepan and heat over a medium flame, stirring constantly with a wooden spoon. After 5 to 10 minutes, the mixture will thicken, then become lumpy, and finally form a mass. Remove from the flame and beat until the dough is very smooth. Spoon into the oiled saucers or plates and allow to cool. (You need not spoon out equal amounts.)

When the *panisse* dough is cool, cut it into little sticks (½ inch wide and about 2 inches long) as you would potatoes for French fries.

In a heavy pot, heat 1 inch of peanut oil, and when it is very hot fry the little sticks in the same manner as you would French fries, not cooking too many at one time. When they are crisp and golden, turn them very carefully with a spatula. (They will be done in about 4 minutes.) Remove and drain on paper towels. Put them on trays in a slow oven (250°) while you fry the remaining *panisses*.

Sprinkle with salt and pepper and, if you like, a little grated Parmesan cheese and serve.

Pâtes aux Oeufs

Fresh Egg Noodles

This is my favorite recipe for egg noodles. Children and adults alike love this dish. I serve it with *Pistou* (p. 86), *Sauce aux Noix* (p. 84), warm *Coulis* (p. 79), *Saussoun* (p. 52) or a meat sauce. I also serve it plain with sweet butter and freshly grated

Swiss cheese. Delicious with *boeuf à la niçoise, agneau à la niçoise,* or *porc à la sauge et aux câpres.*

For 8 people:

4 cups unbleached flour
6 eggs, slightly beaten
1 tablespoon salt
2 tablespoons water
2 tablespoons olive oil
1 teaspoon peanut oil

Put the flour in a large bowl and make a well in the center. Put into the well the eggs, salt, water, and olive oil, and with your fingers work it gradually into the flour. Place the dough on a counter or table and knead it for 15 to 20 minutes—flouring your hands and the counter or table often, push the dough away from you with the heel of your hand, then gather it back into a mass, and repeat until the dough is smooth and elastic. Let it rest, covered with a towel, for 1 to 2 hours.

Divide the ball into eight parts (each the size of a fist). Roll each part through the pasta machine into thin layers, starting at No. 1, then 2, then skipping to 4, and finally 5 or—if you like thin noodles—6. Sprinkle a little flour on the machine every time you put in a new layer of dough so it will not stick to the metal. In using No. 6 be sure to reach underneath and pull out the thin strip as it is being rolled. If allowed to pile up under the machine, it will stick together. Sprinkle flour on all the trays you have (use counters and tables also) and let the sheets of thin pasta dry on them for 30 minutes. Then cut the sheets in the machine into thin or wide strips, as you prefer. Dust lightly with more flour and let them fall loosely onto the floured surfaces.

Bring a large pot of salted water to a boil. Add the peanut oil and drop the noodles in the pot. Cook, stirring twice, for 5 to 10 minutes over a medium flame. Drain them in a colander and pour into a shallow dish. Add whatever you wish: olive oil or butter and freshly grated cheese, or any of the following sauces—*pistou,* tomato, walnut, or your own meat sauce of the day).*

* Your meat sauce could be the juices from either *Boeuf à la Niçoise* (pp. 140–41), *Agneau à la Niçoise* (pp. 137–38), or from *Porc à la Sauge et aux Câpres* (p. 154). Or you can make it by pouring ½ cup of white wine or vermouth into the pan in which chicken or a leg of lamb has been cooked, scraping up the bottom of the pan, and simmering the liquid for 3 minutes.

Note: Raw fresh pasta can be left overnight in a refrigerator, but will lose most of its quality. Better cook them *al dente* and reheat the leftovers with ½ cup of milk the next day.

Pâtes aux Moules
Pasta with Mussels, White Wine, and Garlic

Mussels, olive oil, and garlic make a pungent combination with noodles. This is a simple dish you can prepare all year round, since all the ingredients are readily available. It takes 15 minutes to prepare if you already have the pasta at hand.

For 6 people:

> *3 pounds mussels*
> *salt*
> *½ cup dry white wine*
> *3 tablespoons olive oil*
> *4 garlic cloves, minced*
> Pâtes aux Oeufs (*p. 216*) *or good com-*
> *mercial egg noodles*
> *3 tablespoons chopped parsley, basil, or*
> *mint*

Scrub the mussels thoroughly, remove the beards, and leave them in a bowl of cold water for 10 minutes. Discard all the opened ones. Meanwhile, set a large pot of water to boil with salt and 1 tablespoon of the olive oil.

In another pot, cook the mussels, covered, over high heat with the wine for 3 to 5 minutes, or until their shells open. When cool enough to handle, discard the shells and strain the mussel broth through a piece of cheesecloth that has been dipped in cold water and wrung out and then spread over a sieve. Heat 2 tablespoons of the olive oil in a heavy skillet and cook the garlic over a low flame for 3 minutes. Stir in the drained mussel broth and cook for 5 minutes more.

Cook the noodles in a kettle of boiling salted water until tender but still firm. Drain at once and put in a heated serving dish. Put the mussels into the skillet and heat briefly. Pour the mixture over

Farineux

the noodles and toss with two forks. Garnish with parsley, basil, or mint.

Pâtes Rouges et Vertes

Noodles with Ham and Herbs

The texture and flavor of fresh herbs, good ham, and olive oil complement the subtle taste of the noodles. This is a beautiful, lively dish made in a few minutes. Don't ever attempt it with dried herbs.

For 6 people:

½ cup olive oil
⅓ cup chopped Virginia ham, country
  ham, or prosciutto
2 large garlic cloves, finely minced
1 cup finely chopped basil, mint, chives,
  thyme, or parsley (or in whatever
  amount you like)
salt
freshly ground pepper
Pâtes aux Oeufs (p. 216) or good commercial noodles

Heat the olive oil in a heavy-bottomed pan and add the ham, garlic, and herbs. Cook, stirring, for 3 minutes over a medium flame.

Meanwhile, cook the pasta and drain it. Pour in a warm shallow dish and spoon the ham-and-herb mixture over the noodles. Sprinkle with pepper and taste before adding any salt. Toss lightly with two forks and serve.

Pâtes à la Verdure

Fresh Herb Pasta

Pasta and
Grain Dishes

This is a delicious pasta. The addition of fragrant fresh herbs—mint, basil, chives, thin scallions, Italian parsley—to the dough gives a lively flavor to the noodles. The dish can be served as a main course with a little olive oil and some grated cheese. Sauces should not be used, as they would smother the fragrance of the herbs.

For 6 people:

*1 to 2 cups minced fresh herbs (choose
one or two: mint, basil, chives, very
small scallions, Italian parsley)
4 cups unbleached flour
6 eggs, slightly beaten
3 teaspoons salt
4 tablespoons olive oil
1 teaspoon peanut oil
freshly grated Parmesan or Swiss cheese
(optional)*

Dry the minced herbs thoroughly in a paper towel. If you prefer a paste, pound the herbs in a mortar.

Place the flour in a large bowl. Make a well in the center, add the eggs, salt, and 2 tablespoons of the olive oil, and gradually work the flour into the eggs and mix well. Add the herbs and place on a counter or table and knead for about 20 minutes. Flour your hands and the work surface as often as necessary to prevent the dough from sticking. Keep pushing the dough away from you with the heel of your hand, then gathering it back into a mass, until the dough is smooth and elastic. Make a ball of the dough, cover with a towel and let it rest for 1 hour.

Divide the ball into three parts. Roll each part through the pasta machine to make thin layers. Pass it through the No. 1 plate, then 2, then 4, then 6, adding flour each time so the dough will not stick to the metal. If No. 6 seems too thin for your taste, set it on 5 instead. Let the layers of dough rest on a floured surface (trays, tables, counters) for 30 minutes, then pass them through the machine to cut them in strips. Let them fall loosely on the floured tray. Sprinkle with flour.

Add salt and peanut oil to the water in a large pot and bring to a boil. Add the pasta and cook, uncovered, for 5 to 10 minutes, depending on how tender you want it to be.

Pour the pasta into a colander to drain well. Pour into a large bowl, add 2 tablespoons of olive oil, and toss with two forks. Serve with a bowl of cheese.

Farineux

Pâtes aux Courgettes
Pasta with Zucchini

This is a fresh and pleasant dish that can be prepared in a flash. Make sure the zucchini are very crisp and very small and don't overcook the pasta.

For 6 people:

> 3 *small zucchini, unpeeled (try to find*
> *those that are 2 to 3 inches long)*
> 1/2 *cup olive oil*
> 2 *teaspoons thyme*
> *salt*
> *freshly ground pepper*
> *good commercial noodles or spaghetti*
> 1 *garlic clove, finely chopped*
> 1/2 *cup freshly grated Parmesan cheese*

Wash and scrub the zucchini and slice them on the bias. Pat dry with paper towels. Heat the olive oil in a heavy-bottomed pan and add the zucchini. Sauté them, stirring with a wooden spoon, over a medium flame until they are golden brown. Sprinkle with thyme, salt, and pepper.

Meanwhile, cook the pasta and drain it. Put the zucchini on top of the pasta and sprinkle with 1 tablespoon of the olive oil and the garlic and cheese. Toss with two forks and serve.

Polente aux Champignons
Corn Meal Mush with Mushroom Sauce

Polente comes from Italy (where it is called *polenta*). In Nice it is accompanied by good pork sausage, small wild birds, or vegetables. Americans, who are so used to eating corn meal in many interesting ways, may find plain *polente* rather dull, so I am giving the recipe for a mushroom sauce to go with it.

Pasta and
Grain Dishes

For 6 people:

Polente

1 to 2 teaspoons salt
6 cups water
10 tablespoons coarse corn meal

Add salt to the water in a heavy pot. When the water comes to a boil, slowly add the corn meal while stirring with a wooden spoon. Lower the heat to medium and stir frequently for 25 to 30 minutes. It should be quite thick and detach itself from the sides of the pan. Pour it into a shallow dish oiled with peanut oil. When cool, cut into 2-inch squares

Mushroom Sauce

2 tablespoons olive oil
1 pound mushrooms, sliced
3 onions, minced
3 fresh or 1 cup canned tomatoes,
    chopped
2 garlic cloves, minced
3 tablespoons chopped parsley
2 bay leaves
½ teaspoon thyme
salt
freshly ground black pepper

Preheat the oven to 350°.

Heat the olive oil in a heavy-bottomed frying pan. Add the mushrooms and sauté briskly for 3 minutes, stirring often. Add the onions, tomatoes, garlic, parsley, bay leaves, thyme, salt, and pepper and cook for 5 minutes.

Pour the sauce over the squares of *polente*. Sprinkle with about 2 tablespoons of grated Swiss cheese and bake for 15 minutes.

Ravioli à la Niçoise

Beef and Spinach Ravioli

Farineux

Inspired by the dish Marco Polo brought back from China, *raïoles* have been a traditional treat in Provence for centuries. The little

squares of dough can be filled with beef, veal, ham, lamb's brains, pumpkin, and rice. The Niçois version is truly superb—it is as light as it is fragrant. The secret here is the savory combination of *boeuf à la niçoise* (with its wine and orange flavor) and spinach.

This is not a quick dish to prepare, but it is well worth the time. Frozen spinach and a pasta machine are great helpers. The *boeuf à la niçoise* must be prepared a day ahead, then chopped for the ravioli.

So with recipe in hand and a little time, you can now produce a most wonderful dish.

For 6 people (about 80 ravioli):

Filling

¾ pound beef stew (Boeuf à la Niçoise, *pp. 140–41*)
½ cup lean salt pork
2 10-ounce boxes frozen spinach
1 onion
1 tablespoon olive oil
1 garlic clove, peeled and crushed
½ teaspoon freshly grated nutmeg
2 eggs, lightly beaten
½ cup freshly grated cheese
1 teaspoon thyme
salt
freshly ground black pepper

Prepare the beef stew, then dice the beef. Reserve the stew sauce. Chop the salt pork. Blanch and drain the spinach; squeeze it dry and chop. Grate the onion.

Heat the olive oil in a heavy skillet and add the salt pork and onion. Cook for 5 minutes. Place the beef, spinach, onion, and salt pork in a blender in three batches until it becomes a paste. Or chop them on a board as finely as you can. Pour into a large bowl and add the garlic, nutmeg, eggs, cheese, thyme, salt, and pepper. Check the seasoning and stir well. You should have a smooth and fairly dry mixture.

Pasta

3 *cups unbleached flour*
1 *tablespoon olive oil*
2 *eggs, beaten*
5 *to 6 tablespoons water (or more as*
    needed)
2 *teaspoons salt*

Sift the flour into a large bowl. Make a well in the center and pour in the olive oil, eggs, water, and salt. Mix with a fork until all the flour is absorbed, adding another tablespoon of water if necessary. Knead for about 10 minutes, either in the bowl or on a floured table or counter, until the dough becomes smooth and elastic. Form a ball of dough, place it in an oiled bowl, cover with a clean cloth and let it rest for 1 hour.

Put your pasta machine on the table or counter and flour it. Divide the dough into 4 balls the size of small apples. Roll each ball through No. 1, then 3, then 5, then 7. Reach underneath and pull out the thin strip as it is being rolled. If allowed to pile up under the machine it will stick together. Lay the paper-thin sheets of dough on a floured tray or table to dry for about 10 minutes.

If you do not have a pasta machine, roll each small ball of dough on a floured board as thinly as you can. Let the sheets rest for 10 minutes. (Left longer they will become difficult to work with.)

Filling the Ravioli

Place a sheet of dough on a floured surface. Put a teaspoon of filling every 2 inches along the entire sheet, making two long rows. Place another sheet of dough on top of the mounds and carefully press around each little heap with your fingers, sealing the two layers together. With a pastry wheel cut around each heap so that you have neat little squares that look like plump cushions. If the pasta strips have become too dry to adhere to one another, dip the pastry wheel into warm water and work them together. When all the squares are cut, sprinkle them with a little flour and allow them to rest for 1 hour before cooking.

To Serve

Bring a large kettle of water to a boil. Add 2 tablespoons of salt and 1 tablespoon of olive oil. Lower the flame and gently slide the ravioli in. Simmer them gently for 5 to 10 minutes. When they rise to the surface they are ready. Take them out with a slotted spoon and drain them in a colander.

Farineux

Arrange the ravioli in a warm dish, alternating layers of ravioli with a layer of warm beef stew sauce or grated cheese and olive oil (or *sauce aux noix*).

Variation:
If you have roasted a chicken or leg of lamb, deglaze the pan with a little white wine while scraping the bottom of the pan. Use this sauce with the ravioli, which can accompany the chicken or lamb.

Note: With the leftover filling prepare *Tout-Nus* (p. 227) for the next day.

Riz aux Herbes
Rice with Herbs

Use long-grain Carolina or converted rice for this dish.

For 6 people:

> 7 *quarts salted water*
> 1½ *cups raw rice*
> 3 *bay leaves*
> 2 *teaspoons thyme or rosemary*
> 3 *tablespoons olive oil*
> *freshly ground pepper*

In a large kettle, bring the water to a boil and add the rice while slowly stirring with a fork. Add the bay leaves and 1 teaspoon of the thyme or rosemary. Boil, uncovered, for 20 minutes. Rinse under cold running water and drain in a colander. Transfer to a saucepan, add the olive oil, and fluff the rice with two forks. Sprinkle with the remaining thyme and pepper.

Reheat, stirring lightly with the two forks a few times, for 5 minutes just before serving. (Do not remove the bay leaves.)

Pasta and
Grain Dishes

Riz au Safran

Saffron Rice

For 6 people:

a large pinch of saffron
2 *tablespoons olive oil*
1 *large onion, finely chopped or grated*
1 *cup raw rice*
2 *cups hot water*
½ *teaspoon freshly grated nutmeg*
2 *bay leaves*
salt
freshly ground black pepper

Crush the saffron into 2 tablespoons of hot water and let it stand.

Heat the olive oil in a heavy-bottomed pan. Add the onion, cover and cook slowly for 3 to 5 minutes, or until the onion becomes transparent. Add the rice and stir over a low flame until all the grains are coated with oil. Add the dissolved saffron and 2 cups hot water and stir. Add nutmeg, bay leaves, salt, and pepper. Bring to a boil, then reduce the heat and simmer, covered, for 15 minutes. All the liquid should be absorbed and the rice tender. Fluff the rice with a fork and remove the bay leaves. Just before serving, add a dash of olive oil and check the seasoning again.

You can keep this warm over simmering water until ready to serve.

Tout-Nus

Spinach, Rice, and Meat Balls

These little balls are called *tout-nus* (all naked) because basically they are the filling for ravioli, but without their coats of dough. You can prepare them from leftover ravioli filling made of spinach and *boeuf à la niçoise,* or else with spinach and any leftover meat or with spinach and lean salt pork or ham. In all cases, children will love them and they are wonderful for a buffet.

For 6 people:

½ cup cooked rice (2 tablespoons raw)
2 cups minced stewed beef and cooked
  spinach
2 tablespoons chopped parsley
1 egg, beaten
3 tablespoons grated Swiss or Parmesan
  cheese
salt
freshly ground black pepper
3 tablespoons flour
2 tablespoons olive oil
3 tablespoons grated cheese

Put the rice in a large bowl and add the spinach and beef, the parsley, egg, and cheese. Stir and add salt and freshly ground black pepper to taste.

Taking a tablespoonful of the mixture at a time, make small round balls. Sprinkle the flour on a tray and roll the balls in it.

Bring a large pot of salted water to a boil. Drop the balls in and cook over a medium flame for 8 to 10 minutes (they are cooked when they rise to the surface). Drain them on paper towels and arrange them in a shallow dish. Sprinkle with olive oil and cheese. Check the seasoning and serve.

These balls can be cooked ahead and reheated in a 350° oven for 10 minutes.

Les Plats de Festin

Festive Dishes

Aïoli, bouillabaisse, and *couscous* are the perfect party dishes. They each represent the menu itself. An assortment of *crudités* can precede them, and the dessert could be a basket of fruit—but nothing else is needed.

These superdishes require exuberance in the planning, many guests to enjoy them, a certain solemnity at the table, and a long siesta to recover from them.

Perhaps Brillat-Savarin was thinking of these culinary joys when he wrote that "the discovery of a new dish does more for the happiness of mankind than the discovery of a new star."

Aïoli Monstre

A Rich Variety of Vegetables, Fish, and Meats Served with a Garlic Mayonnaise

"*Aïoli* intoxicates gently, fills the body with warmth, and the soul with enthusiasm. In its essence it concentrates the strength, the gaiety, of the Provençal sunshine," said Mistral, the Provençal poet. One of the most beloved dishes in Provence, *aïoli* is a legend, a festival. It offers a whole banquet by itself.

Traditionally, *aïoli* is eaten on Christmas Eve with boiled snails and on Ash Wednesday with dried cod, and its elaborate *monstre* version is always the star of village festivals.

In the summer every village and town in Provence celebrates its saint's day festival. The parades, dances, and games last three days and end with the appearance of a huge *aïoli monstre,* shared by all on the village green. Long tables are set up on the plaza, and shopkeepers, farmers, dignitaries, tourists, and children sit side by side to enjoy the virtually endless variety of fish, squid, meat, snails, eggs, and raw and cooked vegetables. The *aïoli* sauce is passed separately in a bowl or in the marble mortar in which it was made.

When you prepare your own *aïoli* sauce, remember to allow about two cloves of garlic per person. It has to be almost unbearably strong to enhance the very bland food it accompanies. (If your guests fear for their breath, offer a sprig of parsley, a few mint leaves, or a piece of dark chocolate after the meal.) The crisp garlic, the mortar (either marble or china), the pestle (either wood or china), and a good olive oil are the essential elements in making *aïoli*. Serve ice water or a full-bodied red wine with this most exhilarating of dishes and be prepared to take a long siesta after the meal.

Remember that germinating garlic cloves, drafts, or disloyal wives are supposed to cause an *aïoli* to fail.

For 8 people:

Sauce

14 garlic cloves
salt
2 egg yolks
1 teaspoon Dijon mustard
2 cups oil (1 cup peanut, 1 cup olive)
juice of 1 lemon
freshly ground black pepper

Make sure all the ingredients are at room temperature. Peel the garlic cloves and push them through a garlic press into a mortar. (Do not use the blender because it makes the sauce too fluffy.) Add the salt. Pounding steadily with the pestle, reduce the garlic and salt to a paste. Add the egg yolks, and mustard, then very slowly add the oil. Put your left thumb (if you are right-handed) over the oil bottle top to control the thread of oil you dribble into the sauce. As the sauce becomes firmer you may increase the stream of oil.* When the sauce becomes firm and shiny, beat in the lemon

* If your *aïoli* curdles, you may start again by putting an egg yolk into another bowl and very slowly beating in the sauce, or you may add a teaspoon of boiling-hot wine vinegar and stir vigorously until it becomes firm and smooth again.

juice and pepper and taste to see if you need more salt. Cover with plastic wrap and refrigerate on a low shelf until ready to use.

Aïoli Garni

*a variety of the following to set the tone for
    the feast:*
*2 pounds snails, blanched in water flavored
    with herbs*
2 chickens, boiled or roasted
1 pound bottom round of beef, boiled
1 leg of lamb, roasted
1 large striped bass, baked
3 pounds octopus or squid
2 bay leaves
salt
freshly ground black pepper
2 pounds dried cod
8 carrots
8 potatoes
8 beets
1 bunch celery
4 fennel bulbs
3 pounds green beens, trimmed
8 zucchini
1 large cauliflower, trimmed
2 pounds chickpeas, boiled
8 artichokes
4 hard-boiled eggs, cut in halves
4 tomatoes
1/3 cup chopped Italian parsley
1 pound canned tuna or salmon
4 lettuce leaves
2 bunches parsley
1 lemon, sliced

Prepare the snails, chickens, beef, lamb, or bass. Wash and cut squid or octopus into ½-inch strips; heat 3 cups of water, add bay leaves, salt, and pepper and simmer for 25 minutes. Drain and set aside.

Soak the dried cod overnight (follow instructions on the package). Place it in a pan of cold water, bring to a boil, reduce the flame, and let it cook for 20 minutes in barely simmering water. Peel the carrots, potatoes, and beets. Cut the celery and fennel bulbs into sticks and refrigerate until ready to serve. Heat a large pot of water (or better, a *couscoussière*) and cook the carrots for

Les Plats
de Festin

15 minutes, then add the potatoes and green beans and cook for 15 minutes more. Add the unpeeled whole zucchini and cook for another 15 minutes. Keep covered until ready to serve.

Boil the cauliflower and the beets separately. Heat the chickpeas, and if the artichokes are not tender enough to be eaten raw, cook them for 20 minutes in boiling water. Hard-boil the eggs, then peel and halve lengthwise. Slice the tomatoes.

Place all your cooked vegetables in large round dishes according to color and texture. Serve the raw vegetables surrounded with the eggs. Put the squid in a shallow dish, the cod on a platter sprinkled with chopped parsley, and the chilled canned tuna on a bed of lettuce. If you serve a boiled chicken or beef or poached fish, place this on a large platter with bunches of parsley at both ends and slices of lemon.

Pour the *aïoli* sauce into one or two bowls to be passed along with the various platters. *Bonne sieste!*

Note: You may also make an eggless *aïoli,* which is lighter. Peel the garlic cloves and boil and peel 1 potato. Crush the garlic and the potato in a mortar. When they have become a paste, slowly add the oil while stirring constantly. Add salt, pepper, and lemon juice.

Bouillabaisse
The Supreme Fish and Vegetable Stew

Bouillabaisse is the noble "golden soup" which embodies not only a whole region's ambience but a whole philosophy. You must invite at least eight guests, since *bouillabaisse* requires a large variety of fish and must be abundant. The success of a good *bouillabaisse* depends on the contrast of flavors and textures. Every home, every town, every restaurant has its own "authentic" version, but remember, it originated as a simple stew made with whatever the fishermen brought home and quickly boiled with saffron, herbs, and garlic. Although its preparation requires two separate operations, the process is very simple and the result truly superb.

Although many of the Provençal fish, such as *rascasse, fiela, grondin* are not found in the United States, there is enough variety here to make a delicious *bouillabaisse*. Three types are essential: a firm, lean, strong-flavored fish; a soft, delicate fish; and a hearty

Festive Dishes

231

fish stock (I use the *soupe de pêcheur*). The stew must cook quickly (no more than 20 minutes)—*bouillabaisse* means "to boil at top speed"—so that the olive oil becomes slightly emulsified.

Serve the stew accompanied by *rouille*, a garlic and cayenne pepper mayonnaise. It should be eaten in a relaxed, informal atmosphere with only a light appetizer to start with and fresh fruit to finish the meal. Serve with a strong dry white wine or a light red wine.

For 8 people:

2 pounds flavorful fish (sea bass, striped bass, snapper, cod, haddock, halibut, hake), cut into thick slices

2 pounds delicate fish, such as flounder, whiting (as big a fish as possible), and red snapper, with skin left on

salt

freshly ground pepper

5 tablespoons olive oil

2 tablespoons pastis or 1 teaspoon anise extract

Rouille (*p. 89*)

2 onions, chopped

1 fish head and backbone

8 large potatoes, sliced ½ inch thick

3 tomatoes, fresh or canned, chopped

1 teaspoon thyme or rosemary

a pinch of fennel seed or a branch of wild fennel

5 sprigs parsley

2 2-inch pieces dried orange rind

1 bay leaf

2 celery stalks, chopped

2 leeks, chopped (optional)

2 quarts water

4 cups white wine

2 or 3 hard-shell crabs, whole

1 teaspoon Spanish saffron

8 slices French bread or 6 slices firm white bread for making Croutons (p. 12)

1 tablespoon Pernod or 2 tablespoons anise extract

Les Plats
de Festin

Fillet the fish (save 1 fish head and 1 backbone) and sprinkle with salt, pepper, 1 tablespoon of the olive oil, and the *pastis* or anise extract. Set aside. Prepare the *rouille* sauce.

In a heavy frying pan, heat 4 tablespoons of the olive oil. Add the chopped onions and sauté gently for 3 minutes. Add the fish head and backbone and sauté for another 3 minutes. Add the potatoes, tomatoes, thyme or rosemary, fennel seed or wild fennel, parsley, orange rind, bay leaf, carrots, celery, leeks, salt, and pepper. Cook for 5 minutes. Add the water and 3 cups of the wine (some claim white wine gives a bitter aftertaste, so you may use water instead) and bring to a boil. Simmer for 20 minutes. Crush the saffron between your fingers over the soup. Cook for 2 minutes and remove from heat. Place a Mouli food mill over a pan and pour two ladlefuls at a time of the soup mixture into it. Grind, adding a little broth whenever the mixture becomes too dry. Place a sieve over a large bowl and force the ground mixture through with a pestle or a large wooden spoon. Discard the residue.

Put the soup in a large kettle, add the firmer fish, and cook for 5 minutes, then add the potato slices and the more delicate fish, crabs, 1 tablespoon of the olive oil, 1 cup of the wine (the fish should be covered with liquid). Simmer gently for 20 minutes. Meanwhile, prepare the croutons (you may want to rub the bread with garlic).

Just before serving the soup, add the Pernod or anise extract and check the seasoning. (The dish should be highly seasoned.) The traditional way to serve *bouillabaisse* is to place two or three croutons in each soup plate and to ladle the soup, fish, and potatoes on top of the croutons. Serve the *rouille* in a separate bowl. Leave the tureen of *bouillabaisse* on the table throughout the meal so that the guests can help themselves to the soup, fish, and potatoes and pour some *rouille* in the soup itself, or else spoon it over the fish.

You may also serve *bouillabaisse* as two separate courses: first, the soup over the croutons; then the fish on a warm platter surrounded by potato slices with a ladleful of warm soup poured over them and served with a bowl of *rouille*.

Note: If you have any leftover fish, soup, or potatoes, pass it through a Mouli food mill, add ⅓ cup of white wine, a dash of olive oil, and freeze—a thick soup will be ready for another day.

Festive Dishes

Variations:

Bouillabaisse de Martigues
A black *bouillabaisse* with a very tasty, thick bouillon. Little 1-pound squids (together with their ink bags) are added to the fish.

Bouillabaisse Borgne
Add a poached egg to each plate. (*Borgne* means one-eyed.)

Bouillabaisse de Morue
Sauté in 3 tablespoons of olive oil: 2 leeks, 1 quartered tomato, 3 peeled garlic cloves, 2 pounds dried cod (after soaking in water for 3 hours), 2 diced potatoes, a bouquet garni, a pinch of salt, and freshly ground black pepper. After about 5 minutes, add a glass of water per person and boil it for 10 minutes.

Revesset
This is a green *bouillabaisse*. To a big pot of boiling salted water (2 quarts) add ½ pound Swiss chard, ½ pound spinach, and a few sorrel leaves. Boil for 10 minutes, then add 2 tablespoons of olive oil, 1 pound of sardines, and cook for 10 minutes. Prepare Croutons (p. 12) and place in each soup plate. Pour the broth with the greens over them. Serve the fish separately with a sprinkling of red wine vinegar or lemon juice.

Bouillabaisse aux Poissons d'Eau Douce
Use eels, crayfish, trout or other fresh-water fish. Follow the main recipe for *bouillabaisse*.

Bouillabaisse de Toulon
Add 3 more potatoes and 3 pounds of mussels to the main recipe for *bouillabaisse*.

Couscous
Couscous with Chicken, Meat, Vegetables, and a Hot Sauce

Although *couscous* is originally a North African dish, it has been incorporated in the Provence repertory for so long that it is now a traditional part of the cuisine.

Like *aïoli* and *bouillabaisse*, *couscous* is a spectacular creation, a feast in itself. It consists of many foods served on different platters containing meat and vegetables, chicken and carrots, the couscous

Les Plats
de Festin

grain itself, and the chickpeas. The assortment of dishes is served with a bowl of broth and a bowl of very hot red pepper sauce.

The dish derives its name from the grain (hard wheat semolina) which is its principal ingredient. In North Africa a special semolina is rolled to prepare couscous, but in France and the United States, packages of ready-made couscous grain are available in stores selling health food or in stores with imported food items. It is also available through mail order. The Harissa sauce is available under that name in special grocery shops, but it can also be prepared at home.

The dish will take about 2 hours to cook. You will need three pots: a pan for cooking meats and vegetables, one for cooking the chicken and carrots, and then a *couscoussière* (see Techniques and Tools, p. 21). If you do not have a *couscoussière*, line a sieve with a linen towel, place this over a large pot, and cover the sieve with a lid.

For 10 people:

2 pounds lamb, shoulder or breast
2 pounds short ribs of beef
1 cup Sauce Tomate (*p. 91*)
1 can Harissa sauce or Tabasco sauce
3 tablespoons olive oil
2 beef or lamb bones
5 onions (1 minced, 4 peeled and left whole)
4 tomatoes, fresh or canned, chopped
4 chili peppers, minced, or 2 teaspoons cayenne pepper
salt
8 medium-sized turnips, peeled
10 zucchini, seeded, or 1 pumpkin, peeled, seeded, and cut into large pieces
1 clove
1 6-pound chicken
1 celery stalk, cut into 2-inch sticks
5 carrots, peeled
freshly ground pepper
2 pounds couscous grain
3 large heads green cabbage, quartered
½ pound of chickpeas, cooked or canned
¼ pound sweet butter

Festive Dishes

Cut the lamb and beef into 1½-inch pieces, trimming as much fat and gristle as possible.

Prepare the *sauce tomate* and add Harissa sauce or Tabasco sauce to taste.* Set aside.

The following instructions for cooking the meat, chicken, vegetables, and couscous grain should be followed in such a way that everything will be ready at about the same time—this means that at some point you will have three pots cooking on the stove.

Heat 3 tablespoons of the olive oil in a large heavy-bottomed pan and sauté the meat for 5 minutes. Add the beef or lamb bones, minced onion, tomatoes, chili peppers, and salt. Pour in enough hot water to cover and simmer for 1 hour. Add the turnips and cook for 15 minutes. Add the zucchini or pumpkin and cook for 20 minutes over a low flame. Remove from heat and set aside.

Stick a clove in one of the whole onions and put it in a large pot with the chicken, bones, celery sticks, and carrots. Add salt and pepper and cover with cold water and bring to a boil. Cook for 1 hour. Remove the chicken, take off the skin with a sharp knife, and cut into pieces. Put the chicken back in the broth until ready to use.

Meanwhile, pour the couscous grain into a large bowl and sprinkle it with ½ cup of cold water. Toss it with your hands and let it rest for 30 minutes.

Take your *couscoussière* (or a large pan and a sieve) and fill the bottom part with 6 quarts of water, the remaining whole onions, the cabbage, salt, and pepper. Place the couscous grain in the top part (or the sieve if you are not using a *couscoussière*). Bring the water to a boil and steam the couscous, covered, for 30 minutes. Remove the grain from the pot, sprinkle it with ½ cup of cold water, 1 tablespoon of salt, 2 tablespoons of olive oil, and mix gently with your hands or two forks (the grains should not stick to each other). Allow to rest for 15 minutes. Put the grains back in the top of the *couscoussière* or pot and cook above the boiling broth for 30 minutes. Just before serving, heat the chickpeas with a little olive oil.

To prepare for serving, place the couscous grain in a large shallow dish. Dot with butter or sprinkle with olive oil and keep covered with a lid until ready to serve. Place the meats and vege-

* Or else prepare a different sauce: Crush 2 peeled garlic cloves into a mortar. Add ½ teaspoon cayenne pepper, ½ teaspoon ground cumin, ½ teaspoon crushed coriander seed, ¼ teaspoon ground ginger, and salt to taste. Pound and stir. Slowly add the olive oil and stir, then add 1 cup of *Sauce Tomate* (p. 91). This sauce can be kept refrigerated for a few days.

Les Plats
de Festin

tables on one or two platters—discard the two bones. Pour hot broth over them. Place the chicken on a large platter and pour some of the broth over it also. Pour six ladlefuls of the hot broth in a large bowl. Put the hot Harissa sauce in another bowl to pass around for pouring on all the various foods. Each person will put a ladleful of couscous grain onto his or her soup plate (this must be large and shallow), then take some of the meat, chicken, and vegetables, and then spoon some hot broth and tomato sauce over everything.

Variations:
The ingredients and the proportions will vary according to what you have on hand and according to your taste. Follow the general process as described in the main recipe and remember this is a simple dish you can improvise on and in which nothing needs to be absolutely precise.

Couscous aux Sept Légumes
Made with cabbage, yellow and red squash, carrots, tomatoes, eggplants, chili peppers, fresh lima beans, and onions, with 2 teaspoons of saffron crumbled and sprinkled over the cooked vegetables a few minutes before serving.

Couscous aux Courgettes, Fèves et Navets
Made with zucchini, fresh lima beans, turnips, onions, and lamb stew, flavored with saffron and coriander.

Couscous aux Onions et au Miel
Made with chicken and lamb, onions, cinnamon, and honey.

Couscous aux Raisins Secs et Pois Chiches
Made with raisins, chickpeas, lamb, onions, and saffron.

Couscous Medfon
Made with lamb, chicken giblets, onions, saffron, and cinnamon.

Couscous aux Boulettes
Served with little meatballs seasoned with cumin and simmered in the broth for the last 15 minutes of cooking.

Les Desserts
Desserts

Most meals in the South of France end with cheese and fresh fruit. In fact, the Niçois word for dessert is *la frucha* (the fruit), and most of the time it comes from the family orchard. Fresh, stewed, dried, *confit,* or kept in brandy, they usually replace the elaborate cream-rich desserts of haute cuisine.

There is a traditional pastry based on honey, almonds, and, of course, fruits, but it is not for everybody's taste.

There are *pompes,* shaped like plump crowns; *chichi fregi,* little circles of fried dough; *pogne,* the sweet brioche of Easter; *pan coudoun,* in which a whole quince wrapped in plain dough is slowly baked in the oven. There is *pain de Sainte Agathe,* in the shape of a breast (*le martyre de Sainte Agathe*); *oreillettes,* little ears of dough fried until crisp; *navettes,* little boats flavored with orange blossom water, *muscardins, pignolats, tourtillons,* and, of course, there is confectionery: *les calissons d'Aix,* made with candied fruit and almonds; *berlingots de Carpentras,* delicious hard mint candy; the *chiques d'Allaud,* soft honey candies; *suce-miel d'Aubagne,* a caramelized honey candy; and the famous *nougat de Montélimar.*

So, though they are simplicity itself, Provençal pastry and sweets do exist, and dessert can be other than the more prevalent *grata queca,* or baskets of seasonal fruit. The selections here represent only the recipes we think would please the American palate.

Beignets de Fruits

Apple Raisin Fritters

This apple-raisin *beignet* recipe is an old Niçois dessert. The lovely crisp fritters can also be made with bananas, peaches, apricots, or acacia blossoms. Rum brings out the flavor of tart apples and raisins and enlivens this dessert. Since the fruit must marinate for 3 hours and the batter rest 1 hour, this is not a last-minute dish.

For 6 people:

Fruit and Marinade

    6 tart apples
    ½ cup raisins
    ½ cup dark rum
    ⅓ cup sugar

Peel, core, and dice the apples. Combine them with the raisins, rum, and sugar and let them stand for 3 hours.

Batter

    2 eggs, separated
       about ⅔ cup warm beer
    1 cup unbleached flour
       salt
    2 teaspoons butter, softened, or peanut
       oil
    ¾ cup (or more) vegetable oil
    1 cup confectioners' sugar

Separate the egg whites from the yolks and reserve them. Blend the yolks and beer and stir in the flour, salt, and butter or oil. Stir well until the batter is smooth. Leave in a warm place (such as a turned-off oven) for 1 hour.

Preheat the oven to 300°. In a saucepan heat the vegetable oil. Beat the egg whites until stiff but not dry. Pour off the rum marinade from the apples and stir it into the batter, then very gently fold in the egg whites. The batter must be smooth. (It will be very liquid with the addition of the marinade. If you want slightly heavier, more rounded *beignets*, stir in 1 to 2 teaspoons of

Desserts

flour before you add the apples and raisins.) Very delicately but thoroughly fold the fruits into the batter and drop by tablespoon-fuls into the hot oil. Fry the fritters until they are golden on both sides, turning them over with tongs after 3 minutes. Remove with a slotted spoon and drain on paper towels. Bits of the batter will break off and burn at the bottom of the pan. You will have to fish them out with a slotted spoon. Keep warm in the oven, changing the paper towels twice.

When all the *beignets* are ready, arrange them in a long basket or a platter line with a napkin. Sprinkle confectioners' sugar (or crushed crystallized sugar and a little dark rum) on top and serve.

Cloche Amandine
Bell-Shaped Almond Brittle

Croquante, or *cloche amandine,* is usually served at Christmas and Easter in Provence. It is placed in the center of the table and everyone breaks off little pieces of it to nibble on. Leftovers are crushed and used on top of baked apples or pears or on ice cream.

> *enough shelled nuts to make 1½ cups*
> *finely minced almonds or a mixture*
> *of hazelnuts and almonds*
> 2 *cups white sugar*
> 1 *cup brown sugar*
> ½ *cup honey (the best you can find)*
> ½ *cup water*
> 1 *lemon, cut in half*
> 8 *tablespoons butter*

Preheat the oven to 300°. Place the shelled but unpeeled almonds on a cookie sheet and bake for 10 minutes until brown. Remove from the oven and mince them finely. Put them back in a turned-off oven.

Bring the sugars, honey, and water to a boil and stir with a wooden spoon. When the mixture has heated to 300° add the butter and the warm nuts and pour onto a greased surface (marble or formica counter, aluminum cookie sheet, or aluminum foil). Smooth out and push with the 2 halves of the lemon until the en-tire sheet is very thin—from ⅛ to ¼ inch thick. Lift off the sheet before it is completely cooled and hardened and mold it against the inside of a buttered marble or china mortar or a wide bowl. Let it cool, then unmold on a platter. It will look like a golden bell.

You may decorate it with crystallized violets or mimosa flowers (on sale in gourmet shops) or candied fruits or dribbles of icing. I prefer it plain.

Keep the leftover pieces wrapped in aluminum foil or in a closed glass jar. Never refrigerate.

Compote d'Abricots, de Pêches et de Prunes

Apricot-Peach-Plum Compote Cooked in Lemon and Orange Juice

Peaches in the United States are full of flavor, but the apricots and plums tend to be rather bland. Poached in lemon and orange juice, however, they make a subtle combination perfect for concluding a hearty dinner or a rich lunch.

For 6 people:

6 *peaches*
6 *large or 10 small apricots*
6 *plums*
1 *cup sugar*
1 *cup orange juice (frozen is acceptable)*
1 *lemon*
2 *tablespoons cognac (optional)*
2 *or 3 sprigs mint (optional)*

Peel and pit the peaches, apricots, and plums. Cut the peaches in half. Cut and squeeze the lemon and peel off 2 3-inch strips of the yellow rind. Bring to a boil the sugar, orange juice, and lemon juice and rind in a pan. Add the fruit and allow to cool in a shallow bowl.

Boil the syrup for 10 minutes, or until very thick, and spoon it over the fruit. Chill. Just before serving, you may add cognac and sprigs of mint on top.

Note: In Provence the fruit is never peeled because part of the flavor is lost in removing the skin. But Americans would probably prefer the fruit to be peeled. Try it both ways.

Compote de Fruits

Stewed Fresh Fruit

You don't need jumbo, out-of-season, out-of-state, or exotic fruits for this. It is usually made with fruit that is too ripe, too small, or too blemished to be acceptable for serving in a *panier de fruits de saison* (basket of fresh fruits).

So look around your market for good buys of seasonal fruits. There's no special list to follow, but you do need a varied selection.

For 6 people:

 1 *lemon*
 ½ *cup white or black grapes*
 3 *or 4 ripe pears, peeled and sliced*
 3 *peaches (or apricots or plums), peeled and sliced*
 3 *apples, peeled and sliced*
 1 *cup sugar*
 1 *cup water*
 ⅓ *cup chopped mint (optional)*

Cut the lemon and squeeze it. Peel 2 3-inch strips of the yellow rind. Rinse the grapes and remove the stems. Peel the pears, peaches, and apples; remove the pits or seeds and slice them (quarter the fruit that is very ripe). Bring the rind, juice, sugar, and water to a boil.

Add the fruits to the boiling syrup and lower the flame. Simmer, uncovered, for 10 to 15 minutes. Remove the fruit with a slotted spoon and put in a shallow bowl to cool.

Boil the syrup for 10 minutes, or until it thickens, then pour it over the fruit. Chill. Sprinkle with chopped mint leaves.

Confiture Noire

Preserves Made with a Variety of Fruits

Delicious preserves are made in Provence with interesting combinations of fruits, such as cherries with red currants and watermelon with orange and lemon, but the best is *confiture noire,* or black jam. This can be made in any proportion you want of the following fruits and nuts:

> *fresh figs (if unavailable, use dried figs*
>   *or omit figs altogether)*
> *pears*
> *melons*
> *quinces*
> *lemon rinds*
> *walnuts*
> ½ *pound of sugar for each pound of fruit*

Choose very ripe fruits. Place the whole figs in a heavy-bottomed pan, sprinkle with sugar and bring to a boil. Remove from heat and drain through a piece of cheesecloth. Bring the juice to a boil and add the peeled and quartered pears, quinces, and melons, and the shelled walnuts. Add sugar. Cook for 1 hour or more, or until the mixture is dark and sticky. Return the figs to the pan and cook for 15 minutes. Allow to cool and place in a sterilized jar and seal.

Confiture de Tomates Rouges
Red Tomato Preserves

Curiously, in Aix the tomatoes are mixed with eggplant. For this recipe chose firm, ripe tomatoes.

> *5 pounds tomatoes*
> *4 pounds sugar*
> *rind of 1 lemon*
> *juice of 1 lemon*
> *2 tablespoons dark rum (optional)*

Drop the tomatoes in hot water for 5 seconds to loosen the skin and remove it with a sharp knife.

Cut the tomatoes in half and squeeze out the seeds. Place the tomato halves in a heavy-bottomed saucepan with the sugar and the lemon rind and juice. Bring to a boil and stir with a wooden spoon. Lower the heat and simmer, uncovered, for 1 hour, or until the tomatoes have become transparent and sticky. Remove the

Desserts

lemon peel. You may add rum before putting the preserves in sterilized jars and sealing.

Serve as a dessert with plain cookies or spread on toasted slices of homemade bread for a *goûter* or at teatime.

Confiture de Tomates Vertes

Green Tomato Preserves

> 5 *pounds green tomatoes*
> 4 *pounds sugar*
> *rind of 1 lemon*
> *juice of 1 lemon*

Cut the tomatoes in half and squeeze out the seeds, then cut the halves into thin slices. Put them into a large glass or china bowl and sprinkle with the sugar. Allow to marinate for 24 hours. The next day, cook the tomatoes over a low flame in a heavy pot with the lemon juice and lemon rind for 2 hours. Stir from time to time with a wooden spoon. Allow to cool completely before sealing in sterilized jars.

Serve with thin cookies for dessert or spread on toast for a five o'clock *goûter*.

Délices au Miel

Honey Delights

This is a most unusual dessert, crunchy, sweet, and light—a children's favorite.

> For 6 people:
> ½ *pound flour*
> *a pinch of salt*
> ½ *cup water*
> ½ *cup peanut oil*
> *honey to coat the pastries*

Preheat the oven to 250°. Put the flour in a large bowl, make a well in the center and add salt and water. With floured hands knead well until the dough no longer sticks to your hands. Form a ball and let it rest, covered with a towel, for 2 hours.

Oil a board or counter and knead the dough again for 5 minutes. Pull off a piece the size of a walnut. Pour a little oil in a saucer, dip in the piece of dough and place it on the oiled board. With an oiled rolling pin, roll the dough very thin and fold it in four; again roll it and fold it in four; then roll it out for the third time to a 4-inch square.

Heat the peanut oil to 350° and put in the square of pastry. Cook about 2 minutes, or until golden, turn over with tongs, and cook for a few more minutes. Place on a heated plate, spread some honey on top and keep warm in the oven. Repeat the process, piling the squares one on top of the other.

Galette des Rois

A Crown-Shaped Brioche with Candied Fruits

Epiphany, on the twelfth night after Christmas, is celebrated throughout Provence. Three clay figurines, representing the *Rois mages* (the three kings—Melchior, Balthazar, and Gaspard), are added to the Crèche in each home. Families and friends celebrate *la fête des Rois*, which ends with a big cake in which a tiny china figure or dried white bean is hidden. Whoever finds the figure is the sacred king of the day. He chooses his queen, receives a toast, and must invite the whole group the following week to share a second *galette des Rois* and drink champagne or *vin cuit*. *Tirer les Rois* is a wonderful reason for gathering with friends to chat, drink, and eat throughout the whole month of January.

Children in Nice are told that if they get up at midnight on Epiphany Eve, wear a wet nightgown, hold a tree branch and stand on the roof or on a high branch of a tree, they will see the Kings marching toward the church. A good thing they enjoy the *galette des Rois* before such an ordeal!

This is not a very sweet cake. The sweetness of the candied fruits and sugar on top is enhanced by the fresh, light texture of the cake itself. Start the cake the day before you plan to serve it. You can make the golden crown from some metallic Christmas paper or

Desserts

245

gilded cardboard—wonderful for a children's party. The proportions given here are for two large cakes. Whatever is left over can be frozen.

For 12 to 16 people:

2 *packages dry yeast*
⅓ *cup lukewarm water plus water to cover*
5 *cups unbleached flour*
1 *cup softened butter*
½ *cup lukewarm milk*
2 *eggs*
6 *egg yolks*
1 *tablespoon fresh orange rind, finely grated*
1 *tablespoon fresh lemon rind, finely grated*
1 *tablespoon salt*
1 *cup mixed glacéed cherries, angelica, pineapple, melon, raisins*
¼ *cup lukewarm dark rum*
8 *pieces crystallized sugar or 8 tablespoons sugar*
2 *egg whites mixed with 1 tablespoon milk*
1 *white china figurine (about 1 inch high) or a dried white bean*

Mix the yeast with the lukewarm water and let it sit for 5 minutes. Put ¾ cup of the flour in a bowl, make a well in the center and add the dissolved yeast. Knead for 3 minutes, then make a ball of the dough. Let it rest in the bowl and cover it with more lukewarm water. Let it stand in a warm place about 15 minutes, or until the ball floats to the top.

Put 4¼ cups of the flour in a large bowl, make a well in the center and add half of the butter, milk, eggs, egg yolks, orange and lemon rind, and salt. Blend them and knead well. Add the ball of yeasty dough and knead for 15 minutes. Knead in the remaining butter until the dough is smooth and no longer clings to the bowl. Place this in a greased bowl and cover with a damp towel. Heat the oven to 200° for 2 minutes, turn it off, and place the bowl there (or another warm place) to let the dough rise until double in bulk

—about 1½ hours. Punch it down. Let it double in size again—1 more hour. Punch down and refrigerate overnight.

The next day, soak the glacéed fruits in the rum for 2 hours. Remove the dough from the refrigerator and let it warm to room temperature.

Drain the fruits. Reserve about 10 cherries and some angelica to decorate the top. Flour the rest so they will not sink to the bottom of the batter during baking. Reserve the rum for garnish.

Knead the floured fruit into the dough and form two balls. Place each ball on a floured table and make a hole in the center of each with your fingers, then stretch the dough to form a 2-inch-wide ring with a diameter of 6 to 8 inches. Place both rings on buttered cookie sheets with a custard cup or something similar in the center to keep the hole open. With kitchen shears, cut little notches all around the edge of the rings. Place in a warm place about 1 hour, or until doubled in size.

Preheat the oven to 400°. With a wooden mallet or a bottle, coarsely crush the crystallized sugar (or use plain sugar instead) and add to the rum used for soaking the fruit.

Paint the surface of the rings with the mixture of egg whites and milk and sprinkle the sugar and rum on top. Bake for 30 minutes.

Carefully hide the figurine or bean inside the cake. Garnish the top with the cherries and angelica. Make golden paper crowns to fit the center of each cake and place them in the hole before serving.

Gâteau aux Fruits

A Soft Bread and Candied Fruit Dessert

This cake, originally intended for children's snacks, will become dressier and seem more important if you serve with it a bowl of *sabayon niçois, purée de fruits frais,* or a *sauce à l'abricots.*

It is quick and easy to prepare, since you probably have all the ingredients at hand and simply cannot fail. You may use a good firm bread or a slightly stale pound or marble cake or even madeleines or cupcakes.

For 6 people:

>   2 *cups diced candied fruits and raisins or*
>   2 *cups diced dried fruits* (*peaches,*
>   *apricots, pears, prunes*)
>   1 *cup dark rum*
>   6 *slices good firm white bread*
>   (*preferably homemade*) *or stale*
>   *cake*
>   *grated rind of* 1 *lemon*
>   4 *egg yolks*
>   2 *cups milk*
>   ¾ *cup sugar*
>   4 *egg whites, beaten until stiff*
>   *a bowl of* Sabayon Niçois (*p. 256*),
>   Purée de Fruit Frais (*p. 256*), *or*
>   Sauce à l'Abricot (*pp. 257–58*)
>   3 *tablespoons sugar or a little confec-*
>   *tioners' sugar*

Place the fruits in a bowl and cover with the rum to marinate for at least 2 hours. Cut the bread or cake into small cubes and sprinkle the grated lemon rind on them. Preheat the oven to 350°

Butter a baking dish and place one thin layer of bread cubes, then a thin layer of the marinated fruits. Repeat until all the ingredients are used up.

Put the egg yolks, milk, and sugar in a bowl and beat vigorously. Add to them the beaten egg whites and blend well. Add the rum marinade and pour over the fruits and bread cubes in the baking dish. Place the baking dish in a pan of hot water (reaching a level of 2 inches from the edge of the dish) and place in a 350° oven for 1 hour. Serve slightly warm or cold, with a bowl of *sabayon niçois, purée de fruits frais,* or *sauce à l'abricot,* or simply sprinkled with sugar.

Glace à la Fleur d'Orangers

Orange Blossom Water Ice Cream

This is the most delicate and exquisite of desserts. You may sprinkle it with a few curls of bitter chocolate to provide contrast in color and flavor with the light ice cream and surround it with mint leaves. Keep the leftover whites for *soupirs aux amandes*.

For 6 people:

3 *cups milk*
7 *egg yolks, beaten*
⅓ *cup sugar*
2 *tablespoons orange blossom water* (*or more for a stronger flavor*)
½ *tablespoon vanilla*
1 *ounce dark bitter chocolate*
mint leaves

Scald the milk. In a heavy saucepan, beat the egg yolks and sugar until very thick and lemon-colored. Stirring constantly, slowly pour in the hot milk. Put over a moderately low flame and stir constantly with a wooden spoon until the mixture thickens and coats the back of a metal spoon. Let the custard cool at room temperature, then chill it in the refrigerator. Stir in the orange blossom water and vanilla. Taste to see if the mixture is sweet enough and flavored enough (freezing diminishes the taste so it should be fairly strong). Place the mixture in an ice cream freezer and turn until smooth and thick. Pack in a mold, cover with foil, and place in the freezer for several hours or overnight.

Put a piece of chocolate on a sheet of waxed paper on the top of the stove near the pilot light. When it has softened somewhat, shave off little curls of chocolate with a potato peeler or a sharp knife. Decorate a large platter with mint leaves. Run the mold quickly under hot water and invert on the platter. Sprinkle the chocolate curls on top and serve with a sweet wine (*vin cuit* or *vin à l'orange*) and *Soupirs aux Amandes* (pp. 263–64).

Glace au Miel

Honey Ice Cream

For this recipe you must use honey that is strongly flavored but not too sweet. The mixture of honey ice and toasted almonds is wonderful. Keep the leftover egg whites for *soupirs aux amandes*.

For 6 to 8 people:

> 3 *cups milk*
> 7 *egg yolks*
> 1½ *cups honey (the best you can find)*
> ½ *teaspoon salt*
> 3 *teaspoons thyme (optional)*
> ½ *cup coarsely chopped unpeeled*
>   *toasted almonds*
> *fresh mint leaves*

Scald the milk. Beat the egg yolks in a heavy saucepan until the mixture is thick and lemon-colored. Very gradually stir in the hot milk and then the honey and salt. (You may stir in the thyme for a more accented flavor.) Put over a moderately low flame and stir constantly with a wooden spoon until the custard thickens and coats the back of a metal spoon. Do not let the mixture come anywhere near a boil (a "thermospoon" is perfect for checking the temperature). Cool at room temperature, then refrigerate for 1 hour, or until thoroughly chilled. Pour into an ice cream freezer and turn until the custard is very thick and smooth. Dip a mold in cold water, pour in the honey ice cream, cover tightly with foil, and freeze several hours or overnight.

Just before serving, run the mold quickly under warm water and invert on a chilled plate. Sprinkle with almonds and decorate the platter with mint leaves. Serve with *Soupirs aux Amandes* (pp. 263–64).

Grata Queca

Snow Flavored with Fruit Syrup or Liqueur

This is a perfect light dessert to serve after an *aïoli, couscous,* or a hearty stew. Children love it. In Nice it is sold on all street corners. Easy to make, it is a refreshing substitute for brandy after dinner.

Good French and German fruit syrups are sold in specialty shops and the gourmet departments of most large stores; most liquor stores have the fruit liqueurs.

Ingredients:

---

ice
fruit syrup (sirop de fraise, de cassis *or* de
    framboises) *or fruit liqueur* (liqueur de
    cassis, *or* d'abricots, *or* crème de menthe
    or de cassis) *or homemade berry syrup*
    or fruit purée
fresh mint leaves (*optional*)

Shave a block of ice or crush ice cubes wrapped in a towel. Fill individual glasses with the shavings only, not the mush. Pour into
them the syrup or liqueur of your choice and garnish with fresh
mint.

For an elegant occasion, serve in tall sherbet glasses with long-
handled spoons.

Nougat Blanc
Honey, Almond, and Egg-White Confection

Christmas in Nice is not conceivable without having on hand at
least two kinds of nougat—the black and the white. Since commercially made nougat is so remote from what it should be, it is
well worth learning how to make this delicious and healthy con-
fection. Besides, the whole process of making it—the smell, the
color, the taste—is a delightful experience.

> 1½ *cups almonds, peeled and quartered*
> ⅔ *cup hazelnuts or pistachios, peeled*
>   *and chopped or quartered*
> ½ *cup water*
> 1⅓ *cups sugar*
> ⅔ *cup honey*
> 3 *egg whites, stiffly beaten*

Place the almonds and hazelnuts or pistachios on a baking sheet in
a 300° oven. Stirring with a wooden spoon, heat the water and
sugar until the candy thermometer reads 290°.

Meanwhile, in another pan, heat the honey, stirring with a
wooden spoon until the thermometer also reads 290°.

Desserts

Mix the honey and the sugar syrup slowly and carefully add the beaten egg whites. Pour the mixture into one of the saucepans and heat over a very low flame for a few minutes. Add the warm nuts and stir with the wooden spoon.

Oil a bread pan. Place a sheet of waxed paper on it and butter it (you may use baker's wafer instead of waxed paper). Pour the nougat mixture into it and place a buttered sheet of waxed paper on top. Wrap a piece of cardboard or wood the size of the bread pan with aluminum foil. Put it on top of the nougat, then weight it down with something heavy (canned food, bricks, or heavy pebbles). Or pour the mixture into a loaf pan and push another loaf pan into it and then weight it down with heavy jars.

Let the nougat cool at room temperature. Unmold, cut into 2-inch strips, and wrap in aluminum foil. This will keep well at room temperature. Do not refrigerate.

Nougat Noir
Black Honey and Almond Confection

For 8 to 10 people:

1½ cups shelled almonds and hazelnuts, cut in half (do not remove the skins)

1 to 2 tablespoons sweet butter

1⅓ cups honey (the most fragrant you can find)

3 teaspoons rosemary or thyme (optional)

1 lemon, cut in half

Place the almonds on a baking sheet and heat them in a 350° oven for about 5 minutes. Reserve in the warm oven.

Butter two long and narrow bread pans, or if you own one, a wooden nougat mold, and line with baker's wafer (available at candy supply stores) or waxed paper (butter this also).

Heat the honey in a heavy-bottomed pan made of copper, cast-iron or enamel. Stir with a long wooden spoon until it reaches the boiling point. (You may stir in the rosemary or thyme at this point.) Add the warm almonds and stir for about 30 minutes, or until the honey turns brown and the almonds begin to crackle. At this point the candy thermometer should register 300°.

Pour the hot mixture into the prepared molds and push it down with the lemon halves. The layer should be about ½ to ¾ inch thick. Cover with a sheet of baker's wafer or buttered waxed paper. Cut a piece of cardboard or wood to fit the inside of the mold, wrap it in aluminum foil and weight it down with two cans. Let the nougat cool at room temperature overnight.

The next day, release the sides of the nougat with a knife. Unmold by holding the bottom of the mold over a burner for a minute. Peel off the waxed paper. Cut the nougat into 3 long strips or leave it whole and wrap in aluminum foil. Or you may cut it in pieces and store it in a closed jar. It will become chewy and easy to eat. Keep in a cool place but not in the refrigerator.

Petits Biscuits aux Noix
Crumbly Walnut Cookies

Like most of the pastry in Nice, these sinfully rich cookies are made with walnuts. But pecans may be used instead if necessary. Make them small—the size of a walnut.

Makes 24 to 50 cookies:

> 1 cup finely chopped walnuts
> ¼ pound butter
> ¼ cup sugar
> 2 teaspoons vanilla extract
> 1 cup unbleached all-purpose flour
> 2 tablespoons granulated sugar
> 2 tablespoons confectioners' sugar

Preheat the oven to 300°. If you use a blender to chop the walnuts, chop only a little at a time to prevent turning the nuts into butter. Cream the butter and stir in the sugar. Add the vanilla, nuts, and flour. (All this can be done in the Cuisinart food processor in a few seconds.)

Butter two baking sheets and dot with teaspoonfuls of dough, (about two-thirds of a teaspoon) spacing them 2 inches apart. Bake for 20 to 30 minutes. When the cookies begin to turn pale

Desserts

brown, they're done. Remove from the oven, and with a spatula, lift the cookies carefully onto a plate, table, or tray to cool. Sprinkle at once with granulated sugar. When cool, sprinkle with confectioners' sugar.

Poires au Vin Rouge

Pears in Red Wine and Lemon Juice

One of the easiest desserts to prepare. You can make it ahead of time and all the ingredients are often at hand. Quickly made, impossible to do poorly, always delicious. Serve it warm or chilled with *petits biscuits aux noix*.

For 6 people:

6 *large, ripe, firm pears*
1 *lemon*
    rind of 1 orange
2 *cups strong red wine (California Burgundy is good)*
1 *cup sugar*
2 *tablespoons fresh strawberry or raspberry purée (see* Purée de Fruits Frais, *p. 256) or 2 tablespoons preserves*
sprigs of mint or a handful of mint leaves

Peel and core the pears. Wash and dry the lemon and orange, and with a potato peeler, remove the rind, taking care to peel off only the zesty surface. With kitchen shears, cut the orange rind and half of the lemon rind into fine strips. Squeeze the lemon and reserve the juice.

Simmer the wine, sugar, and rind in a heavy pan, uncovered, for 5 minutes. Add the pears and simmer, covered, for 35 to 45 minutes, basting from time to time and turning gently with a wooden spoon so that they cook and color evenly. Prick with a thin skewer to test for doneness. The pears should be tender but not mushy. Remove them with a wooden spoon and put in a serving dish. Add the fruit purée or preserves to the wine and simmer for

15 minutes. Stir in the lemon juice and pour over the pears. Or you may discard the wine syrup and simply serve the pears in fresh fruit purée. The pears may also be sprinkled with sugar and caramelized under the broiler before serving. Garnish with fresh mint.

Pommes Surprise
Baked Apples with Raisins, Honey, and Rum

This is a simple country dessert made with simple ingredients. You can make it more sophisticated by replacing the honey and the preserves with fresh strawberry or raspberry purée.

For 6 people:

> 1 *cup raisins*
> 3 *tablespoons dark rum*
> 6 *large Rome Beauty apples*
> *rind of 1 lemon, grated*
> *juice of 1 lemon*
> 6 *tablespoons honey*
> 12 *almonds (with skins left on), chopped*
> *or slivered*
> 6 *tablespoons apricot preserves or red*
> *currant jelly*

In a bowl, soak the raisins in the rum for 1 hour. Preheat the oven to 375°. Wash and core the apples, but don't peel them. Cut off a thin strip at the base so the apples will remain upright. Put them in a baking dish and fill the center with the raisins and the rum and the grated lemon rind, lemon juice, and honey. Sprinkle with the almonds. You can prepare this much ahead of time and cover with plastic wrap or aluminum foil and set aside until ready to cook.

Pour ½ cup of warm water around the apples, cover with a sheet of aluminum foil and bake for 1 hour in a 375° oven. Remove the foil, pierce the skin of each apple two or three times with a sharp knife and bake for 10 to 15 minutes. Transfer the apples to a serving dish. Stir the preserves or jelly into the cooking-pan juices and pour over the apples. Serve warm or cold.

Desserts

Purée de Fruits Frais

Fresh Fruit Sauce

Serve this fresh sauce with *Semoule aux Fruits Confits* (p. 258) or *Gâteau aux Fruits* (pp. 247–48).

> ½ *cup sugar*
> ½ *cup strawberries*
> ½ *cup raspberries*
> 3 *tablespoons kirsch*

Put all the ingredients into a blender or through a Mouli food mill.

Sabayon Niçois

Nice's Own Sabayon

This is delicious served with *Gâteau aux Fruits* (pp. 247–48), *Semoules aux Fruits Confits* (p. 258), or *Soupirs aux Amandes* (pp. 263–64). If you serve it by itself, pour it into tall glasses.

> For 6 people:
>
> 6 *egg yolks, beaten*
> ½ *cup sugar*
> *juice and grated rind of 1 lemon*
> 1 *cup white wine, sherry, port, Marsala,*
> *or a mixture of dark rum and water*

In a bowl, beat the egg yolks and the sugar with an eggbeater. When the mixture turns pale and frothy, add lemon juice, grated lemon rind, and the wine and beat for 1 minute. Place the bowl over a pan of hot water and cook for 8 to 10 minutes, stirring constantly with a wire whisk or a fork. The mixture will thicken and become creamy. Don't overcook or it will curdle.

Pour into a warm bowl or into individual cups. Serve at room temperature—not chilled.

Salades de Fruits

Fresh Fruit Salads

Select as many fruits as you can, varying the flavor, color, and texture as much as possible. Serve the salad in a glass bowl—this will look very cool on a hot summer day—with perhaps a few mint leaves to decorate it.

Slice the large fruits but leave the small ones whole. Arrange the fruits in layers in a bowl, sprinkle with sugar, red wine, rum, kirsch, and orange or lemon juice. Chill well, then toss gently just before serving.

Each of these combinations is a sample of the variety a salad bowl can have:

—Peaches, oranges (sliced, with rind left on), and strawberries with red wine

—Apricots, strawberries, pears, and maraschino cherries with lemon juice

—Apples (sliced), bananas (sliced and quickly covered with lemon juice to prevent discoloring), and oranges with dark rum and orange juice

—Strawberries, raspberries, and red currants with lemon juice and kirsch

—Black and white grapes (each grape washed and dried, but not peeled), pears, and blackberries with red wine

Note: Never combine melon or watermelon with other fruits—they lose their crisp freshness.

Sauce à l'Abricot

Apricot Sauce

Delicious on baked apples, semolina cake, bread cake, or plain ice cream.

> 1 *cup apricot preserves*
> 6 *tablespoons dark rum*

Place the preserves and half of the rum in a heavy-bottomed pan and bring to a boil. Lower the flame and simmer, stirring with a wooden spoon, for 5 minutes. Add the rest of the rum and cook for 3 minutes more. Use this sauce warm or hot. It can be reheated.

Semoule aux Fruits Confits

A Semolina Dessert with Candied Fruits

Prepared with the simplest of ingredients, this light, velvety dessert is also one of the healthiest. It is always a children's favorite. Adults will also love it when it is accompanied by *sabayon niçois* or fresh fruit purée or with apricot or red currant preserves heated with lemon and sugar.

For 6 people:

1/4 *cup raisins*
2 *tablespoons dark rum*
4 *cups milk*
1/3 *cup medium-grain semolina (a hard*
   wheat semolina wheat product) *
2 *whole eggs, beaten*
3/4 *cup sugar*
3/4 *cup diced candied fruits (cherries,*
   melon, apricots)

Soak the raisins in the rum for 1 hour.

Bring the milk to a boil, then lower the flame and sprinkle the semolina into the milk while stirring constantly with a wooden spoon. Cook for about 10 minutes, or until the mixture thickens. Remove from heat.

Preheat the oven to 350°. In a large bowl, beat the eggs with a fork. Add the sugar, diced fruits, raisins, and rum marinade. Add the mixture to the semolina and stir. Pour into an oiled baking dish and place it in a large pan filled with about 2 inches of water. Bake for 20 minutes.

This can be served warm, spooned out on individual plates and

Les Desserts

* Available at health food shops, at all Greek, Italian, and Spanish markets, and in some supermarkets.

garnished with *Sabayon Niçois* (p. 256), fresh strawberry or raspberry purée (see *Purée de Fruits Frais* (p. 256), or *Sauce à l'Abricot* (pp. 257–58). It can also be chilled and unmolded before serving. It will keep a few days in the refrigerator.

Suce-Miels

Honey Candies

Virtually impossible to eat, not easy to make, but these little sticks of cooked honey are a favorite in Provence.

Heat 1⅓ cups of honey in a heavy enamel saucepan or a copper pan, or even better, in a metal mold used for making caramelized custard. Stir with a wooden spoon over a medium flame. For a more fragrant *suce-miel,* you may want to stir in 2 tablespoons of dried thyme. When the honey turns dark brown and liquid after about 15 minutes, remove from heat.

Spread in little sticks on a buttered sheet of waxed paper. Cover with another buttered sheet and let them cool. Keep in a dry, cool place. With scissors, cut into pieces a few sticks at a time.

Tian au Rhum

Rum and Milk Custard

This is a delicate and exciting traditional dessert, yet very easy to prepare. You can use the whites of the eggs later for *Soupirs aux Amandes* (pp. 263–64); you will like the lovely combination of rum custard and almond wafers.

For 6 people:

1 cup sugar
2 tablespoons water
1 quart milk
3 whole eggs and 3 yolks
5 tablespoons dark rum

Desserts

259

Boil ½ cup of the sugar with the water in a 1-quart mold over a medium to high flame. Shake the mold from time to time. When the syrup turns from golden to amber in color, place the bottom of the mold in a pan of cold water for 1 minute, then rotate the mold so the caramel runs and coats the entire bottom and part of the sides. Let it cool upside down for a few minutes over a plate that has been buttered to prevent the caramel from sticking.

Preheat the oven to 350°. Heat the milk in a large pot. In a large bowl, beat the eggs and yolks, gradually adding the remaining ½ cup of sugar. Very slowly pour in the hot milk while stirring vigorously. Stir in 4 tablespoons of the rum and pour the custard into the caramel-coated mold.

Place the mold in a large pan and pour 2 inches of hot water into the pan. Bake for 40 to 50 minutes, or until a knife inserted in the center comes out clean.

Allow to cool, then run a knife around the edge of the custard to unmold it more easily. Place a flat dish over the mold and then, holding both dish and mold, turn them upside down to unmold the custard.

If some caramel is still on the mold, add 1 tablespoon rum to the mold and heat the caramel to dissolve it again. Pour this over the top of the custard. No garnish is needed.

Les Treize Desserts de Noël
The Thirteen Desserts of Christmas

Christmas, or *Calena*, in Nice is celebrated with a rich variety of rituals. It all starts on the fourth of December, when children place wheat and lentils in saucers and cover them with a little cotton wool so that they will sprout. The budding green is used for the Crèche.

Displayed in the Crèche are *santons:* little hand-painted clay figurines representing the most characteristic of Provençal villagers. There is the fish vendor with a large, flat basket of sardines on each arm, the miller carrying a bag of flour, the wine merchant with a barrel of wine on his shoulder, the simpleton, *ravi,* with his dried cod, the housewife with a full mortar of *aïoli,* the baker and his *pompe à l'huile,* the hunter carrying rabbits and a hare, the

Les Desserts

shepherd with a white lamb on his shoulder, and the old peasant women dressed in black and wearing shawls, the chair-cane weaver, the knife grinder. Curiously, there is also a drummer, a postman, and a mayor.

A week before *Calena,* all the *santons* are unpacked and placed on a mantelpiece, a chest of drawers, or a table. Rocky hills (brown wrapping paper), green meadows (the wheat and lentil sprouts), and snowy lanes (flour) create the setting. The little stable with Jesus, Mary, and Joseph in it is put in, and then, from all sides come the villagers, dressed in nineteenth-century Provençal costumes.

The theaters during that week play little pastorals (*presepi*) in which all the characters of the Crèche take part: the gossipy linen washer, Tanta Giana, the Bastian Countrari (a sort of Mary contrary), Don Boutifa, the greedy monk, and many others.

Decorations in the streets are minimal and food is the most colorful part of Christmas in Nice. On Christmas Eve the *gros souper* or *souper maigre* takes place. It is *gros* (big) because it is a celebration of all the good things we are thankful for and because it is an important family affair; it is *maigre* (lean) for religious reasons—no meat is allowed.

Before the meal begins, the master of the house places in the fireplace a log (usually taken from a fruit tree) kept from the previous Christmas. He adds some pine cones and vine branches. Surrounded by all the guests, he lights the fire, dips a branch of celery in a glass of *vin cuit* and sprinkles the fire with it. The guests sip the wine as the glass is passed around.

The table is set with three white tablecloths. A large candle is brought to the table and throughout the meal everyone—from the youngest to the oldest member of the family—takes turns blowing it out and lighting it again.

The *gros souper* may begin with *aïgo bouido,* the light garlic and herb broth, or with raw celery dipped in an *anchoïade* sauce. Then there might be little gray snails or dried cod cooked in *raïto* or served with *aïoli.* A warm vegetable salad will follow—either cauliflower or chickpeas or lentils. Lean ravioli made with vegetables or *tians* of vegetables will come next. A crisp green salad, either endives or celery, follow, along with garlicky *chapons* seasoned with newly pressed olive oil.

The meal is long but is composed only of healthy natural foods and it ends with the traditional *treize desserts,* presented on a large tray or in little earthenware bowls.

Fresh Fruits

pale oranges from Nice
tangerines
wintermelon (carefully turned to ripen
evenly in the cellar since the autumn)
pears
apples
pomegranates

Dried Fruits

grapes that have been hung since the
autumn and are wrinkled and sweet, al-
most like honey
figs, dried first in the sun, then kept in-
doors on screens and then between
peach-tree and bay leaves
hazelnuts
almonds, both the soft sweet kind and the
hard-shelled bitter ones
walnuts
dates en branche, *from Africa, candied on*
their branches

Sweets

calissons d'Aix, *made with candied fruits*
and almonds
fruit tourtes
black and white nougats
quince paste (pâte de coing)
candied fruits
pompes à l'huile, *a sweet cake enriched*
with orange blossom water and olive oil

The guests nibble on the thirteen desserts, sip the sweet *vin cuit* (prepared in the fall), gather around the Crèche and sing while waiting for midnight mass.

Before leaving for church, the lady of the house places some of the thirteen desserts on a clean tablecloth ready for neighbors, beggars, or even the souls of ancestors to taste while she is at church. She then pours the leftover wine on the fire, removes the log, wraps it, and places it in a closet for the following Christmas.

Back from the mass the children are put to bed. Their shoes—

Les Desserts

262

here it is shoes and not stockings that Father Christmas fills—are stuffed with oranges, dates, and sweets of all kinds.

Then the grownups sit down for the *réveillon*. It can be either a small snack taken before going back to one's home or a large elaborate affair—*boudin blanc*, foie gras, and other delicacies—lasting until dawn.

Traditionally on Christmas Day the godfather brings his godson a cake in the shape of a rooster, and his goddaughter a cake in the shape of a doll. The meal is also a family gathering; it often starts with chopped turkey heart and kidneys sautéed with olive oil, celery, and black olives. Then comes the turkey or the goose, filled with chestnuts and ham, followed by a tart endive salad seasoned with newly pressed olive oil. There may be a large tray of goat's cheese—creamy ones and little dry ones set on leaves. And finally, some of the thirteen desserts left over from the previous night. It ends with homemade liquors—*ratafia, liqueur de coings* —and songs.

Soupirs aux Amandes
Wafers with Almonds

These crisp little cookies (they indeed deserve their name—*soupirs* means sighs) are made in Nice with a mixture of sweet and bitter almonds. Since there are no bitter almonds available here, I add almond extract to the dough and leave the skin on the nuts. The cookies go wonderfully well with *Glace à la Fleur d'Orangers* (pp. 248–49), *Tian au Rhum* (pp. 259–60), and all the fruit desserts.

Makes about 35 wafers:

> 1/2 *cup almonds, with the skins left on*
> 3 *tablespoons sweet butter at room*
> *temperature*
> 1/2 *cup sugar*
> 2 *or 3 egg whites*
> 5 *tablespoons unbleached flour*
> 3/4 *teaspoon almond extract*
> 1/4 *teaspoon salt*

Preheat the oven to 450°. Grind the nuts in a blender at high speed for 2 minutes, or pass them through a Mouli food mill, or chop them very fine by hand.

Cream the butter and sugar until the mixture is light and fluffy. Stir in the egg whites and blend well. Add the flour, almonds, almond extract, and salt.

Butter a baking sheet and drop the batter onto it by small teaspoonfuls, 2 to 3 inches apart. Lower the oven heat to 400° and bake for 5 to 6 minutes, or until the edges turn light brown.

Remove the cookies immediately with a spatula and let them cool on wire racks or on a cold surface. When cold, store them in an airtight container to keep them crisp.

Tourte de Blettes

Apple, Spinach and Pine Nut Pie

This is a curious blend of apples, raisins, and spinach or Swiss chard (this is what is used in Nice) baked in a light pie. It is one of Nice's traditional and most beloved desserts, and although it may seem odd to you at first, it will probably become one of the staples for your picnics and buffets. It can be eaten warm or cold.

For 8 people:

Pastry

> *3 cups unbleached flour*
> *2 eggs, beaten*
> *1 cup sweet butter, softened*
> *½ cup sugar*
> *about 1 tablespoon salt*

Working quickly with the tips of your fingers, mix all the ingredients together on a well-floured board. Pound and stretch the dough away from you with the heel of your hand to be sure all ingredients are well blended. Shape the dough into a ball, cover with a clean cloth, and leave for 2 hours at room temperature.

Filling

> *4 large Golden Delicious or Granny Smith apples*
> *3 tablespoons raisins*
> *2 tablespoons dark rum*

<blockquote>
*1 cup cooked and thoroughly drained
chopped spinach (2 10-ounce packages frozen chopped spinach or 2
pounds fresh spinach)*

4 tablespoons pine nuts

½ cup confectioners' sugar

*¼ to ½ pound bland cheese, such as
Gouda or a mild Cheddar, diced*

*2 beaten eggs
grated rind of 1 lemon*

2 tablespoons currant jelly

3 tablespoons confectioners' sugar
</blockquote>

Peel the apples and cut two of them into small cubes. Put the raisins and rum in a pan and bring to a boil. Cook for 2 minutes.

Preheat the oven to 375°.

In a large bowl, mix the spinach, raisins, apple cubes, pine nuts, sugar, cheese, eggs, and lemon rind. Slice the remaining two apples. Divide the pastry into two unequal parts, the smaller being about a third of the larger amount. Roll the pastry as thin as you can.

Butter a deep mold and spread the larger circle of dough in the bottom, molding it around to fit the bottom and sides. Prick it all over with a fork. Spread the currant jelly on the bottom and add the filling. Cover with the apple slices and then with the other small circle of dough. Fit together smoothly and cut off the excess dough. Prick the top crust with a fork and bake for 30 minutes, or until golden. Remove from the oven and sprinkle with confectioners' sugar.

Tourte aux Noix et au Miel

Walnut and Honey Pie

This recipe comes from the hills above Nice where bees have fields of lavender and rosemary for making honey, cows have good pasture, and walnut trees are luxuriant. It is a superb, richly flavored dessert. Make sure when you prepare it that you have crisp walnuts (always keep them in the freezer so that they remain fresh) and flavorful honey. It must be made 3 to 4 hours before it is served to allow the taste to mature. Cut the pie in small slices, since it is quite rich. It will keep well.

For 8 to 10 people:

Crust

1¾ cups unbleached flour
1¼ sticks sweet butter, chilled and cut
    into pieces
2 tablespoons peanut oil or lard
1 teaspoon salt
2 teaspoons sugar
4 to 6 tablespoons cold water, as
    needed

Put the flour on a counter and make a well in the center. Add the butter, peanut oil or lard, salt, and sugar. Blend with your fingers for 3 minutes, then add the cold water and knead briskly, pushing the dough down and then away from you with the heel of your hand, for a few minutes, or until all the water is incorporated. When the dough is smooth, form a ball and wrap it with plastic wrap or a towel. Chill it for 1 hour.

Filling

1½ cups sugar
½ cup water
3 cups chopped walnuts
1¾ sticks sweet butter
1 cup milk
⅓ cup honey

Put the sugar and water in a pan and heat it over a low flame for a few minutes. When the syrup turns light brown, immediately remove from heat (it can turn into caramel). Add the walnuts and the butter to the pan and stir. Add the milk and put the pan back on the stove. Simmer over a low flame for 15 to 20 minutes. Stir in the honey and remove from heat. Set aside.

Preheat the oven to 400°. Roll the dough on a floured surface into two 11-inch circles. Place one of the circles in a well-buttered 10-inch pie pan and pour in the filling. Place the other circle of dough on top and seal the edges. Press and pinch the two layers together. With a thin knife, trim the crust and cut a few slits on top to allow the steam to escape.

Les Desserts

Place in the center rack of the oven and bake for 20 minutes. Let cool for several hours. Sprinkle with confectioners' sugar and cut into thin slices.

Note: You may use strips of pastry on the top in a lattice pattern rather than a full crust.

Boissons de Ménage

Homemade Beverages

Most liquors and sweet wine were first prepared and their use justified as medicines. Quinces, cherries, oranges, herbs, and blossoms were marinated in brandy or wine and prescribed (most of the time self-prescribed) for melancholy, toothache, gout, and spring fever—anything from senility to growing pains.

I remember they were so good that every afternoon someone in my family would suddenly feel faint and whisper, "I am hot and cold—I don't know what . . ." in full expectation that a delicious beverage would instantly appear to cure the mysterious discomfort.

As a child my passion was *ratafia d'oranges*. When my ailments became "overwhelming," I was allowed to dip a lump of sugar in a glass of *ratafia*. The curative effect was very slow. Only after the third lump of sugar did I feel a barely perceptible improvement.

Now my two daughters seem to draw immense benefit from *vin de noix*. So every June I prepare a large jar of it. I also prepare grated quince marinated in brandy and sugar for my husband (he cannot quite explain how it helps or what it helps, but he knows it does help); lavender blossoms in white wine to fight severe winters; the *liqueur de lait* to fight severe summers, and a wide variety of *liqueurs de fenêtre* (called "window liquors" because the fruits, brandy, wine, and sugar are left on the window sill to marinate and to let the sun mellow them).

Thus no malaise ever catches us unprepared.

Ratafia d'Oranges

Orange Liqueur with Coriander

Ratafia can be made with sour cherries, strawberries, quinces, or oranges. They are always served in ornate glass decanters and sipped in the afternoons or after dinner. They are good when one feels melancholy, anxious, or even merry—truly wonderful for all occasions.

Makes 1 quart:

6 *oranges*
1 *pound sugar*
1 *pound whole coriander seed*
1 *quart brandy or cognac*

Wash and dry the oranges. With a potato peeler, peel off only the zesty part of the rind and discard the white part. Chop it into small pieces. Squeeze the oranges and put the juice and rind in a bowl. Add the sugar, coriander seed, and brandy or cognac, and stir. Pour into a large jar or a small barrel or a demijohn and close tightly. Let it rest in a dark, cool place for two months. Pass through a sieve, pour into bottles, and store them, tightly capped, in a dark, cool place.

Vin Cuit

A Sweet Dessert Wine

Vin cuit is served at Christmas with the *treize desserts,* at epiphany with the *gâteau des Rois.* In former times most families made their own *vin cuit,* but now it is made commercially and few bother to concoct it. Here is the recipe, however, for those who may be interested.

First of all, one must always choose the ripest black grapes (preferably *muscat de malaisie*) picked during the heat of the day.

Crush the grapes. The unfermented grape juice, called must (*le moût*), is the base of the *vin cuit.* Pour 10 quarts of must in a large

Homemade
Beverages

copper cauldron. Simmer it until it has been reduced to 6 quarts. From time to time remove the scum that rises to the top. Pour the must into a large barrel or an earthenware jar. Stir vigorously with a long stick or spoon. When the liquid is cold, add 3 cups of brandy. Let it rest for 48 hours. Pass it through a sieve and pour into bottles. Seal and keep in a cool, dark place.

To this basic recipe, many additions can be made. While the must is boiling, 2 unpeeled quinces cut in half may be added. Anise seed, coriander, cinnamon, and apricot pits may also be added to the must as it cools before the brandy is added. The proportions can be what one likes best. Each housewife in Provence prided herself on her own inimitable version of *vin cuit*.

Vin de Noix

A Sweet Red Dessert Wine Flavored with Green Walnuts

This is the most delectable of wines. It is prepared on the first day of summer and is ready at Christmas. Unbruised green walnuts can be picked during the month of June. Both the green kernels and the beige shells will be soft, so it should be possible to pass a long knitting needle through the whole fruit.

Makes 5 quarts:

40 *green walnuts with their shell,*
　　quartered
5 *quarts strong red wine*
2 *pounds sugar*
1 *nutmeg, grated*
1 *clove*
1 *vanilla bean*
1 *quart brandy*

Quarter the walnuts and place them in a large container. Add the wine, sugar, nutmeg, clove, and vanilla bean. Cover the container tightly. Place in a dark room and let it rest for fifty days, shaking it a bit every two weeks. Add the brandy and pass the mixture through a sieve. Pour into bottles, seal tightly and leave them for about six months in a dark, cool place.

Vin d'Orange

An Orange-Flavored Dessert Wine

━━

This is a lovely wine to serve chilled with cookies in the afternoon or as a dessert wine after dinner.

Makes 5 quarts:

> 5 *large oranges*
> 1 *large lemon*
> 5 *quarts white wine, preferably dry, or red wine*
> 2 *pounds sugar*
> 1 *quart brandy or cognac*
> 1 *vanilla bean (optional)*
> 1 *4-inch piece dried orange rind*

Wash the oranges and the lemon and grate their skins onto a plate. Quarter the fruits into a demijohn or preserve jars or any other large glass containers. Add the grated rind, wine, sugar, brandy, vanilla bean, and the piece of orange rind. Close the top and let it rest for forty days.

Pass through a sieve and pour into bottles. Seal tightly and keep in a cool place. Serve chilled.

Homemade
Beverages

Menus

Menus

Escoffier wrote that like music, the grand structure of gastronomy is built upon the harmony and sequence of its elements. Preparing a menu is as important to me as preparing any given dishes. The seasonal fresh ingredients I find available always determine the core of the meal, and I organize the rest around them.

But the circumstances and the guests are also important. Do I want to prepare a substantial dinner for robust gourmands, an elegant lunch for dainty gourmets, a picnic *à la bonne franquette* for cozy friends? Do I have time to prepare only one dish? several dishes? Shall I have someone in the kitchen, someone to wait on table, no help at all?

I don't attempt more than one challenge a meal; the rest are easy and often-tried reliable recipes. With the tone and core of the meal decided, I think about the sequence in which the courses will be served. I never have a Chinese-style series of delicious unrelated dishes. To me, not only the sequence but also the color, texture, flavor, and temperature are important. Each dish must contrast with the next. A crisp tossed lettuce salad in the middle of the meal will refresh the guests and allow a pause. I try to avoid repetitions. No *loup farci*, with its tomato sauce, after a *salade niçoise*. No meal starting with a *pissaladière* and finishing with *tourte de blettes*.

I usually plan not only special meals but also the whole week's menus to make sure of the variety of the meals, and because in the long run it is less time-consuming. Since so many good Niçois dishes are based on leftovers, I double the proportions of *gigot à l'aillade, boeuf à la niçoise, poisson court-bouillon,* and then prepare *salade de riz,* ravioli, and *tian* the next day. The transformation of the basic ingredients is so total that nobody can guess they are making a second appearance.

Cooking and planning ahead also prevent impulse buying, the falling back on easily prepared but expensive cuts of meat and on convenient processed food, or subsisting on a boring repetitious diet.

While the pots and pans, the knives, and Mouli food mill are being put to use anyway and the kitchen has become something of a battlefield, I feel I may as well win two or three battles simultaneously. The cleaning up will take only a little more time but the interesting menus we will have for days will take only a moment to produce—I will only need to add a tossed lettuce salad, a vegetable omelet, a tray of cheese, or some of the cold salads I keep in the icebox.

So the soup cooks while the *boeuf à la niçoise* simmers and the *tian* bakes next to the *gâteau à la semoule.* Instead of a boring routine, a chore, those big cooking sessions are full of joy. My children love the excitement, the mess, the fun —they see me kneading and cutting, and they jump about helping me gather up peels, chop nuts, rinse vegetables. And they compose their own strange mixtures.

The kitchen is full of delicious smells—vinegar, thyme, lemon, garlic—and all the rituals of cuisine become vitalized by this magical chemistry practiced *en famille.* Food and love always mingle easily. And children soon begin to realize the respect they should have for the variety and quality of food, and learn that like all other pleasure-giving activity, cooking and eating are serious matters.

When I serve my Niçois dishes, I always try to please the eye as well as the palate. Pretty earthenware, an assortment of baskets, bright napkins on which to place a *terrine* or *beignets*—everything is fresh, cheerful, and more than merely functional.

However, keep the *Faites simple* motto. Don't fuss, don't

overdo. Gain confidence, plan carefully, consider your guests and the time you can spend, then enjoy yourself.

Here are a few suggested menus you may like to try. Soon you will learn the quality of each dish and you will enjoy creating the delicate balance each menu demands.

Le Déjeuner
Lunch

Soupe de Moules
Salade de Chou-fleur (Salade Blanche)
Compote de Fruits
Soupirs aux Amandes

Terrine de Campagne
Salade Amère
Tian au Rhum

Champignons Farcis
Tian d'Épinards et de Morue
Compote de Fruits
Petits Biscuits aux Noix

Artichauts à la Barigoule
Tian de Navets Rosés
Salade de Fruits
Soupirs aux Amandes

Pois Gourmands en Marinade
Pâtes aux Moules
Plateau de Fromages Variés

Caillettes de Nice
Tian de Navets Rosés
Salade Mélangée aux Noix
Pommes Surprise

———

Crique (Omelette Jardinière)
Salade de Haricots Verts
Gâteau aux Fruits

Le Diner
Dinner

Moules aux Épinards
Canard comme à Nice
Champignons Provençale
Tian de Navets Rosés
Salade de Fruits

———

Salade de Moules
Poulet à la Niçoise
Gnocchis
Salade Verte
Tourte aux Noix et au Miel

———

Soupe de Moules
Brochettes à la Niçoise
Riz au Safran
Glace à la Fleur d'Orangers
Soupirs aux Amandes

———

Ratatouille
Boeuf à la Niçoise
Salade Mesclun
Poires au Vin Rouge

———

Poisson Mariné
Farcis à la Niçoise
Glace au Miel
Petits Biscuits aux Noix

Poulet en Gelée
Salade de Riz Variée
Beignets aux Fruits

Barba Jouan
Estockaficada
Salade Mesclun
Pommes Surprises
Soupirs aux Amandes

Asperges Vinaigrette
Loup Farci à la Niçoise
Courgettes Râpées
Poires au Vin Rouge

Pois Gourmands Paysanne
Rôti de Porc Provençale
Tian de Navets Rosés
Compote de Fruits

Soupe de Lentilles
Agneau à la Niçoise
Épinards aux Pignons
Févettes à l'Ail
Tian au Rhum

Anchoïade
Estouffade
Pâtes aux Oeufs
Févettes à la Verdure
Panier de Fruits

Nu et Cru
Gigot d'Agneau à l'Aillade
Pommes de Terre aux Herbes
Tomates Provençale
Beignets de Fruits

Soupe de Pois Chiches
Caillettes de Nice
Riz aux Herbes
Céleri Paysanne
Pommes Surprise

Brandade
Artichauts à la Barigoule
Tourte de Blettes

Terrine de Campagne
Suppions à la Niçoise
Salade Amère
Glace à la Fleur d'Orangers
Soupirs aux Amandes

Plateau de Hors-d'Oeuvre Variés
Merlan Magali
Riz aux Herbes
Compote d'Abricots, de Pêches et de Prunes
Petits Biscuits aux Noix

Menus

Pissaladière
Gigot de Mer
Riz au Safran
Salade Verte
Poires au Vin Rouge

Soupe de Pêcheurs
Troucha
Beignets aux Fruits

Pâtes à la Verdure
Capilotade
Courgettes Râpées
Grata Queca

Escargots à la Provence
Tian de Courges
Gâteau aux Fruits
Sabayon de Nice

Soupe de Courges
Capoun
Salade Verte
Tian au Rhum
Petits Biscuits
aux Noirs

Nu et Cru
Ravioli de Nice
Salade Amère
Plateau de Fromages
Glace au Miel
Soupirs aux Amandes

Pissaladière
Merlan aux Moules
Riz aux Herbes
Salade Mélangée aux Noix
Pommes Surprise

Sardines au Vinaigre
Daube d'Avignon
Courgettes Râpées
Tian au Rhum
Petits Biscuits aux Noix

Papeton d'Aubergines
Poisson au Court-Bouillon, Sauce Verte, Sauce Rouille
Salade de Riz Variée (au Fenouil)
Semoule aux Fruits Confits

Crudités et Bagna Cauda
Couscous
Plateau de Fruits

Anchoïade
Bouillabaisse
Salade Mesclun
Plateau de Fromages

Socca
Aïoli
Poires au Vin Rouge

Le Pique-Nique
Picnic

Food for a picnic can be prepared ahead of time or barbecued on the spot. It must always be appetizing and easy to handle.

Salty Dishes

Pissaladière
Farcis à la Niçoise
Omelettes Jardinières
Brochettes Niçoise
Pan Bagna
Terrine de Campagne
Sardines Grillées
Caillettes de Nice
Pietsch
Crudités (with salt instead of sauces)

Sweet Dishes

Tourte de Blettes
Tourte au Miel et aux Noix
Soupirs aux Amandes
Petits Biscuits aux Noix
Paniers de Fruits Frais
Plateau de Fromages
Nougat Noir
Nougat Blanc

Le Goûter
Snack

The most cheerful of meals for children. We call it *la merenda* in Nice.

Salty Dishes

Socca
Pan Bagna
Anchoïade
Saussoun
Pissaladière
Terrine
Toasted slices of bread spread with congealed olive oil and eaten with raw vegetables

Sweet Dishes

Panisses au Sucre
Beignets aux Fruits
Tourte de Blettes
Tourte au Miel et aux Noix
Semoule aux Fruits
Grata Queca
Nougat Noir
Nougat Blanc
Délices au Miel
Confiture de Tomates Rouges
Confiture Noire

Le Buffet

Buffet

There must be a rich offering of colors, textures, and flavors, and there must be both hot and cold dishes. Variety is important and easy to have because all the dishes can be prepared ahead of time.

Salty Dishes

Anchoïade
Crudités et Saussoun
Crudités et Sauce Verte
Caviar Provençale
Bagna Cauda et Crudités
Plateau de Hors-d'Oeuvre Variés

Poisson au Court-Bouillon (with three sauces)
Pissaladière
Terrine de Campagne
Pan Bagna
Salades Blanches
Salade Niçoise
Pois Gourmands en Marinade
Salade de Riz Variée

Sweet Dishes

Salades de Fruits
Pommes Surprise
Poires au Vin Rouge
Tourte de Blettes
Tourte aux Noix et au Miel
Tian au Rhum
Les Treize Desserts de Noël
Soupirs aux Amandes
Petits Biscuits aux Noix
Confiture de Tomates Rouges
Confiture de Tomates Vertes
Confiture Noire
Semoule aux Fruits (in individual dishes)
Panier de Fruits Frais
Plateau de Fromages

Spécialités

Special Treats

Some Niçois dishes depend on local products and are impossible to recreate outside their home ground. The mushrooms of a certain wood, the fish from a particular cove, the ham from a village in the area—these are unique. And the traditional ways of curing meats, pressing olive oil, and candying fruits are unique, too.

Can *poutine* (tiny undeveloped fish) be found anywhere but between Antibes and Menton? The privilege of fishing for these quarter-inch-long sardines, herring, and other minute fish dates back a hundred years. It is only valid for a month and each boat is entitled to bring back only two hundred pounds of *poutine*. The *poutine* is rather thick and pasty; the *nonat,* another group of tiny fish, is transparent and slightly bigger. They are both prepared in various ways. Dusted with flour, they are fried in olive oil and served with lemon wedges. Fried as an omelet or a pancake, they form a golden crisp flat mass, which is sprinkled with red wine vinegar and chopped parsley and cut in sections like a tart. They can be cooked in individual dishes with little chili peppers and garlic or be part of a *tian* made of vegetables, eggs, and cheese. They can also be prepared in *beignets* and in soups. The closest American counterpart to these Mediterranean fish would be whitebait or minnows.

The *poutargue,* made with mullet roe, is another delicacy impossible to find outside Provence. It is called "the caviar of Martigues" (a small fishing town), and is gathered every spring when the sea is calm. Every year between the fifteenth

Special Treats

of July and the end of August, the mullet leave their eggs along the Berre Pond, near Marseilles. Gathering the eggs is a delicate operation because great care must be taken not to tear the membrane surrounding the roe. The eggs are placed in a bowl and covered with rough salt. A heavy board is left on top of them for forty-eight hours to press out as much moisture as possible. After being rinsed with clear water, they are spread in the sun for four days, until they are perfectly dry. Then they are hung inside a large fireplace and smoked slowly (the wood is covered with sawdust to increase the smoke). After one hour of smoking each day for four consecutive days the *poutargue* is ready. It is eaten with oil and red wine vinegar as an hors d'oeuvre, or is added in small pieces to chickpeas, then covered with a light nutmeg-flavored mayonnaise mixed with minced onions and parsley.

Snails in Nice are small and either pale gray or striped. Fed on fragrant herbs, such as fennel and thyme, they are often cooked in a hot tomato sauce with herbs or barbecued outdoors over an open fire. *Limaçons à la sucarelle* are first cooked in an herb-flavored court bouillon, then mixed with a spicy sauce and put back in their shells, the bottom of which has been opened so that it makes it easier to suck the snail out of its shell. It is interesting that the Chinese use the same technique with periwinkles.

Some of the specialties are based on simple ingredients, easily available everywhere, but are prepared in ways that might startle most Americans. Among these is *galito denti* (which means a chicken with teeth), a curious dish loved by all. The head of a lamb is opened and washed, surrounded with quartered potatoes, sprinkled with herbs, and broiled; the brain and cheeks are great delicacies, and the potatoes cooked around the bones have a superb flavor. A goat's head, spread with a paste of parsley and garlic, is broiled the same way. A calf's head, simmered in tomato sauce with a little wine, is also delicious. A boar's head is more robust and also more elaborately prepared. The skull is emptied and washed carefully, and is filled with onions, thyme, chopped carrots, chopped tongue, ham, and cheeks and seasoned with cognac and white wine. It is first marinated, then cooked for eight hours in white wine.

There is *fressure d'agneau* (lamb kidneys, liver, heart and lungs simmered with olives and mushrooms); cockscomb stew; *bala de mouton* (by no means symbolic of "women's lib's revenge"—this has long been considered a delicacy), sliced and fried and served with lemon wedges and parsley.

Anchovies in vinegar are a staple in a Niçois kitchen. Here is the way the Niçois housewife prepares it:

Place a pound of fresh anchovies on a board and remove the heads and insides. Dry with paper towels. Bring to a boil 1 quart of red wine vinegar, add 2 cloves, 1 tablespoon of thyme, 1 teaspoon of savory, and 3 peeled garlic cloves. Add the anchovies, bring back to the boiling point, then lower the flame and simmer for 15 minutes. Remove from the stove and let cool in its liquid. Place the anchovies in a glass jar. Close tightly and wait for two weeks before testing. These are served as hors d'oeuvre, in sandwiches, and as an accompaniment.

Pissalat is sold everywhere in Nice packed in small jars with elaborate old-fashioned labels, but most Niçois still prepare their own. Here is the recipe in case you want to try it. Rinse and dry 1 pound of fresh sardines and 2 pounds of fresh anchovies. Remove the heads and the insides. Place a layer of fish in a large bowl and sprinkle with rough (kosher) salt, a few peppercorns, a few cloves, branches of dried wild fennel, and bay leaves. Repeat the procedure with the rest of the fish. Stir the mixture every day with a long wooden spoon. After a few days, the fish will turn pasty. After a month, push the fish paste through a sieve with a pestle. Fill glass jars with this purée and cover with a little olive oil before closing the top. Keep in a cool place. Serve with hot toast, cold meat, hot boiled potatoes, or sliced tomatoes.

Baby thrushes and baby larks are called *chachas*. The insides (except for the gizzard) are kept, and the birds are stuffed with a little butter, a few juniper berries, and a grape or two. Wrapped in thin slices of salt pork or caul, they are cooked in white wine seasoned with crushed juniper berries. The stuffed birds are served on warm croutons. With their little beak tucked under the wing, they can also be skewered and broiled over a fire of pine cones, vine prunings, or rosemary sprigs. Toward the end of the cooking, large slices of bread are placed under them to gather the delectable juices, and the whole dish is served with a crisp bunch of watercress.

Panier de Fruits Niçois

A Look at Nice's Fruits

There is a staggering variety of fruits offered all year round in Nice's marketplaces. In summer, there are melons and watermelons, rounder and more compact than the American variety. There are *cantalous, charentais, Verdons.* Madame de Sévigné, on her visits to the South of France, was fond of saying that "it is indeed a strange thing, but if by an odd whim we were to demand a tasteless melon, we would have to have it sent from Paris. There are *none* here!" And Southern melons are so fragrant that Alexandre Dumas offered his four hundred volumes of books in exchange for twelve Southern melons a year.

There is also an abundance of peaches: the yellow peach of Nice with its pointed tip, strong delicious flavor, and firm flesh; little vine peaches; the red peaches. There are yellow freckled apricots, *les muscats,* and big orange ones. There are pears with disconcerting names: *le trompe chasseur* (how can a pear cheat a hunter?); *cuissette de dame* (lady's little thighs), with a thin yellow-striped skin; and the *cuisse de dame* (lady's thighs), with a coarser skin but a melting flesh; and the *bon chrétien,* a very sweet but not very tasty summer pear. There are plums, the yellow *pistole* (after the Spanish money), the purple *perdigon,* with its mother-of-pearl flesh, the *reine claude* (the green gage), translucent and delicious. There are more than twenty varieties of figs: the purple-brown *belone;* the *barnissotte,* which looks like a black spinning top; the small green *marseillaise;* the big black *col de dame* (lady's neck). All are picked the very morning they are sold; dried in the sun, they are preserved with bay leaves in wooden cradles for the winter months and Christmas. There are grapes: the large white *Saint Jeannet* which grows on lattices until February; the large white *Servan;* the delicious white *muscat d'Alexandrie;* the black *muscat d'Hambourg;* the sweet *rolle,* which becomes the *Bellet,* the famous wine of Provence.

In winter there are the oranges of Nice with their thick yellow skin and delicate flavor; the tangerines, the lemons of Menton; the kumquats (called *chinois*), kept in brandy or candied; the little bitter oranges (*oranges amères*), used for preserves and liquors or perfume. There are hazelnuts, walnuts, almonds—the sweet *pausane* and the delicate *princesse,* the hard-shelled bitter almonds (used for making pastry), the *coque dure,* the *Courrières,* the *Capronene,* the *Aberane,* the *Natherane,* the *Molière.* Around the hills surrounding Nice there are chestnuts—five varieties to be roasted in winter and eaten with sweet white wine. There are pomegranates, medlars, arbutus berries, persimmons, quinces for making pastry and liquors.

Les Fruits Confits

Candied Fruits

Nice's confectionery shops are full of baskets piled with *fruits confits*—superb glossy, mouth-watering melons, tangerines, strawberries, and apricots. The fruits are preserved by replacing their own water with a sugary liquid, and remain beautiful and moist for months.

The process of treating the fruits is lengthy. It requires patience and precision and the help of a special instrument, a hydrometer, to determine the density of the liquid.

The first day: The most beautiful, firm, ripe fruits are chosen and the pips removed. They are blanched until a long needle inserted in them draws no water, and are then removed from the fire, rinsed in cold water, and carefully drained.

The second day: Sugar is melted in water (1 quart of water to every 3 pounds of sugar) and brought to a boil in a copper or heavy aluminum saucepan and simmered until a hydrometer dipped in it reads 20° density. The fruits are gently put in the syrup and boiled for a second, then removed from the flame and allowed to cool. Both the fruits and the syrup are then poured in a large bowl and left to rest for a day.

The fourth day: The fruits are removed from the syrup, and sugar is added to the syrup to raise the density to 22°. The fruits are again cooked briefly in the syrup and then removed.

The sixth day: The same procedure is followed as the day before, but the syrup must now be at 24°, so sugar is added accordingly. The fruits rest for a day.

The eighth day: The syrup must be at 28°. The fruits rest for two days.

The eleventh day: From this point on, glucose is added instead of sugar. The syrup must be at 32°. The fruits rest for four days.

The fifteenth day: The syrup must reach 36°. The fruits rest for six days.

The twenty-first day: The syrup must reach 37°. The fruits rest for eight days.

The twenty-ninth day: The fruits are removed from the syrup and drained. The syrup (at 37°) is brought to a boil for a few seconds. The fruits are placed on a flat surface and the syrup poured over them is allowed to drain off. The fruits are now *confits* and will keep.

Whole melons, pears, apricots, lemons, oranges, figs, and strawberries are candied by the above process until they become totally impregnated with sugar and glucose. The last pouring of syrup over them is to make them shiny. Flowers, such as violets, roses, and mimosa, are also candied.

Fruits confits must be kept in a dry place and are usually sold in baskets or in wooden boxes.

Le Miel

Honey

Every spring the beehives are taken to the mountains around Nice and the bees feed on heath and on herbs—lavender, thyme, rosemary, sweet marjoram, sage—and on eucalyptus and flowering almond, apple, pear, and orange trees. In September the honey is gathered and allowed to ripen for a whole month so that it will lose its excess of water. In November the hives are taken back to their original places, usually after the vine harvest is over. The liquid honey, which is blond at crop time, is poured into cardboard containers, where it solidifies and crystallizes. In winter the bees cease all activity. All through winter and spring they are fed with syrup and some of their own honey.

Lavender honey is amber-colored and strongly flavored. Rosemary honey is white and highly flavored also. Acacia honey is pale yellow with a delicate taste, and heath honey is dark yellow. The best is thyme and wild thyme (*serpolet*) honey.

Honey is the base for most of Nice's desserts. It is used to cook fruits with, to make *Nougat Noir* (p. 252), *Nougat Blanc* (p. 251), and *Suce-Miels* (p. 259), and to sweeten *tisanes* (herb teas).

Huile d'Olive
Olive Oil

Olive oil is at the core of Provençal life. It is not only its most essential culinary element, but it is also treasured as a universal remedy, and is thought to restore vitality to hair and skin. It is the only oil which is the natural juice of a ripe fruit rather than of a seed or nut.

A healthy olive tree is a thing of beauty—its silver-gray leaves are like delicate lace. In Nice, where the trees are not regularly pruned, they grow in romantic shapes, like weeping willows, but in Provence they are tight and trim because of careful shaping. Around Nice the big trees produce small black olives with a bitter flesh, while the small trees bear larger, plump olives.

There are a great many kinds of olives: *olivière, lucques, pigale, verdale, rougette, picholine, saillerne, amelan, argentale, croniale, blancale, arabane, dent de Verrat, rose, redonale, moirale, caillet, rubeyro d'Antibes,* and *coucourelle,* to name only a few. Olive trees produce only from their twenty-fifth year on. *Caillet* is the most widely found around Nice and Grasse. It has a purplish flesh, produces a fine pale-yellow sweet oil, and comes from big pyramidal trees.

Around Marseilles, fleshy green olives grow on small, stocky trees and produce a very tasty oil. Big, plump olives growing in the lower Alps make a heavy, very tasty green oil which is considered superb by some but unpalatable by others. There is a wide range of flavor, from the sweet yellow to the strong green, but the best oil is always made from perfectly ripe fruit. The more an olive matures and the more its water content diminishes, the better its oil will be. In August there is 40 percent oil in the olives but the acidity is high, and oil made from these is of low quality. Olives picked too early taste too strong. The crop continues from August to September, and the oil is processed from November to April.

For picking eating olives, a double ladder (*caracons,* or *escaracons*) is raised for the picker and the olives 'are received in an apron with a big pocket in the center. Then they are spread on a large sheet in the shade of the tree. Olives to be used for making olive oil are knocked down with a long, flexible pole. Since the trees are in bloom in late spring, most of the blossoms are hurt by this method of picking and so a crop is available only every other year.

There are still some 150 olive mills in France and sixty of them are around Nice. Olives are brought to the mill (about a hundred pounds from each tree) and put under a granite millstone, which reduces the pulp and the pits of five hundred pounds of olives to a thick paste in about an hour and a half. The paste goes into a large "mixing bowl" before being spread in large *scourdins* (round flattish sacks made of coco fiber). As many as sixty mats are piled five feet high under the heavy hydraulic press, which is usually run by water—only occasionally by electricity. All this must be done in a well-ventilated space. The first juice squeezed out is darkish. It is pumped into an *écrémeuse,* running six thousand turns a minute, which separates the oil from the water. When the water is gone, what remains is a totally pure oil—the finest—officially labeled *Huile Vierge Première Pression à Froid.* Then comes the second pressing. The dried paste from the first pressing is covered with hot water and the process is repeated. This oil is labeled *Huile Vierge Deuxième Pression* and is sold in grocery stores either in pure form or mixed with other vegetable oils. The paste left over is covered with cold water. The pulp is used for soap, while the hard part, *les grignons noirs,* is burned in factories as fuel.

For purposes of cooking, oil from the first pressing must be bought because its acidity is never more than 1 percent, whereas the *vierge fine* has 1 to 1½ percent acidity and the *vierge ordinaire* has as much as 3 percent, which makes for a harsh, bitter taste. The pale-yellow oil from Nice or Grasse is low in acidity and can be either very fine and sweet or more fruity, if green olives are added to the local black ones. One should beware of all the other oils. *Olive Pure* means (legally, that is) that it is mixed with Tunisian oil. *Huile de Table* is made from leftovers, chemically treated oils, and by-products of various things, such as colza, soy, and sunflower.

Because olive oil is such a fine product, it is best not to leave rosemary or basil leaves in it, or if used, to keep them in for only a short time. Grape-seed oil or peanut oil, which have very little flavor of their own, are better for flavoring in this way.

In Provence and in Nice we not only season almost every dish with olive oil, but we also nibble the olives as an appetizer, we stuff them with anchovies and capers, we use them in stews, *farcis,* and dips. Also, the pits left over from the process of crushing olives to extract the oil are used as fuel for cooking in the winter.

There are many ways to prepare olives, most of which you would find possible here, since some American grocery stores sell uncured olives every fall.

Olives Cassées

Green olives have a very bitter taste when picked, so they must be cured. They are broken with a heavy piece of wood or a stone or gently squashed with a bottle, then thrown into water for nine days. The water is changed every day to hasten the curing. On the tenth day they are put in brine—salt water in which a bay leaf, a sprig of fennel, an orange rind, and a few coriander corns have been boiled.

Olives à la Picholine

Very plump, firm green olives are plunged into water. They are taken out when the flesh can be detached from the pit easily with a nail. The same weight of wood ashes as the olives is put in enough water to make a paste. The olives are left in the paste to neutralize their acidity. Then they are put in pure water for nine days, the water being changed every day. On the ninth day they are washed and put in brine made with 10 quarts of water for 10 pounds of olives and 2 pounds of salt, a bay leaf, an orange rind, a fennel branch, coriander, and a clove and boiled for 5 minutes and then cooled before the olives are added. Completely covered with the marinade, the olives are kept away from light.

Olives Farcies

First, *olives à la picholines* are prepared with very plump olives. The pit of each olive is removed and replaced with a caper wrapped in an anchovy fillet. Then the stuffed olives are put in a glass jar and covered with a good olive oil. They are kept in a cool place in the closed jar.

Olives Piquées

Olives that have reached perfect maturity and are quite fleshy, oily, and sweet are used for this treatment. They are put in a basket and pricked with a fork, then sprinkled with salt. Tossed from time to time and left in the basket for eight days, they lose some of their water. After fifteen days, when they have lost their bitterness, olive oil, pepper, and bay leaves are added.

Olives en Saumure

For this, not-too-ripe black olives are used. They are pricked with a needle and left in water for ten days, with the water changed every day. Finally, they are put in a cool brine spiced to taste and left there for five days.

Mail Order Sources

California

Haig's
441 Clement Street
San Francisco, CA 94118

Georgia

Atlanta Municipal Market
209 Edgewood Avenue, S.E.
Atlanta, GA 30303

Happy Herman's
4300-A Banker's Circle
Atlanta, GA 30360

Illinois

La Preferida, Inc.
3400 West 35th Street
Chicago, IL 60632

Louisiana

Central Grocery Company
923 Decatur Street
New Orleans, LA 70116

New Mexico

Las Cosas de Sante Fe
125 Lincoln Street
Sante Fe, NM 87501

The Winery
510 Montezuma
Sante Fe, NM 87501

New York

Balducci's
424 Sixth Avenue
New York, NY 10011

Bloomingdale's
337 Second Avenue
New York, NY 10022

Dean and De Luca
560 Broadway
New York, NY 10013

Manganaro's Foods
448 Ninth Avenue
New York, NY 10018

Paprikas Weiss Importer
1546 Second Avenue
New York, NY 10028

Todaro Brothers
555 Second Avenue
New York, NY 10016

Zabar's
2245 Broadway
New York, NY 10024

Tennessee

Good Life Natural Health Foods
3125 Poplar Street
Memphis, TN 38111

Lipsey's Fish Co.
5041 Summer Avenue
Memphis, TN 38122

Sessel's
1761 Union Avenue
Memphis, TN 38104

Index

Index

301

Index

304

Index

305

Index

Index

About the Author

MIREILLE JOHNSTON was born in Nice, educated in France and America, and now divides her time between the two countries. She is the author of *Central Park Country: A Tune Within Us* and the translator of the film script for *The Sorrow and the Pity*, by Marcel Ophuls, and *Criticism of Everyday Life*, by Henri Lefèvre. She is married and has two daughters, Margaret-Brooke and Elizabeth.